FAITH IN THEIR OWN COLOR

RELIGION AND AMERICAN CULTURE

IN AFFECTIONATE REMEMBRANCE OF THE
REV. PETER WILLIAMS,
THE FOUNDER AND DURING TWENTY YEARS
THE FAITHFUL MINISTER OF THIS PARISH.
HE DIED OCT. 18TH 1840, IN THE
54TH YEAR OF HIS AGE.

ERECTED BY HIS BEREAVED PARISHIONERS.

R.E. Launitz, N.Y.

Faith in Their Own Color

Black Episcopalians
in Antebellum New York City

CRAIG D. TOWNSEND

COLUMBIA UNIVERSITY PRESS
NEW YORK

COLUMBIA UNIVERSITY PRESS

Publishers Since 1893

NEW YORK   CHICHESTER, WEST SUSSEX

Portions of chapters 6 and 7 were previously published in
Anglican and Episcopal History,
2003 the Historical Society of the Episcopal Church.

Library of Congress Cataloging-in-Publication Data

Townsend, Craig D., 1955–
Faith in their own color : Black Episcopalians in antebellum
New York City / Craig D. Townsend.
p. cm. — (Religion and American culture)
Includes bibliographical references and index.
ISBN 0–231–13468–1 (cloth : alk. paper)
0–231–50888–3 (e-book)
1. African American Episcopalians—New York (State)—
New York—History—19th century.
2. New York (N.Y.)—Church history—19th century.
I. Title. II. Religion and American culture (New York, N.Y.)

BX 5979.T68   2005
283'.7471'08996073—dc22   2005045584

To Terry and Sara Townsend and Jean Finn
who have been so patient

CONTENTS

ACKNOWLEDGMENTS

I would like to thank the Rev. Brenda G. Husson and the people and vestry of St. James's Church in Manhattan for giving me the time and support to write this book.

I would like to thank the people of St. Philip's Episcopal Church for welcoming me into their midst and supporting my research and work in so many ways.

Thanks to David D. Hall, who oversaw the dissertation that was the original form of this work and encouraged me in so many ways; thanks also to Bill Hutchison and Evelyn Higgenbotham for their critiques of that version.

The research for this book was funded in part by the Lilly Endowment, Inc. and by the Episcopal Church Foundation. I am extraordinarily grateful for their support.

I am particularly indebted to Diana Lachatanere, curator, and her staff in the Rare Books and Manuscripts division of the Schomburg Center for Research in Black Culture of the New York Public Library. I also appreciate the time and support given to me by Madeline L'Engle, librarian of the Cathedral of St. John the Divine, New York City; by the General Theological Seminary, which at one point gave me a carrel even though I wasn't a student; by the New-York Historical Society; and by the John Jay Homestead.

Portions of chapters 6 and 7 were previously published in *Anglican and Episcopal History*; my thanks to their editorial board for their gracious encouragement.

I owe an enormous debt of gratitude to my editor, Wendy Lochner, for wanting this book to see the light of day.

Thanks to John Davis, who has supported this project with his interest and friendship for what must seem like forever. Thanks also to Dan Bergner and to all the friends, family, and colleagues who read portions of this work in various stages.

Finally, thanks beyond words to Cathy, Caleb, and Asher.

FAITH IN THEIR OWN COLOR

CHAPTER I

Improper Associates

By 1853, slavery in America was legally confined to the Southern states, and Northerners often basked in a sense of righteousness that they were free of the "peculiar institution." Yet slavery had only been abolished in the state of New York twenty-six years earlier, and few African Americans living in New York City felt Northern governments had much right to feel proud. The passage of the Fugitive Slave Law three years earlier had effectively removed any rights to security free blacks had gained in the North, and prejudice in both gross and petty forms was the societal norm. African Americans were only permitted on the public horse-drawn trolleys and omnibuses at the whim of the driver or conductor. They were excluded from restaurants, theaters (unless the balcony was designated as separate seating for "colored persons"), and cultural and professional institutions. They attended segregated schools and had largely established their own churches, rather than attend the separate services to which white congregations had relegated them. Their right to vote was encumbered by residency and property requirements significantly different from and more difficult to meet than those in effect for whites. And despite the existence of their own fancy balls, elegant restaurants, cultural institutions, and a growing bourgeois class, African Americans were still assumed to be uniformly lazy, poor, uneducated, bereft of all virtues, and unworthy of mingling with white citizens in any setting.[1]

Yet on a Thursday afternoon in September of that year, three black men walked into St. John's Chapel in Manhattan, an Episcopal parish that operated under the auspices of the august Trinity Church on Wall Street, and took their seats among some five hundred wealthy and powerful white men.[2] It was the second day of the Convention of the Episcopal Diocese of New York, an annual gathering to conduct diocesan administrative and canonical business.[3] The convention was attended by the clergy and appointed lay representatives of each parish in the eastern half of the state. These three men were the delegation from St. Philip's Church, the first African American Episcopal church in the city. The congregation had been excluded from the convention for over thirty-five years by a variety of procedural maneuvers, but the question of the delegation's admission had finally come to a vote that afternoon, and the convention had no longer been able to deny them the right to attend.

The three men were Peter Ray, supervisor of the Lorillard tobacco factory and keeper of its secret recipe for snuff; Henry Scott, owner of a successful pickling concern that furnished foodstuffs for the seagoing trade; and Philip White, who ran a pharmacy and was thus a de facto physician. Ray was warden at St. Philip's, meaning he was one of the two leaders of the vestry, the board of laymen who directed the affairs of the parish. Scott was treasurer of the parish, and White was secretary of the vestry. Ray and Scott had held their church positions for most of the previous ten years, and White had been elected to his post for the past two years. Within the severe constraints of being African American in mid-nineteenth-century New York City, these were successful and important men in their own right, with real standing in their church and in the wider community.[4]

Their identities and accomplishments, however, were immaterial to the vast majority of the men gathered at the convention. What mattered to them was that these three men in their midst were black, representing a black church that had been consecrated by an Episcopal bishop and legally incorporated as an Episcopal parish. It was only the second such congregation in the country, after St. Thomas's in Philadelphia. The existence of the church did not disturb the delegates; they were in fact proud of how their denomination had reached out to bring the gospel to such "unfortunates." What was disturbing to these white clergy and laymen, however, was that Ray, Scott, and White were the first black delegates to be admitted to New York's diocesan convention. In other words, they were the first African Americans with whom these Episcopalians were to conduct their church business as equal partners. Though the convention had voted overwhelmingly to admit the delegation that day, few of the voters actually welcomed their presence. The racism that had kept St. Philip's segregated from the diocese all those years and had kept all African Americans from any real sense of freedom in these Northern cities was so ubiquitous, unquestioned, and unapologetic as to be casual. These three men cannot have felt very comfortable walking into that church.

Yet they must have felt a sense of triumph nonetheless. Ray, Scott, and White represented not just their parish, but their parish's history of moving slowly and inexorably toward full recognition as an Episcopal congregation. They represented the history of their church's paradoxical struggle for, on the one hand, autonomy and independence as a black congregation, and on the other, acceptance by a white hierarchy and a white denomination. And they represented the reality that despite the racism and oppression endemic to the life of African Americans in New York City, and despite the efforts on every ecclesiastical, political, social, and economic level to segregate and isolate black New Yorkers from the lives of their white counterparts, interaction between black and white Episcopalians was as much a result of white leaders enforcing their hierarchy as it was of black parishioners demanding their right to full participation.

St. Philip's had its beginnings in 1809, when the black congregation attending separate services at Trinity Church decided to become independent. It took them ten years to build a church and have it consecrated, incorporate as an Episcopal congregation, and have one of their own members, Peter Williams Jr., ordained as their liturgical and spiritual leader. The church burned to the ground once, and it was ransacked and nearly destroyed during the 1834 antiabolitionist riots. Its rector was humiliated by denominational leaders at each step of his career, as were the young men the congregation occasionally raised up for ordained ministry. After Williams's death, the parish was forced to make use of part-time white priests, as there were still so few black clergy. The congregation's every communication with the diocese requesting full inclusion was treated with patronizing contempt, culminating in the public response by one convention that because of their color the people of St. Philip's were "socially degraded, and . . . not regarded as proper associates for the class of persons who attend our Convention."[5] In the face of these trials, St. Philip's refused to give up its belief that it was an Episcopal parish deserving of denominational recognition. The Episcopal Church was not welcoming to them—but it did not succeed in isolating or ignoring them either.[6]

The story of St. Philip's Church underscores two opposing developments in the relations between black and white New Yorkers in the first half of the nineteenth century. First, the oppressive measures imposed formally and informally by white citizens created both strictly parallel black and white cultures and the simultaneous necessity for interaction between those cultures in order to regulate or negotiate their relationship. Second, the desire of black Americans to be accepted as equals by white Americans led to the creation of separate and autonomous institutions by the black community in order to demonstrate their equal capabilities. These paradoxical movements do not resolve over the course of this history. Instead they remain sources of conflict and creative adaptation for everyone involved. It is perhaps true that the people of St. Philip's were more aware of the existence of these paradoxes than the white leaders, who tended to believe their actions and choices to be guided by straightforward and clear motives.

Above all, what the struggles of St. Philip's Church illuminate are the extraordinary difficulties of being African American in the first half of the nineteenth century. All efforts to operate within those difficulties—let alone attempt to ameliorate them—by African Americans must be seen in that most basic context. To be of African heritage during this period was to live with unrelenting prejudice, racism, injustice, and oppression. It was to belong to a minority that was patronized, reviled, feared, pitied, or simply ignored by the white majority, from the newest of immigrants to the oldest of families. And it was to have all aspects of one's life shadowed by the existence of slavery as a legal institution, either immediately at hand or as a dominant factor in one's national life and consciousness.

Between 1800 and 1850, the decades that roughly frame this history of St. Philip's, the United States saw the massive growth of its urban centers. This was especially true in the North, where, for example, Pittsburgh grew from a village of a bit more than 1,500 people to a city of well over 46,000, Cincinnati mushroomed from 750 to more than 115,000, and Boston and Philadelphia, among the larger cities at the turn of the century, both quintupled in population over this period, with Philadelphia nearly reaching 400,000 people. During the same period, Brooklyn went from a small town of some 2,400 to a city of 97,000, and New York itself grew more than eightfold, from 60,489 to 515,547, becoming the largest city in the country.[7]

African Americans followed this urbanizing trend to a proportionally greater degree than white Americans: between 1800 and 1850, across the nation, the growth in the population of African Americans living in urban settings increased almost one thousand percent, more than triple the urban growth rate of the population as a whole. By 1850, more than one in five black Americans lived in the fifteen largest cities, compared to fewer than one in twelve white Americans. Yet despite these increases, the number of African Americans as a percentage of the total populations of these cities declined—in some cases, quite dramatically. The percentage of African Americans in Pittsburgh dropped from around 6.5 percent in 1800 to 4.2 percent by 1850; in Philadelphia, from 10.33 percent to 8.85 percent; and Boston's black population decreased from nearly 5 percent of the total in 1800 to less than 1.5 percent in 1850. In Brooklyn, African Americans, both free and slave, were almost 27 percent of its small population in 1800, but by 1850, they were only 2.5 percent of what had become a good-sized city. New York City's black population declined proportionally as well, dropping from over

10 percent at the beginning of the century to only 2.67 percent at mid-century. Across the northern landscape, though real numbers were increasing impressively, the African American communities in urban centers were nonetheless becoming increasingly marginalized, as white populations grew even more precipitously.

This increasing urban marginalization was accompanied, however, by some seemingly significant strides toward greater freedom for African Americans. The abolition of slavery in the North was by far the most important step. By the turn of the century, slavery was nonexistent in Boston and Cincinnati, and the number of slaves in such cities as Providence, Pittsburgh, and Philadelphia was either meaningless or negligible. The presence of slavery nearby, however, made such signs of freedom tenuous. New York State's abolition of slavery did not fully take effect until the Fourth of July, 1827; as late as 1820, there were still over 7,500 slaves in the state, 518 of whom lived in New York City. Baltimore, of course, was the northernmost city where slavery remained legal throughout this period; its slave population hovered around 3,000 during most of these decades. Kidnapping escaped slaves to return them to their owners, or free blacks to sell into slavery, was not geographically difficult during this period and was, both before the Fugitive Slave Act as well as after, a ubiquitous aspect of life for urban African Americans throughout the North.

Slavery was effectively gone from the Northern states by 1830, however, and suffrage laws in some areas even meant that African Americans had reasonable access to the vote (Massachusetts was the early leader in this area).[8] New York State enacted laws that permitted black suffrage, but then restricted the right in 1821 to those who could demonstrate three years of residency in the state and unencumbered ownership of property worth at least $250— making it nearly impossible for anyone to qualify. Legal restrictions on public transportation were challenged in several cities and as a result were abolished; rights to incorporate and assemble were affirmed. These gestures of progress, however large or small and however widely ranging or constrained, were all understood by African American leaders as signs that American society could be moved in the right direction.

Yet many of these official freedoms, restricted as they were, were honored more in the breach than the observance. The experience of New Yorkers was not unique in this regard, and its African American leaders were quick to point out the discrepancies between freedom promised and freedom given. The issue of suffrage was a sore point, attacked by petition and politicking year after year. As has been noted, public transportation had been made officially available to all, but in reality was usually segregated quite effectively (black New Yorkers were often forced to ride on the outside running boards, and if allowed inside at all, were expected to take the rear seats), and economic opportunities were barred in a number of ways. The difference, for example, between the incomes of a porter hauling goods with his handcart and a drayman employed in the same activity with a horse-drawn cart was quite large, but the latter cart required a city license that, while not officially restricted, was somehow generally unavailable to African Americans.[9]

It has been amply demonstrated that the employment opportunities for free black Americans in Northern cities were significantly scarcer than for those in Southern ones.[10] In the North in 1850, anywhere from two-thirds to three-quarters of African American men were engaged in menial employment, and under ten percent made their incomes as artisans or entrepreneurs, while the proportions were nearly the reverse in such cities as New Orleans or Charleston. What this meant was that the majority of urban African Americans lived in crushing poverty. The reality of this condition has been eloquently conveyed by one historian:

> Antebellum urban poverty was wholly unlike anything conveyed by the term "below the poverty level" in the last quarter of the twentieth century. . . . [The poor] lived in cramped and congested quarters, frequently rendered more crowded still by the presence of boarders (sometimes whole families) whose minute payments somewhat reduced the burden imposed by even the lowest rents. Their dwellings were stifling in summer and frigid in winter, when the cost of firewood became an intolerable additional expense. They had inadequate or no access to sanitary facilities. Their food was inferior in both quantity and quality and the facilities for its preparation and preservation were usually unsatisfactory at best. Their clothing rarely offered sufficient protection against the elements. . . . They had almost no financial resources, and a serious illness, an accident, or the loss of one or two weeks of employment by the principal breadwinner could well mean eviction, starvation, and utter destitution. This group lived on the knife-edge of existence, and doubtless included most blacks in every city.[11]

While African Americans were hardly alone in occupying such status, they were vastly more likely to do so than the average white American.

Beyond the difficulties that such actual economic conditions caused, however, was the social attitude that multiplied the weight of poverty. In the first half of the nineteenth century, a distinction was drawn between the poor who were deserving of assistance and those who were not. Widows, orphans, and the aged or infirm were understood to be dependent on society for support through no fault of their own. As for the rest, they were understood to be poor because of their own moral defects: laziness, drunkenness, or a lack of character. In other words, it was their own fault.[12] Poverty, then, was another sign of moral and intellectual inferiority in the eyes of those who were not poor, and since most African Americans were poor, the condition simply amplified the prejudice to which they were already subjected. The fact that the same society that was restricting their economic opportunities was also blaming them for their poverty and ascribing it to their faulty characters was an irony seldom lost on black New Yorkers.

During the second quarter of the century, however, there were also growing middle and upper classes within the African American populations of these cities. Some artisans, entrepreneurs, and professionals had created secure and even wealth-producing businesses. Ray, Scott, and White were all examples of such successes. Educational and cultural institutions had been created, modeled on and paralleling such institutions in white society. Victorian values and assumptions about human progress were permeating African American culture as well as American culture as a whole. In New York City, schools, newspapers, political and abolitionist organizations, mutual societies for death and unemployment benefits, and clubs of learned men reading papers to one another were all flourishing black institutions. And in all of the Northern cities, the religious life of black communities was growing, creating churches that served as sources of inspiration and support for the people and the political, social, and religious causes of those communities.

The first three decades of the nineteenth century saw a number of black congregations form separate churches and even denominations in the urban North. In New York City, the Abyssinian Baptist Church was founded in 1808, the African Free Meeting Methodist Society was incorporated in 1812, and the First Colored Presbyterian Church (later renamed Shiloh Presbyterian) began services in 1822. In addition, the African Methodist Episcopal Church became an independent denomination in Philadelphia in 1816 and founded a New York City congregation in 1820. A second independent denomination, the African Methodist Episcopal Zion Church, developed at the church of the same name that was founded in 1797 as the first black Methodist congregation in lower Manhattan. It existed in an odd relationship with the Methodist hierarchy until finally incorporating as a separate denomination in 1820.[13] All of these churches shared, to varying degrees, the paradoxical ten-

sions between African American autonomy and racial interaction and negotiation that marked the history of St. Philip's. All of them, however, achieved
some accommodation with their denominational structures (or created their
own) long before the Episcopal parish.

As indications of the religious commitment of the city's black population,
these churches paint an active picture. By the 1850s, St. Philip's was claiming
a membership of around 700, while Zion Church had grown to 2,000. Bethel
Church (AME) had dropped to only some forty congregants from over 400
in the 1830s, but Shiloh Presbyterian had over 450 members and Abyssinian Baptist and Zion Baptist (a newer congregation) were about the same
size. These numbers point to thriving institutions. Yet they were thriving as
separate institutions, defining themselves by their racial identity even as their
members were decrying the use of that identity, by the white society that surrounded them, for restrictive purposes. It was a dilemma that was constantly
debated in the churches and in the black community.

Urban life for African Americans, then, was fraught with legal, social, and
economic obstacles, with paradoxes of racial autonomy and interdependence,
and with dilemmas of separation and assimilation. These were the circumstances at the beginning of the nineteenth century when St. Philip's took its
first tentative steps toward existence. These were still the circumstances, much
changed and yet much the same, more than forty years later, when Peter Ray,
Henry Scott, and Philip White walked into St. John's Chapel as full members
of the diocesan convention of an otherwise white denomination. It is difficult
to convey both the enormity of the parish's accomplishment and simultaneously how limited that accomplishment was. It was enormous because this
band of African Americans had negotiated its own identity and acceptance
by a white hierarchy with minimal interest in granting them either, and they
had done so by wielding nothing more powerful than religious faith and
theological conviction. It had limited effects beyond the confines of the parish, however: the earth did not move, society at large did not shudder and
change, and their fellow Episcopalians felt little need to treat them as any less
isolated or separate than before.

The triumph of St. Philip's story, then, lies not in bringing about any
great societal or even denominational changes. The triumph lies in the fact
of their presence. St. Philip's created its own religious identity, and forced
a rigid and racist hierarchy to accept that identity. Even in their segregation they remained a presence in the diocese, for all the years that it took
to get that presence recognized by the diocese. They believed themselves to

be Episcopalians, and they refused to take anyone's word otherwise. Most of their fellow Episcopalians did not consider them proper associates, and would never change that opinion—but they were going to have to associate with them nonetheless.

CHAPTER 2

Freedom's Defects

Preaching on Independence Day in 1830, Peter Williams announced, "Alas! the freedom to which we have attained is defective."[1] He was speaking in general, regarding the conditions of African Americans in the nation and especially in his own city on this third anniversary of the abolition of slavery in New York State. Those who were now "free" found themselves in a quagmire of constraints and restrictions, caught in the tension between areas of personal autonomy and exclusion from full participation in the society in which they lived. But Williams could just as easily have been speaking personally, for his life at this point was representative of both the promises of what came to be known as the "American dream" and the obstacles to that dream that came from being black. Born in slavery, he had raised himself up through education and religious faith to a position of significant power and importance in the city's black community. He had been the spiritual leader of St. Philip's since its inception, and achieved the title of rector on his ordination to the priesthood seventeen years later. Yet his isolation from his denomination and his fellow clergy was a lifelong source of disappointment and shame, and gave him a strong sense of the defective nature of the freedom of black New Yorkers.

Williams could have been speaking of his family history as well, for that too was a story of the struggle for both control over one's religious practice and inclusion of that practice within an established institution. Williams's father, Peter Williams Sr., was intimately involved with the creation of the church that eventually anchored a denomination, the African Methodist Episcopal Zion Church. But while Williams Sr. was one of the original organizers of the independent black Methodist congregation, he was not willing to go as far down the road to autonomy as the others.

Peter Williams Sr. was born a slave in New York City in 1749 or 1750, one of ten children of George and Diana Williams, who had been brought from Africa and were owned by a family named Boorite.[2] The children were all sold and scattered, with Williams ending up owned by a tobacconist in the city named James Aymar. Sometime in the 1770s, Williams was converted to Methodism and began attending the Wesley Chapel, the first incarnation of what was to become the John Street Methodist Church. The chapel had a number of African Americans who attended services, sitting in the gallery. It was there that Peter met Mary Durham (known as Molly), a slave from the West Indies who was two years older than he, and married her. Williams Jr., Peter and Molly's only natural child, was born in 1786.[3] A number of years later, they adopted a year-old girl, Mary, but that was the extent of the family.

During the Revolutionary War, Aymar's sympathies lay with the British, so he removed himself and his effects to Brunswick, New Jersey, a less confrontational setting. He returned to Manhattan by the end of the war, but gave up the new nation in 1783 to return to England. Williams went to the trustees of what had by then become the John Street Church and proposed that they purchase his freedom from Aymar for £40, and then allow him to repay them. The trustees agreed, and arrangements were made, including personal loans from congregants. The family was given the basement of the church's parsonage, and Molly worked upstairs as cook and maid. Williams was hired to be the sexton (in charge of buildings and maintenance) and undertaker, and he paid off the loans over the next two years. His freedom was achieved on Evacuation Day, November 25, 1783, when the British officially left New York City at the conclusion of the war. The younger Williams said that the day "always gave a double joy to [my father's] heart, by freeing him from domestic bondage and his native city from foreign enemies." Oddly, Williams did not receive his emancipation papers until thirteen years later; apparently the trustees at the church "thought it was sufficiently understood that he was his own free man."[4]

Williams continued as sexton for many more years, but by the middle of the next decade he was also established as a tobacconist on William Street, apparently having learned a few things from his former owner. His business moved to Liberty Street shortly thereafter, and Williams was described a century later as "proprietor of the largest tobacco manufactory then in the city of New York, and . . . the first to introduce steam power to drive its machinery." He was unable to read or write, however, so his son Peter kept the books for the business. A portrait, painted around 1810 by an unknown artist, shows a formally dressed man with a full head of dark, curly hair and strikingly piercing eyes. It must be acknowledged, however, that he wore a wig for the portrait, as "his hair had come out, and the top of his head was as smooth as a glass bottle."[5]

While achieving this impressive business success, the religious life of Williams Sr. was going through exciting times.[6] In late 1795 and again in the summer of 1796, he was among a group of black men at John Street Church who petitioned the nation's first Methodist bishop, Francis Asbury, for permission to hold separate meetings for John Street's black members while remaining under the auspices of that church. James Varick was the primary leader, and Williams was part of the inner circle. They were unhappy at their treatment by the white leaders of both the church and the denomination, particularly over the fact that some of their number had been licensed as preachers but then were not permitted to preach, even to the black members. They asserted to Asbury, however, that they were completely satisfied with the polity and liturgy of the Methodist Episcopal Church, as the denomination was then known. Thus the movement was initially designed only to create an independent black congregation.

Permission to meet separately was granted in October of 1796, and the congregation began gathering first in a cabinet shop owned by one of their number, William Miller, and then in a rented house. Asbury ordained three of the members, Varick, Abraham Thompson, and June Scott, to serve as ministers, and by the next year the group had built their own house of worship, Zion Church. The next few years saw a great deal of confusion and dispute, however, as the congregation tried to decide how best to take control of their own affairs and establish their denominational identity. From the very beginning, many of the leaders were bent on creating their own denomination to ensure their independence from white meddling. Others saw the future differently.

The ensuing developments demonstrate that no clear path lay before the Zion Church members to retain control over their own affairs. Asbury placed the congregation under the oversight of one John McClaskey, a white preacher whose tenure with the black members of a congregation in Philadelphia was already notorious in New York City. Dissension quickly arose among the congregation's leaders as to whether they should continue as Methodists under McClaskey or move toward forming their own denomination. In February of 1801, Peter Williams Sr. and Francis Jacobs, at McClaskey's urging, incorporated the church as "the African Methodist Episcopal Church in New York City." There was no intention of connecting with Richard Allen's fledgling movement in Philadelphia, though, for it is clear from the Articles of Agreement to which Williams, Jacobs, and two others acquiesced, and which were drawn up by McClaskey, that the incorporation was as a church under Methodist jurisdiction. A meeting of Zion's trustees in April, however, repudiated the Articles of Agreement and the power that they granted to white Methodist leaders to make decisions for the church. Those who had signed them, including Williams, were voted off the board. Zion Church managed to exist in a largely independent state, though technically still Methodist, for nineteen more years, until Varick and his members gave up completely and incorporated in 1820 as the African Methodist Episcopal Zion Church, an independent denomination.

Williams had returned to John Street Church along with those who did not see a black denomination as the most useful direction to go long before the movement actually came to fruition. Perhaps he felt a particular allegiance to the church that had enabled him to obtain his freedom, or perhaps he found it hard to imagine that African Americans, many of them still slaves or barely removed from slavery, could possibly create an independent denomination that would last.[7] It is easy to forget that America was not yet renowned for religious pluralism at the beginning of the nineteenth century, and the idea of leaving a denomination to create a new one was understood at the time to be the sin of schism. The Methodist Episcopal Church itself was so named because its separation from the Church of England, and from the Episcopal Church in the United States, was still not perfectly defined or even agreed to by all Methodists.

It is also possible that Peter Williams Sr. felt that the strongest course of action for the improvement of the religious life of African Americans was to remain in a white denomination and try to change it from within. After all, he and his cohorts had been able to negotiate with a white bishop over these issues; this indicated that the racial divide within the denomination was not impervious. Indeed, Williams and his wife regularly entertained in their home white ministers and their wives who were visiting the John Street Church. According to the widow of one such guest, "the table, spread with taste, [was] bountifully covered with specimens of . . . Molly's culinary art in viands and confectionary."[8] Such interracial intimacies were extraordinarily rare and would only have encouraged Williams in thinking that the Christian faith might provide room for change in its white-led institutions. He would not have been alone in this feeling; in the long run, black denominations did not supply the major black religious leaders of the nineteenth century in New York City. Henry Highland Garnet, Theodore Wright, Samuel Cornish, J. W. C. Pennington: these were the best-known black churchmen, and they were all members of predominantly white denominations. A pattern emerges, then, from Peter Williams Sr. to Peter Williams Jr. and through him to the congregants of St. Philip's: the future of race relations in America, these men felt, lay in first forming an autonomous African American body while remaining within an existing white-run institution, and then seeking to negotiate for full acceptance by that institution. Williams Sr. was not able to persuade his fellow Methodists of this wisdom, however, so he returned to the John Street Church. He died in 1823; his wife had died two years earlier.

None of this explains how Peter Williams Jr. ended up in an Episcopal church, rather than staying with his father at John Street. Apparently a Rev. Thomas Lyell was briefly assisting at John Street Methodist, but then decided to move to the Episcopal denomination.[9] Somewhere around 1803, he became rector of Christ Episcopal Church, founded ten years earlier by a group of white parishioners that had left Trinity Church, Wall Street. Still a teenager, Williams had been impressed with Lyell, and followed him to Christ Church. Lyell took Williams under his wing and provided religious instruction. Whence this adolescent independence on Williams's part it is impossible to say. Nor is it clear when or why he then transferred his allegiance to Trinity Church, the first and grandest of the city's Episcopal parishes; yet by the end of the decade, with Lyell still at Christ Church, Williams had become part of the black congregation meeting at Trinity.

However he arrived at Trinity, Williams found himself at a most opportune spot. The church had been one of the earliest to actively proselytize to the city's slave population. By the time Williams joined them, there were perhaps two hundred African Americans, both slave and free, attending services in a small chapel on Sunday afternoons and being taught the fundamentals of the Episcopal faith by an assistant minister of the parish. It was a separate congregation, and it was outgrowing what Trinity was willing to make available to it.

The legendary Elias Neau had launched this distinct congregation in 1704 under the auspices of the Society for the Propagation of the Gospel in Foreign Parts (SPG), the newly created missionary arm of the Church of England, which was designed to bring the Anglican faith to the colonies' slaves and Native Americans. Neau was an unlikely person for the post, having arrived in New York in 1691 as a French Reformed Protestant (a Huguenot) fleeing the enforcement of the Roman Catholic faith in his native land. He was not, therefore, an Anglican (though he had been granted British citizenship by this time) nor was he ordained. Yet the SPG forced his appointment on Trinity's rector, the Rev. William Vesey, overcoming one objection by requiring Neau to join the Church of England. The SPG also agreed to pay his salary.[10]

Neau's zeal for the post was born of his experience of religious persecution and exacerbated by terrible misfortune. Serving on a merchant ship shortly after coming to New York, he was captured by French privateers, who then botched the ransom payment and instead returned him to France. He refused to renounce his Protestant beliefs, and as a result spent a harrowing year as a galley slave and four more years in prison. Returning to this country through British intercession, he was convinced that the faith in God that had sustained him through these awful events was now compelling him to bring that faith to others who were enslaved. His eloquence in describing this compunction won Neau the SPG appointment as "catechist," or religious instructor.

Neau was not immediately successful, as he had to overcome slaveowners' concerns that making Christians of slaves might be construed as making them legally free. Neau and Vesey set this obstacle aside by persuading the British governor to obtain an act confirming the status of slaves as such after baptism. Other forms of official support brought more and more African Americans into his small flock, and by 1720, despite setbacks including a violent public backlash after the slave uprising of 1712, there were almost eighty students coming to him for religious instruction. When Neau died in 1722, his work was continued by a series of assistant ministers at Trinity Church. Unlike Neau, most of his successors were priests; like him, however, their salaries continued to be paid by the SPG.

This early missionary work of Elias Neau had two significant and opposing long-term implications for American attitudes about race. On the positive side, the proselytizing, educating, and baptizing of black Americans stated clearly that they were believed to possess an eternal soul in need of salvation. The Christian faith, at least in the form of the Church of England, could be seen then as affirming the basic humanity of the Negro race in the face of popular white (especially slaveowner) sentiment that Africans and their descendants were less than human and that their enslavement therefore was not morally or theologically wrong. Unfortunately, Neau's zeal for converts led him also to affirm that baptizing a person did not alter that person's social or civil status, and so did not confer any obligation, legal or religious, for that person to be freed. As the Bishop of London put it at the time, "Christianity . . . continues persons just in the same state as it found them. . . . So far is Christianity from discharging men from the duties of the station and condition in which it found them, that it lays them under stronger obligations to perform those duties with the greatest diligence and fidelity."[11] In other words, a Christian slave should be a better slave. One was freed in baptism from the bondage of sin and death, but not from the bondage of property law.

Thus it was denied that the Christian faith took any actual stand on the issue of slavery. (It would, soon enough, be asserted to be firmly in support of both sides of the issue by more than enough learned and pious folk.) In fact, the roots of its use as a means of keeping slaves in their place are clearly visible here. Of greatest relevance to the story of St. Philip's Church, however, was that the issue of slavery and thereby of race was made for the sake of convenience a civil and social question, divorced from the spiritual state of the people involved. Neau was not alone in bringing about either of these perspectives, of course, but his work helped to codify them in New York and in the Church of England in the colonies, which would become the Episcopal Church after the American Revolution.

The ramifications of these contradictory perspectives would be played out in a variety of ways in American religion and politics for another century and a half, but the immediate effect was to entrench a theological oddity: an entire race was accepted as needing Christianity, but their status in the faith was to be one of inequality. Though this appeared untenable to many even then, for the majority of Americans the seeming paradox was resolved by the long-held belief that God himself had ordained human society to be hierarchical, with some kinds on top and others below. The desire to spread the faith to all did not obligate one to associate with all who happened to be faithful.

In practical terms, the manifestation of this approach was the segregation of black Christians—whether slave or free—into separate bodies, first within the churches and then within the denominations of which they were members. The corollary of this segregation, however, was the need for negotiation among black and white members of those churches and denominations. For white leaders, that negotiation was made necessary by the desire to regulate and control the religious life of all members and to maintain the social boundaries they felt were proper and divinely ordained. But those negotiations became ever more constant and those boundaries ever more slippery, as African American Christians worked to establish their presence and autonomy within existing institutional structures. Such efforts may have encountered obstacles of prejudice and resistance, but the encounters themselves were manifestations of how religious practice brought racial interaction.

Peter Williams Sr. had encountered segregation at John Street Methodist, and had attempted, however briefly, to create in response a separate church that could determine its own affairs rather than be controlled by those who felt themselves placed over others by God. Though he relinquished those efforts when he saw how they developed, his son would soon find himself pursuing a similar course. Peter Williams Jr. would also chafe at segregation by his denomination, and he too would be part of a black congregation that would find no clear and simple path to religious self-determination. The freedom that had been earned by the father and given to the son was not all it was cracked up to be.

CHAPTER 3

Hobart and the High Church

The Episcopal Church that Williams and his compatriots were to press for acceptance was in an awkward period at the beginning of the nineteenth century, an awkwardness destined to lead to a bifurcation from which it has not yet—and may never—recover. The advent of "High Church" and "Low Church" as designations of theological, ecclesiastical, liturgical, and ultimately even sociopolitical positions during this period was to both hinder and help the nascent congregation throughout its early history. Two factors contributed most immediately to the developing awkwardness: the American Revolution, which forced the denomination to re-create itself; and what is known as the Second Great Awakening, a Protestant fervor that swept the United States at the beginning of the nineteenth century and lies behind much of today's "evangelical" Christianity.

Prior to the Revolutionary War, the Church of England was a significant force in the colonies, as it was still the national church of the mother country. It was a hierarchical church, governed by bishops, the archbishop of Canterbury, Parliament, and finally the Crown. To be ordained as a deacon or priest was to swear allegiance to this chain of authority. This occasioned some difficulty during the Revolution, as clergy were forced to choose between their ordination vows and their fealty to the Book of Common Prayer, which mandated prayers for the monarch as head of the church, and their fellow citizens' repudiation of that political authority. Many clergy and lay members fled to Canada or England, while many others reconciled themselves to the dilemma and served nobly in the revolutionary cause.[1]

Following the Revolution, then, the remaining Anglican clergy and laity found themselves cut off from their chain of leadership. They could no longer acknowledge the Crown as the head of the church, and they had no bishops, for the English bishops had never consented to consecrate anyone to serve the colonies. There were administrative difficulties from the very beginning, for it was impossible to say who was in charge of these "Anglicans." But there was a more significant theological issue, for the very legitimacy of the denomination rested on its understanding of the office of bishop. The doctrine of apostolic succession had undergirded the Church of England's claim to validity as a Christian church when it separated from Rome under Henry VIII, and the new Americans needed it to serve the same purpose for them.

This doctrine asserts that the human representatives of the church, the bishops, can trace their lineage—their consecration by the laying-on of hands upon them by other bishops who had been so consecrated themselves—in an unbroken chain back to Jesus's apostles. In other words, the belief is that the apostles passed on their leadership in the teachings and practices of Jesus to their successors by laying hands upon them, who did the same to the generation first designated "bishop" (in Greek, *episkopos*, or overseer), who have continued the ritual (with at least three bishops present) in each succeeding generation. The English bishops who broke from Rome during the English Reformation had already been properly consecrated in this sequence, so those they consecrated were (they argued) still in order. It would be impossible, of course, to document the unbrokenness and liturgical propriety of this history, but theologically it serves to establish an absolute link to the authority of Christ himself.[2]

Without such bishops the Americans were in trouble, and obtaining them became the first post-Revolution order of business. A group of New England clergy chose to send Samuel Seabury of Connecticut to England to request consecration in 1783, but he was unsurprisingly rebuffed. He made his way to Scotland the following year, where there were a group of bishops who felt themselves sufficiently independent of the monarch that they consented.[3] Seabury returned triumphantly to the United States as its first bishop, and rather pompously began styling himself "Bishop of All America." Meanwhile, clergy from the middle states had selected William White, Rector of the United Parish of Philadelphia, and Samuel Provoost, Rector of Trinity Church, Wall Street, and sent them to England as well, where they bided their time. In 1786, Parliament passed legislation providing for the consecration of bishops for the American church, and White and Provoost were duly made bishops the next year. With three American bishops, more could now be consecrated on home soil; Thomas Claggett of Maryland was the first to receive that honor, in 1792.

A problem remained, however: to whom were these new bishops beholden, if not the archbishop of Canterbury, Parliament, and the king? Independent local structures were not consonant with the Anglican perspective on ecclesiology held by these clergy, but the lordliness of the former episcopal hierarchy was not quite in the democratic spirit of the new nation. A new structure was required, one that would constitute a new denomination. Here White, more than any other, helped to broker the theological and political deals that brought resolution in a series of meetings culminating in 1789. A "General Convention" was formed to meet every three years to enact legislation governing all aspects of the denomination. It was deliberately modeled on the new nation's bicameral Congress: a House of Bishops, for all so consecrated, and a House of Deputies, composed of clergy and lay representatives elected from each diocese. The office of "Presiding Bishop" was created not as the ultimate authority but, as the name implied, as one who presided over the implementation of the decisions of the General Conventions and over the House of Bishops itself. Bishops were to be elected; the office of Presiding Bishop was to be assigned to the senior bishop. A revised *Book of Common Prayer* was put together with no references to royalty. And the Protestant Episcopal Church in the United States of America was thus brought into being.

But while the denomination called itself "Protestant," it actually saw itself still as the American embodiment of the Anglican church, which was positioned rather neatly if tenuously between Roman Catholicism and true Protestantism. It was Richard Hooker in the sixteenth century who had articulated the "tripod" approach of Anglican authority: questions of doctrine and practice were to be judged by the standards of "scripture, tradition, and reason": that is, the Bible, the best that the history of Christianity had to offer, and the individual mind judging and interpreting the other two.[4] Roman Catholicism, in this view, was dominated by tradition, by the accretion of councils and theologians and papal pronouncements into doctrine; Protestantism, particularly in America, was dominated by the cry of "*sola scriptura*"—the Bible alone. The new denomination's efforts to find the "middle way" between these influential poles were made particularly tentative by the democratic impulses in religion that greeted the new nation.

The religious life of the new nation in the new century was marked by a combination of camp meetings, revivals, and religious practices that focused on one's individual relationship with God, and came to be known as the Second Great Awakening. A huge, week-long frontier camp meeting at Cane Ridge, Kentucky, in 1801 and the revivals at Yale College led by Timothy Dwight that same year are generally seen as the events that launched this organic, polymorphous set of movements that swept the country in the ensuing decades. They marked a return to the emphases of the first Great Awakening of the previous century, derived from the Calvinist tradition as transformed by Jonathan Edwards, epitomized by the process of "conversion": a focus on a conviction of sin, the need for redemption, and the necessity of a personal experience of God's grace to be accepted as fully Christian. Consciously coinciding with the revolutionary spirit, the movements were characterized by a search for a greater intensity of religious experience, a democratic, anti-authoritarian impulse, and a rejection of "formalist" (meaning traditionally liturgical) religious practices as lacking in true spiritual substance.

By the 1820s, Charles Finney had emerged from western New York as the country's most famous revivalist, largely because of his ability to consistently achieve the desired result of mass conversions. This was accomplished, he asserted, not because of any special spiritual gifts on his part, but because he had brought a rational systematization, which he termed "new measures," to the conduct of revivals. Informally, these included a plainness and bluntness of speech in sermons, the rejection of didactic theological debates, and a willingness to call out sinners by name from the pulpit. More formally, four tactics were established for conducting a revival that would succeed in achieving mass conversions: protracted meetings, the "anxious bench," inquirers' meetings, and separate prayer meetings.[5]

Protracted meetings were efforts to plan and schedule what had begun to occur spontaneously at the beginning of the century, most famously at Cane Ridge: a revival meeting planned for one day had stretched to six or seven, ending only when provisions of food proved insufficient for the throngs that had attended. Finney thus argued that revival sessions should last three to seven days, with lengthy preaching services in the morning, afternoon, and evening of each day, in order to build and sustain a feverish spiritual pitch. During these services, the "anxious bench" was a pew or two placed directly before the pulpit, perpendicular to the rest of the pews, to which those actively seeking conversion could be called, so that preaching and prayers might be addressed specifically to them. The inquirers' meetings were supplementary gatherings to follow up on those who had not yet been brought to conversion by the preaching; their primary purpose was to bring about in invited individuals a conviction of sinfulness and a conversion to God's grace. The prayer meetings were other additional sessions, held before and during the protracted meeting, in which the congregation was gathered briefly to hear appropriate Biblical readings and a short exhortation from the minister, and most importantly, to offer prayers for the success of the revival.

The enormous success of the "new measures"—both before and after their systematization—led to a set of related liturgical emphases in nearly all churches now calling themselves "evangelical."[6] These included the rejection of formal and ancient liturgies, of anything that smacked of medievalism and Romanism, and of the spiritual authority of the minister beyond his own converted nature and his ability to call others to conversion; a focus on extemporaneous prayers from the ministers during the regular services; an attraction to midweek prayer services; and preaching that focused on the theology of the Atonement, the doctrine of Christ's sacrificial death for the sins of humanity. But while there was a strong evangelical movement within the Episcopal Church from the very beginning, it is easy to see how such emphases conflicted with that denomination's self-understanding.[7] Episcopalians treasured their formal, ancient liturgies as ordered by the prayer book, and thereby discouraged spontaneous prayer; they expected their clergy to be educated and to preach accordingly; and they tied themselves to one another and to Christianity as a whole through their bishops, who oversaw all local activities. Evangelical Episcopalians—bishops, clergy, and laity alike—were nonetheless attracted to the fervent spirituality they saw around them, and tried to reconcile their denomination's structures to the "new measures."

The new denomination, having just resurrected itself after being disconnected from its past and traditional self-conception, thus found itself in a culture celebrating the independence and individual orientation of revivalism, and had to define itself once again. Evangelical Episcopalians were happy to work out accommodations, emphasizing preaching, experimenting with adding spontaneous prayers to the services, and downplaying the liturgical and hierarchical structures, but those of a more traditionally Anglican bent were not impressed with the evangelical leanings. They were proud of the capital-P "Protestant" definition of the denomination, but less interested in these lower-case-p "protestant" practices and the democratizing forces behind them. It was New York's first great bishop, John Henry Hobart, who saw himself as the defender of the *via media*, the "middle way" that Hooker had found between Romanism and Reformation but that Hobart now desired to locate between medievalism and revivalism. Drawing on the insights of his mentor, Bishop White of Pennsylvania, Hobart quickly became the staunch proponent of what he termed "the High Church theology."[8]

The problem with the evangelical movement, as Hobart saw it, was that both the "new measures" and the Calvinist theology that underlay them had made grace, the experience of God's love and presence, conditional and restricted. In the context of the Second Great Awakening, grace was understood as the overpowering individual experience of the divine that provided assurance that one was part of God's elect, his chosen ones. This grace could only come about authentically through the experience of conversion, thus requiring a conviction of one's own sinfulness and need for personal redemption through the atonement of Jesus Christ. In Hobart's view, this process amounted to earning God's love through a prescribed set of steps, in contradiction to the long-held tenet that grace is unconditional and unmerited, and therefore cannot be earned (few evangelicals, of course, agreed with Hobart's analysis). In contrast to revivalism and its emphasis on conversion, then, Hobart proffered a "higher" view of the Christian church and a broader view of the experience of grace. The church itself was to be understood as the locus of grace, and God's love was not only to be encountered in overpowering individual experiences, but more mundanely and corporately in the worship of a gathering of Christians as a church. In the Eucharist, the service of Holy Communion instituted by Christ at the Last Supper, Hobart argued, any baptized Christian availed himself or herself of God's grace as embodied in the bread and wine. A confession of sinfulness, an affirmation of faith, solid theological exhortation, and prayers of petition and thanksgiving were all intrinsic to the experience of grace in the service, but they were done corporately, and were not requirements that earned God's favor but rather preparations for and responses to the acceptance and love of God manifested in the actions of worship.

Hobart therefore offered a definition of his denomination that gloried in the formal and ancient dimensions of Episcopal worship and the historical continuity of the apostolic succession, elevated the spiritual importance of the Church as a whole over that of individual congregations or gatherings, and fell smoothly into the gap between Rome and Reformation and between medievalists and budding revivalists. He argued in 1816 that "it is, indeed, the singular glory of the Church from which our Church has descended, that she conducted her reformation from papal corruptions with the highest of moderation and wisdom."[9] The Anglican tradition had, in Hobart's eyes, reformed that which needed reforming and kept that which the history of Christianity had of value to pass along, "rejecting equally Papal corruptions and Protestant errors."[10]

Those Episcopalians excited by the evangelical movements found this all a bit precious, of course, and soon enough hardened into the "Low Church" wing of the denomination. The "High" and "Low" designations would come to focus on the practices of worship, especially in the years after Hobart, and the underlying theological tug-of-war over grace would become more diffuse. The split would also come to play a significant political role in the struggle of St. Philip's Church for acceptance. These denominational factions still exist today, with theological and liturgical differences that can be traced quite clearly to the Hobart era and its aftermath. But at this early stage, it is important to note primarily that in contrast to the evangelical denominations that emphasized local authority and therefore easier (in some ways) admission into the ministerial and congregational ranks, Hobart's view of his denomination exacerbated the formality and rigidity of the processes through which both Peter Williams personally and his congregation as a whole would have to toil to achieve acceptance.

But while the High Church theology worked to solidify the formality of the Episcopal Church, it also laid the groundwork for the recognition of an African American congregation. A view of the church as the highest manifestation of God's presence and benevolence and the valorization of its historical continuity were strenuous arguments for the unity of that church's particular bodies. Such a theology also stressed its denominational distinctiveness in relation to those that understood themselves differently. Thus a congregation calling itself Episcopalian, worshiping according to the Book of Common Prayer, and petitioning the bishop it recognized as its own for properly ordained spiritual leadership could not be long ignored—whatever its race—when such a bishop propounded these High Church views.

CHAPTER 4

One of Their Own Colour

The missionary work of Elias Neau and his successors continued at Trinity Church after the American Revolution, despite the loss of SPG backing (it was, after all, an English church institution, no longer interested in the fate of the upstart nation's downtrodden). In September of 1800, John Henry Hobart, then a young deacon, was appointed assistant minister of the church. The work of preparing interested African Americans for baptism and of leading their religious life was part of his charge. And thus began a connection between the future bishop and the future congregation of St. Philip's that would prove both fruitful and complicated.

By the time Hobart arrived at Trinity, the first three American bishops had been consecrated, providing both leadership for three dioceses and the means of replicating that leadership for the rest. Establishing a pattern that would continue for the next fifty years, Samuel Provoost held the two positions of bishop of New York and rector of Trinity Church simultaneously, as the organizers of the newly independent denomination had not provided for the financial support of a bishop. Hobart thus joined a clergy staff that served both a parish and a bishop. Trinity was now more than just the first parish in the city—it was the center of the diocese itself as its de facto cathedral.[1]

Due to the bishop's ill health, the diocese was not overly surprised when Provoost announced his resignation at the diocesan convention of 1801. They were completely taken aback, however, when following his announcement, he simply walked out of the convention, leaving vacant the position of bishop. There were as yet no provisions for the resignation of a bishop, and the question of Provoost's status was perplexing: Episcopal bishops are consecrated for life. Though the convention hastily elected Benjamin Moore to be his successor, it was never clear while Provoost remained alive just who was the final authority in the diocese. Fortunately, Provoost did not press the issue, and Moore was always properly deferential to him. But the question of who was actually the bishop, raised so early in the history of the diocese, would turn out to be a nearly constant problem for a good portion of the next sixty years.

Hobart was twenty-five years old when he began at Trinity, and he already had assisted in two parishes in Philadelphia (where he was born) and headed two parishes in New Jersey. For someone who had been ordained only two years earlier, by Bishop White in Pennsylvania, this was an impressive start. A man of uncommon energy, it was apparent soon after his arrival in New York that he was bishop material himself. Hobart's elevation to the priesthood in 1801 was Provoost's last ordination. Only months later, Hobart was serving under Benjamin Moore, the new rector as well as bishop.

The African American congregation that Neau and his successors had drawn to Trinity had grown to a sufficient size and stability that, fairly soon after Hobart's arrival, the question of its possible separation began to be raised. There is sketchy evidence that sometime around 1805, Trinity Church set aside funds for the purchase of a cemetery for its black congregation, stipulating that the rights to the burial ground would transfer to any new church they might form.[2] It is unclear whether the African Americans were planning their own parish by this time, or whether the white leadership at Trinity was hoping to encourage them to leave. In 1807, the attitude of the parish toward this group was clarified: Hobart designated the black congregation as the African Episcopal Catechetical Institution.[3] In so doing, he formalized the understanding that these African Americans were not members of the parish; rather, they were a distinct mission field.

Once again, the contradictory impulses of separation and engagement that characterized race relations in these beginning years of the nineteenth century were made manifest. On the one hand, the black congregation at Trinity had always been kept separate from the white congregation: the African Americans worshipped on Sunday afternoons, just prior to the white congregation's evening service. The creation of the African Episcopal Catechetical Institute simply made that separation administratively official by identifying the black congregation as recipients of Trinity's support, rather than identifying them as parishioners. On the other hand, the parish's white leadership remained engaged with this congregation through that support—which took the form of paying for white catechists to instruct them in the faith and providing white clergy to lead their worship. These contradictory impulses resulted in the white congregation finding common cause with the black congregation's desire to move toward independence, but they also helped maintain the relationship of financial support for most of the history of the church that was to emerge.

And emerge it shortly did. In 1809, the African Americans left Trinity and began meeting in a room rented from the African Free School No. 1, the first publicly funded school in the city.[4] (The connection between this school and the eventual St. Philip's was long and fortuitous, as many of the parish's leaders were graduates.) Services were led by a vaguely remembered white layperson named John McCombs (or McCoon), who was under the employ of Trinity Church.[5] Since he was not a priest, services of Holy Communion, weddings, and other sacramental rites were not yet available to the congregation. They therefore sent a request, known as a "memorial," to the diocesan convention that fall, attempting to remedy this lack. The minutes of the convention noted this communication: "A memorial was read from the Africans and their descendants, members of the Protestant Episcopal Church in the city of New York, praying the decision of the Convention on the subject of one of their own colour being admitted to Holy Orders."[6]

Thus the as-yet-unnamed congregation made their priority clear: the first thing they wanted was an African American to lead their services, one who was duly ordained by the Episcopal Church. This would mean they could conduct their own services, of all kinds, without being dependent on volunteer white clergy. An ordained leader would also be a significant step on the road to self-sufficiency as a parish. Finally, it meant they would be recognized by the diocese as an Episcopal body.

The convention's interest, however, is indicated just in the journal's wording—which reports the memorial, rather than quoting it—for the focus is on the congregation's African-ness, their separateness. There is a patronizing tone that bespeaks an assumption that this population was still only a subject for mission, not for inclusion in the norms of the diocese. Note, for example, that the congregation is referred to as having membership in the denomination, but not in any actual individual church. The request was immediately referred to the bishop and his Standing Committee, the board of clergy and laymen responsible for advising and assisting the bishop in conducting the business of the diocese. Their charge could easily have been to begin identifying and preparing someone to serve the congregation, for that was an area specifically under the Standing Committee's jurisdiction. However, in a move typical of this hierarchical and bureaucratic denomination, the convention requested only that the bishop and Standing Committee study the issue and report back to convention the following year.[7] Speedy decision making was not to be a hallmark of this parish's progress.

Hobart was one of those elected to the Standing Committee at the same convention. Over the course of the ensuing year, no records exist of that body's deliberations of the issue in question, but the committee submitted the following resolution to the convention of 1810:

> Resolved, That, for the present, it is expedient that the Clergy of the city of New York be directed to officiate, under the superintendence of the Bishop, in such rotation, and at such times, and in such places as he may appoint, for the Africans and their descendants, members of the Protestant Episcopal Church in the city of New York. And that the Bishop be requested to license a person of colour, to act among them as a lay reader and catechist.[8]

The convention accepted the resolution, and the church hierarchy had now spoken: they were not ready to ordain a black man.

Ordination in the Episcopal Church is understood as being set aside by and for God for particular kinds of ministry. Deacons are ordained to work especially with the poor and needy, and to serve in limited roles in leading worship. Priests are ordained for liturgical leadership of all kinds, making them most useful for the running of a parish: they can offer blessings, consecrate the elements for Holy Communion, and pronounce absolution of sins. Bishops are consecrated to lead a diocese, to be pastors to their clergy, and to embody the continuation of the church since its earliest days. Lay readers are not ordained; during this period, they were licensed by a diocese to serve as leaders where no deacon or priest was available (nowadays they are licensed to assist in a greater variety of roles). Lay readers can conduct services of Morning or Evening Prayer, which are full occasions of prayer, proclamation (reading from the Bible), and preaching. But under a lay reader only, a congregation cannot have a full worship life.

The "Africans and their descendants" were having their services conducted by McCombs, with occasional unlicensed assistance from some of their own black members. It was not a satisfactory situation, as far as they were concerned: they needed someone to celebrate communion for them, bless their marriages, and officiate at their funerals. They did not want to remain dependent on a "rotation" of white clergy to meet these needs. Nevertheless, the convention was offering a step forward: no black man had yet been licensed as lay reader. In response to the convention's decision, they nominated four men for the position. Peter Williams Jr. was chosen.[9]

It was a reasonable choice, for at the age of twenty-four his devotion and his education had apparently set him apart. Williams had graduated from the African Free School and, according to the reminiscences of one parishioner, "had mastered Logic and Algebra, read Latin with some facility, was extravagantly fond of Metaphysics, and, what is remarkable, with the slender advantages he enjoyed, he had formed a style in composition so clear, concise and elegant, that few men of twice his years and with every advantage have excelled it."[10] He had his father to thank for his early religious training, and had received more formal instruction under Lyell at Christ Church. For whatever length of time he had been at Trinity prior to the congregation's leaving, he had surely received instruction there as well, under the African Episcopal Catechetical Institution. Williams had also demonstrated his speaking abilities, having delivered a speech at his father's church two years earlier, on the effective date of the abolition of the slave trade. This work was so well received that some white listeners questioned his authorship, claiming that a white man must have written it for him. The speech was subsequently published in pamphlet form with a certificate of his authenticity as its writer attested by three men—one of whom was Bishop Moore—and it has been anthologized in collections ever since.[11] Certainly Williams was qualified for the limited post of lay reader.

For all his accomplishments and skills, Williams was known even in later years as mild and self-effacing. He was a short man with a high forehead, round face, and his father's prominent dark eyes. While the elder Williams's portrait shows a piercing, forthright gaze, an engraving of Williams Jr. reveals a diffident expression. He asserted in later life that if he could have avoided his own sense of duty, he would have "cheerfully retired to earn my living in some humbler occupation."[12] Fortunately for the nascent parish, that sense of duty overcame his self-doubts, and Williams accepted their call as lay reader and, thereby, as their spiritual leader.

Williams took his duties seriously. In addition to leading worship to the extent allowed, he gathered the children for an hour before the service and undertook their religious training in his capacity as catechist. As many of his congregants were illiterate, he also taught them hymns through the old process of "lining out," which meant singing a line at a time, with the congregation repeating it after him.[13] He pressed the parish's desires to the convention of 1813, which reported that "a memorial was presented by Peter Williams (a coloured man), respecting the necessity of the coloured people of the Episcopal Church in this city having the privilege of separating themselves into a distinct congregation, and of having one of their own colour, to officiate among them, in Holy Orders."[14] Williams, by now, must have sensed that it was his own ordination he was urging.

The convention certainly took it that way, even if its response sounds once again like a delaying tactic: "*Resolved,* That he [Williams] have leave to withdraw his memorial, and that it be recommended to him to submit his application to the Right Reverend the Bishop, and the Standing Committee of the Church, agreeably to the course prescribed by the canons."[15] This was not just a way to avoid the question, however, as the process for ordination did begin with an application to the bishop, not to the convention. That it also let the convention off the hook once again was only an added convenience for that body. Williams must have known that this was the proper course as well, as he (or anyone in the congregation) could have found out how the process worked by asking any of the white clergy who were serving the parish on occasion. Perhaps Williams and the congregation simply wished to test the attitude of the convention (and thus the diocese as a whole) before proceeding any further. Unlike the previous effort, when the convention was clearly against the possibility of ordination, here they found the possibility at least tentatively affirmed.

The timing was also more fortuitous for Williams himself. His original mentor, Thomas Lyell, was elected to the Standing Committee at the same convention, so he would have a potential ally there. And Hobart had been elected "assistant bishop" two years earlier, after Bishop Moore had suffered a paralyzing stroke. Though the diocese now had two retired bishops, either of whom (despite their retirement) could be said to still be the diocesan bishop proper, Hobart was for all intents and purposes functioning in that role, so it would be up to him to make the final decision regarding Williams's ordination.

The Standing Committee reported in its minutes two months later (November 1813) that an application from Williams "to be a candidate for holy orders" had been received. The wording of the committee's response is quite odd, for it postponed consideration of the matter until the resolution of "the late annual Convention" regarding the "memorial presented in behalf of the people of colour" had been "laid before the Board."[16] Since the convention had only resolved that Williams withdraw his memorial and apply to the Standing Committee, it is clear that the committee was stalling. A special meeting of the committee three days later again postponed action on the application. The mysterious delay is cleared up in the December meeting's minutes: the committee was waiting for a reply to their letter requesting the advice of William White, bishop of Pennsylvania, "relative to the admission of a coloured man to holy orders."[17]

White had ordained Absalom Jones to the diaconate in 1795, and to the priesthood in 1804, making him the first African American ordained in the

Episcopal Church. This was, for Episcopalians, the most significant event that followed from the separation of the black members from St. George's Methodist Church in Philadelphia (sometime between 1787 and 1792), when some of that group subsequently followed Richard Allen into founding the African Methodist Episcopal Church. The rest of those members (the majority) left the Methodist denomination, abandoned Allen to his new movement, and formed St. Thomas's Episcopal Church, with Jones as their leader. They then succeeded in persuading White to ordain Jones. Now the Standing Committee of the Diocese of New York wanted to find out how he had handled the ordination process.

Part of what they learned from White was that he had imposed a condition on the ordination that would prove to be of the greatest importance to the future of St. Philip's Church: Jones and his congregation were not to seek admission to their diocesan convention. Having agreed to this condition, Jones was duly ordained, and he and his congregation were thus condemned to exist in a state of segregation within their diocese.[18]

The Standing Committee in New York, however, was not convinced to proceed with Williams's ordination by this information. They decided instead, "after due deliberation," that "it is inexpedient at present to recommend Mr. Peter Williams to the Bishop to be received as a Candidate for holy orders." They did want to be sure that his congregation was receiving the "pastoral attention and care which they require," however, so they created a subcommittee to confer with the bishop on this issue.[19] Their concern is less touching than it is patronizing, given the clarity with which they had determined that they were not ready to ordain a black man in their diocese, whatever Bishop White may have done. The presence of Lyell on the committee had made no difference, and Bishop Hobart was not even present for the conversation. The African American congregation, referred to as Episcopalian by the diocese but still not officially a church, was stymied once again. It would be six years before they would make another attempt to establish their religious identity through their spiritual leadership.

CHAPTER 5

An Orderly and Devout Congregation

With the hope for ordination delayed, the congregation turned in the next few years to seeking a stable place of worship. They left the rented room in the African Free School in 1812, moving to a room over a carpenter's shop on Cliff Street, near the East River. One member from those days later recalled that it was "furnished with only such furniture as was absolutely needed, being lighted up by candles fixed in square blocks."[1] Funds to support the life of the parish were in short supply, demonstrated by an application from the congregation to Trinity Church in 1814 for assistance; a grant was issued for $262 to pay the rent. Trinity recorded the grant as given to the African Episcopal Catechetical Institute, for the congregation still had no official name.[2] No name, no permanent home—small wonder that Trinity's leaders, while willing to support the congregation, continued to think of it as a mission field.

In 1817, the congregation moved again, renting another schoolroom on Rose Street, near Pearl Street. Three locations in eight years points to instability of some sort, but it is hard to say what caused it. Was the congregation outgrowing its space? Were there simply logistical issues? At least one building may have been condemned for city improvements. Or did the congregation have a hard time keeping up financially? Despite the grant in 1814, Trinity did not otherwise help out during this period; is this because the congregation did not ask for assistance, or because Trinity was unwilling to bet on its future? No further funds were forthcoming until 1818, when they were provided in order to support the construction of a church.

George Lorillard, yet another tobacconist and member of Trinity, gave the congregation a long-term lease to three lots of land on Collect Street (soon to be renamed Centre Street; it is the heart of today's courthouse district in lower Manhattan) on June 25 of that year. The rent was $270 per year for sixty years, after which period the land was to become the property of the church. The deed was made to a hastily assembled board of trustees (not yet a parish, the congregation had no official vestry) that reveals the congregation's early leadership: John Marander, John Bees, Andrew Rankin, Thomas Zabriskie, John Kent, William Hutson, Samuel Class, George Lawrence, and Lewis Francis.[3] Marander was listed in the city directory that year simply as "laborer," and was living on Warren Street, near the docks on the west side of the city. Bees was a "fruiter," Zabriskie worked at a livery stable, Hutson ran an employment agency (known at the time as an "intelligence agency"), and the rest went unrecorded in the city directories during this period.

Doing most of the labor themselves, the membership laid the cornerstone for a white wooden church building on August 6, 1818. According to a report in *The Christian Journal*, an Episcopal monthly, the church was sixty feet by fifty feet, thirty-six feet high, with galleries on the sides and in the front. There were 144 pews, and a spacious undercroft for meetings and education. The total cost was slightly over $8,000, of which $3,000 came from Trinity and $2,500 from a Trinity vestryman named Jacob Sherred. The rest was raised through donations from members of the congregation and other Episcopalians. Various furnishings were supplied by individual donors, and as the *Journal* report put it, "the females of the congregation have defrayed the principal expense of the hangings for the pulpit and desk, and are about procuring communion plate."[4]

The congregation's finances remain mysterious during this period: one year they were unable to pay their rent without help, but four years later they were able to raise $2,500 to build their own church. What became a constant, however, was the commitment of Trinity Church, whose rector was still John Henry Hobart. Under his supervision, Trinity agreed to a seven-year grant to cover the ground rent.[5] In fact, the grant was for $330 per year, a bit more than the rent itself, and it was eventually extended almost indefinitely. Such support for fledgling congregations was typical for Trinity in the nineteenth century, as most of the city's parishes received funds from this wealthy benefactor at one time or another. Hobart's successor as rector, William Berrian, spoke proudly of this generous legacy in the history he wrote of Trinity, yet his description does not make any mention of the support for St. Philip's. This lacuna is particularly surprising in that the total amount given to St. Philip's, during the rectorships of both Hobart and Berrian, was greater than what was given to most other parishes.

The finishing touches were put on the building around the end of the year, and on July 3, 1819, Hobart consecrated it as St. Philip's Church, "for the use of a Congregation in communion with the Protestant Episcopal Church in the Diocese of New York."[6] It was the tenth Episcopal church in New York City, and by stating that it was "in communion" with the rest of the diocese, Hobart certainly gave no indication that the parish occupied any different status from the others, or that it would be segregated from the diocese for the next thirty-five years. The service was attended, according to the account in the *Christian Journal*, by "most of the Episcopal clergy of the city."[7] In grand style, Hobart declared that he had:

With the prescribed rites and solemnities, separated it from all unhallowed, worldly and common uses, and dedicated it to the service of Almighty God for reading his Holy Word, for celebrating His Holy Sacraments, for offering to His Glorious Majesty the sacrifices of Prayer and Thanksgiving, for blessing the people in His Name and for the performance of all other Holy Offices according to the use of the Protestant Episcopal Church in the United States of America.[8]

The focus on corporate worship in its various forms is wonderfully representative of Hobart's High Church perspective, for which worship was not merely a characteristic activity of the Episcopal Church, it was the entire point. Worship made God manifest and offered his grace to all. It therefore had to be done properly and in a properly consecrated place. Thus Hobart's sermon for the occasion was on "the great importance of public worship, and the manifold blessings which would certainly result to those, who with pure hearts and fervent zeal, approached the most High in his holy temple," according to a report in one of the city's newspapers. His text was from Psalm 122: "I was glad when they said unto me, Let us go into the house of the Lord."[9]

The *Journal* report offered another perspective on the reason for the existence of the new church, and for its support by the white leadership: "This Church . . . has been erected . . . for the use of the coloured members of the different churches and chapels in the city, who had become too numerous for the accommodations assigned them."[10] The presence of so many clergy, and the wide publicity given to the service, would appear to have been caused not by excitement over a new black parish, but by the excitement of knowing that black Episcopalians had a place to go that was not any of those other clergy's parishes.

That October, Hobart proudly reported the consecration to the diocesan convention, and noted that he had since returned to the church to lead worship. He described the congregation as "remarkably orderly and devout in the performance of the service."[11] This accolade is freighted with the same High Church focus, revealing through the praise of proper worship the fear of "improper" worship tainted by the spontaneity and emotionality of evangelical practices. The "order" of worship was written for Episcopalians in their prayer book, but Low Church adherents were experimenting with ways of moving outside that order. Hobart was reassured that St. Philip's had no such tendencies.

There is also a degree of racial prejudice expressed here, since emphasizing the congregation's orderliness to a convention of white men betrays the opposite expectation. Many denominations were battling over the "excesses," as they were termed by opponents, of revivalism, but there were particular complaints about the demonstrative nature and even physical distress of black evangelical worship. In one incident from around this time in Philadelphia, a black church was destroyed by a white mob from the neighborhood claiming to be angry about the noise and commotion of its services.[12] Yet beyond such specifics, there has remained in history and in many historical perspectives an assumption that black Americans have always been, or ought to have been, more attracted to a spontaneous worship style than a formal one. It is certainly true that many more African Americans joined evangelical denominations than liturgically centered ones, both in the nineteenth century and in the present, but that was also the case for white Americans during this period. And it is also true that Booker T. Washington is credited with the aphorism that "if a black man is anything but a Baptist or a Methodist, someone has been tampering with his religion." Nonetheless, one historian has quite reasonably argued that "the repeated thesis that the emotional make-up of the black psyche makes the Baptist and Methodist worship more appealing than the more restrained and habitual order of worship of the Episcopal Church ... carries the onerous undertone of racism."[13] Hobart, who would almost annually remind the convention of the congregation's "orderliness" in worship, was surely conflating his High Church perspective with the racial assumptions of his time.

Within those standard prejudices, however, Hobart was St. Philip's most active supporter. Just a few months prior to consecrating the new church, he had met with his Standing Committee to discuss ordaining "a coloured man." This time around the bishop took the lead. The conversation was kept on a hypothetical level, with the bishop asking the committee not to approve a specific candidate, but to advise him on the question of policy regarding such an ordination. Williams's name was never mentioned. The committee agreed that "under present circumstances," it was time to proceed. Those "circumstances" centered on the fact that the bishop himself was pushing for approval, but they were accompanied by the setting of certain conditions. As they had learned from William White and his dealings with Absalom Jones, the committee put in writing that a black man could be ordained only if "it . . . be distinctly understood, that neither the person so admitted as a Candidate for Holy Orders . . . be entitled to a seat in the Convention, nor the congregation of which he may have the charge to a representation therein." In addition, they demanded that the hypothetical church of this hypothetical candidate commit to hiring him once he was ordained.[14] The last thing they wanted was a black clergyman wandering around with no connection to a specific black parish, and therefore dependent on the diocese to provide him with employment at a white church.

Hobart continued to play his cards close to his chest. Following this discussion, the committee went on to consider and approve two candidates for ordination—neither of whom was Williams, and both of whom were white. Instead, his application came up with another gentleman's at the following month's meeting, in April: "Testimonials were submitted in behalf of Sands Niles Crumb and Peter Williams Junior, applying to be admitted Candidates for Holy Orders, which being deemed satisfactory and canonical, they were accordingly recommended to the bishop."[15] Williams had cleared his first hurdle, and the bland rhetoric of the minutes of the Standing Committee made it sound as if it had been a simple and straightforward event.

Thirty years later, with Williams dead and gone, his congregation would argue that he had never agreed to any conditions for ordination, and that he had simply avoided the inevitable controversy over attending the diocesan conventions because of his natural reticence. Certainly there is no actual record of the conditions imposed by the Standing Committee ever being officially communicated to Williams, nor is there any written record of his accepting them. Hobart had asked the committee to advise him on policy, and they had done so; a month later he asked them to approve a candidate and they did so. There is no connection made between these two events in the minutes of the committee. The congregation's argument that the conditions were never imposed or accepted is therefore plausible—but highly unlikely. It is most probable that Hobart communicated the conditions to Williams in a less official fashion and with no official record. The only evidence for this assumption is negative: Williams never did attend convention, nor did the parish leadership ever attempt to be admitted to convention during his lifetime.

Williams and Hobart had clearly reached some sort of understanding about the entire ordination process. Some months later, when reporting to the convention about the church's consecration, Hobart acknowledged that services there "are conducted by Peter Williams, jun., a coloured man, who, for some years, under my direction, has acted as a Lay Reader and Catechist among them."[16] Williams was in fact studying with his bishop, which was standard procedure for this period, as the denomination did not yet have a full-fledged seminary of its own, and Hobart had obviously decided that both candidate and bishop were ready to take the process on.[17] Yet he did not mention Williams's candidacy in his report to the convention (as he often did regarding other candidates), instead assuring the presumably nervous delegates that "every measure relative to provision for accommodating the coloured people with public worship and religious instruction has been pursued, and will continue to be pursued, with great caution and deliberation."[18] Such "deliberation" meant the actual ordination would not take place for another eighteen months, presumably so that Williams could finish studying and the bishop could finish gathering the support he would need to take such a step.

Hobart was one of the first bishops to be truly active in administering and expanding his diocese. He was renowned for traveling widely in the western reaches of the state to raise up and encourage new congregations. This was consonant with the High Church goal of bringing proper public worship to all, and he extolled these achievements on that ground in his annual reports to convention. Hence his excitement that year about what was happening at St. Philip's: "The prospect that a numerous class of people belonging to our Church, who have not hitherto enjoyed in their full extent the advantages of public worship and religious instruction, will be furnished with them under the most advantageous circumstances, must give pleasure to every pious and benevolent mind."[19] He manages here to describe St. Philip's as if it were a mission church in some isolated frontier town. But Hobart's theological program was still relatively new and controversial, and he did not want to push it too far, particularly when it involved a black congregation and a black candidate for ordination. His "great caution and deliberation" is, therefore, not hard to understand.

Beside the theology always lurked the racial issue. Hobart never referred to the congregation—or to Williams—without noting that they were "coloured," and the annual diocesan convention journals did the same.[20] His remark about a "class of people" is neatly objectifying, turning a specific group of African Americans into a more palatable abstract concept. Whether this was more palatable only to his audience—as when he turned Williams into a hypothetical case for the Standing Committee—or to himself as well is hard to say.

The same convention journal of 1819 contained a letter from Williams to Hobart reporting on the activities of the newly consecrated church. From this first official communication, Williams established an explanatory tone: "Our morning congregations are but thin, owing to the peculiar circumstances of many of our people, but the afternoon and evening congregations are quite numerous." The reference to "peculiar circumstances" remains historically enigmatic—is this about some aspect of their working lives?—but clarifies how one should judge the robustness of the parish's life. He was also always eager to justify his congregation's validity in the eyes of the denomination, which was most easily done by allusion to its worship: "I have been anxious to have our worship conducted in the best order, and in strict conformity to the instructions of the Church; and have succeeded in good degree."[21] It is slightly ironic to see a reference to "order" in Williams's writing, but conformity in religious practice was the surest assertion of denominational identity an Episcopalian could offer.

Late the next year, on October 20, 1820, Hobart ordained Williams to the diaconate. This was a major achievement for him and for his congregation: the denomination now recognized him as set apart and dedicated to God, marked for spiritual leadership, and called to that leadership by the church. He was only the second African American to be so ordained, and he was the only one in orders at the time, as Absalom Jones had died two years earlier. It had taken the congregation eleven years, but finally "one of their own colour" was accepted by their denomination and designated to lead them. The newspaper account stated that it was an occasion of much ceremony and celebration, with "many of our most respectable [that is, white] citizens present." The Rev. Thomas Lyell, Williams's early mentor, preached on "the duties of a pastor to his congregation, and of his congregation towards him; and also the necessity of members of the same society living in peace and harmony with each other."[22] It was a proud moment for the parish, whatever the denominational leadership's motives may have been.

It must be remembered that there was then as there is now a sharp distinction between a deacon and a priest. As has been noted, the diaconate is an office particularly designated for outreach to the poor and the sick, and a deacon works directly under a bishop. A deacon cannot perform most of the major liturgical functions: he (or she, nowadays—but not in Williams's day) cannot consecrate the bread and wine for communion, cannot pronounce forgiveness of sins, cannot pronounce a blessing and therefore cannot officiate at weddings, and can only baptize in the absence of a priest. The position was meant to directly assist a bishop with the diocese's pastoral needs. It came, however, to be a required step toward ordination to the priesthood as well—reminding all priests that they are also deacons, also called particularly to pastoral work, in addition to the primary liturgical functions of their office. Most priests had served as deacons in the early nineteenth century for no more than a year or two—and the vast majority for six months or less—before being ordained again. Those who remained as deacons (and they were few then, as now) generally were engaged in missionary work.

The parish's triumph, then, was not quite full, for they would still need a white priest to conduct their weddings and their monthly communion services. Williams's triumph was not complete either: he would spend six years, rather than six months, waiting to be ordained a priest. Nonetheless, he was now "the Reverend," which brought him immeasurable respect in his community (if only token respect in his denomination) in addition to the pride of his church. And the priesthood was definitely in the future, even if more distantly than he and his congregation would have liked. Despite this delay, Williams had grown sufficiently in stature to be seen as a public leader as well as a spiritual one.

Now, with a properly consecrated building and a duly sanctioned clergyman, the congregation was ready for the next step: legal incorporation as a church. This could have been accomplished at any time in the past few years, as all the state and denomination stipulated were that the male members be organized into a group governed by an elected board (vestry) and that their worship be conducted according to the Book of Common Prayer.[23] But the congregation had waited for two other pieces—a proper church building and an ordained minister—to solidify their identity as Episcopalians so that they could incorporate as such.

Notice of intent was given for two Sundays, calling upon all male members "of full age" to attend a meeting to elect a vestry and its wardens, decide upon a corporate name, and provide for future vestry elections. Peter Williams chaired the meeting. Lewis Francis and Samuel Class, two of the original trustees in the land lease, were elected wardens, and four more of that original nine were voted onto the first vestry as well: William Hutson, John Marander, Andrew Rankin, and Thomas Zabriskie. They were joined by Michael Johnson, Thomas Sipkins, Richard Tankard, and William Tate. Monday in Easter Week was chosen as the date for future elections, and the corporate name was selected: "The Rector, Church Wardens and Vestrymen of Saint Philip's Church, New York." The name of the church was a reference to the apostle who, according to the Bible's Book of Acts, converted a black African to Christianity. On November 8, 1820, the certificate of incorporation was recorded.[24]

At the convention the following year, Hobart reported rather desultorily on the historic ordination: "On the Friday following the meeting of this body [last year], I ordained Peter Williams, jun., a man of colour, deacon, in the African Church of St. Philip's, in this city, where he still officiates and is collecting a large congregation, who exhibit much order and devotion in the exercise of worship."[25] Such a loaded statement! The ordination took place less than a week after the previous convention, yet had received no mention at that gathering; the ordinand's race is highlighted; the church is referred to as "African," a designation that was not part of the now official name and, by the time of this report, was beginning to be rejected by African Americans as derogatory; and the congregation is once again praised for its formal conduct of worship. The only element untainted by racism is the statement that the congregation had grown quite large. Hobart had every reason to be proud of what he had done, and he surely was, but he also had plenty of colleagues who were not going to be pleased or impressed with this accomplishment, which explains his desire to both downplay the event and locate it carefully within its congregational—and therefore racial—borders.

On December 18, 1821, disaster struck: a defective flue caused the Christmas decorations in the two-year-old church to catch fire, and the building was destroyed. The congregation fortunately had insurance, and they managed to raise an additional $2,000 to replace the wooden structure with one of brick, at a total cost of $10,000. Donations of interior decorations came from Zion Church, which had replaced its burned church five years earlier. Hobart reported on the church's progress at that fall's convention, noting that "the building is nearly completed, and it will give me great pleasure to see assembled in it the decent and devout congregation whom I have often witnessed in the former edifice." On December 31, 1822, he consecrated the new building with all the pomp of the previous occasion, and noted with pleasure how "speedily" St. Philip's had recovered from destruction. The *Christian Journal* described the building approvingly in its coverage of the service: "This church is built upon the same foundation, and is very similar in size, and in the general plan and appearance of the interior; which are characterized by simplicity, good taste, and economy."[26]

True self-sufficiency for this congregation did not come until 1826, when Williams was finally ordained priest. Once that had occurred, Trinity Church began to refer to the annual grant recipient as "St. Philip's Church," rather than as the "African Episcopal Catechetical Institute" that was listed each year through 1825. Recognition of the independence of its former mission field apparently came slowly to the denomination's grand dame.[27] Though deacons in charge of a congregation are at times styled "rector," technically the title can only be held by a priest, for only one so ordained can provide complete liturgical leadership to a parish. With this ordination, then, no more visiting white clergy would be needed for communions, weddings, baptisms at St. Philip's, and no longer would Williams have to hedge the final blessing in the burial service. The church would now be able to function on its own.

This had been a long time coming. Commenting years later on this delay in a letter to his daughter upon the occasion of Williams's death, the abolitionist William Jay asserted, "had he been white he would in a few weeks, or at least months, have been admitted into Priest's orders—but six years elapsed before the pride of caste could submit to his admission into the higher order of ministry."[28] The Standing Committee approved his ordination on July 1, 1826, noting of course for the record that Williams was "a coloured man." They also noted that "the Bishop with the advice and consent of the clerical members of this Committee had dispensed with his knowledge of Greek, Latin, &c"[29]—but why? Did they feel that the same educational standards expected of white clergy were beyond his abilities, or were they simply unwilling to teach him any more? Williams "read Latin with some facility" in addition to his other educational attainments, so it is hard to imagine that Greek or anything else would have been out of his intellectual reach.

The ordination ceremony was held in St. Philip's on July 10, 1826, with Hobart presiding and an odd collection of clergy participating. Morning prayer was led by Benjamin Onderdonk, an assistant at Trinity at the time, but soon to be Hobart's successor as bishop. Onderdonk was assisted by the Rev. Levi Silliman Ives, Hobart's son-in-law, who was serving a church in Philadelphia; the Rev. Cornelius Duffie, Rector of St. Thomas's Church in New York City, was the preacher; and Williams's old friend Thomas Lyell presented him for ordination.[30] Like Hobart, Onderdonk and Ives were staunch High Churchmen (Ives eventually became bishop of North Carolina and then, to everyone's shock, converted to Roman Catholicism), while Duffie's parish was a bastion of Low Churchmanship. These lines were becoming more and more clearly defined, though without being as rigidly divisive as they would be in the next two or three decades.

The process of bringing St. Philip's into existence was now as complete as its parishioners could make it. They had spent some seventeen years working toward their vision of an Episcopal church for African Americans, presided

over by an African American priest. The final step of denominational acceptance—attendance at the diocesan convention and participation thereby
in the life of the diocese of which they were part—was not in their control,
despite their fulfillment of all the necessary requirements. The anomaly of an
Episcopal church existing in such a limbo, in defiance of the canons, did not
even warrant comment in any of these conventions until 1844.

The steps taken by the people of St. Philip's toward self-sufficiency during this period were significant, and each one was a source of pride for the
growing congregation. Yet each also made manifest their dependence on the
benevolence of the white leadership of the denomination, and thus demonstrated the limits of their own power of self-determination. The presumed
conditions required for Williams's ordination, the lengthy interval between
diaconate and priesthood, and the need to demonstrate a desire for "orderly"
worship in the face of expectations to the contrary all signal the burden of
overcoming racial stigmas at each incremental movement toward the congregation's vision of itself. They all signal as well the necessity of careful negotiation by this black congregation with its white environment, in the persons
of the bishop, the Standing Committee, the vestry of Trinity Church, and the
delegates of the diocesan conventions. Such negotiation was not just a result
of the parish's denominational choice; it was a constant element of any efforts
at self-improvement by African Americans in antebellum New York City.

Few of the papers of Peter Williams remain, but one brief letter to his
bishop, written just a month after his ordination to the diaconate, points to
the delicacy of tone this negotiation required. The parish wanted to convince
Trinity Church to continue the grant that had paid their rent for the previous
seven years, and it was now Williams's job to bring this about. He began the
letter by phrasing his request as one for "advice" on a difficult subject, and
placed himself in a submissive position immediately: "Rt. Rev'd. and Dear Sir,
I have called at your house this morning to beg your advice on the subject of
the ground rent of our Church." Recalling the seven-year commitment Trinity had made, he then continued straightforwardly: "As our circumstances are
so poor that we are not able to meet all our other demands, we therefore feel
it necessary to make a new application for assistance on this particular." He
then invoked the white supporter that helped get the church building started:
"This our deceased friend Mr. Sherred advised us to do in case we were not
able to get along without it." As bishop and rector both, Hobart clearly had
the power to bring this about. Williams just as clearly preferred to petition
him as a personal supporter rather than petition Trinity's vestry directly, and
he did so in oblique and apologetic terms:

Rt. Rev'd. Sir, I beg that you will excuse our being so troublesome to you, and that you will befriend us as far as you can in this matter. We stand much indebted to you [referring as much to Williams's recent ordination and Williams and Hobart's past history as colleagues as to past financial assistance] and can make no returns but our thanks and our sincere prayers to Almighty God, that he will reward and keep you. Your Obed't. Serv't., Peter Williams.[31]

It is hard to determine the level of obsequiousness here, given the formalities of nineteenth-century correspondence, but there is a conscious effort being made to establish just the right tone. Apparently Williams succeeded in achieving that tone, as Trinity's grant continued uninterrupted for the rest of his rectorship and for at least twenty years beyond that.

Hobart's address to the convention of 1826 noted the ordination of Peter Williams to the priesthood only in passing. The bishop was more interested in announcing the confirmation service he had held at St. Philip's, where 113 people were confirmed. The parish was thriving: now that a priest was on hand, sixty-seven baptisms and thirty marriages were performed that year, and forty-five baptisms and twenty-six marriages the following year. The funds to purchase a new organ had been scraped together as well. The bishop was clearly pleased at the progress the church was making under his wing, and was especially pleased that the realm of public worship was so carefully and fruitfully tended in this, the most unusual of the churches in his see. Once again he announced regarding the service, "I witnessed an orderly and devout congregation."[32] Four years later, Hobart was dead—and his successor would find the orderly and devout becoming impatient.

CHAPTER 6

A Bitter Thralldom

The American Anti-Slavery Society, less than a year old, gathered in New York City in 1834 to celebrate the Fourth of July. While the rest of the still-young nation was marking Independence Day with the pride of nationalism, however, the Anti-Slavery Society was taking part in what was a rather different celebration among the city's black population: the anniversary of the abolition, in 1827, of slavery in the state of New York. This event had become the cause for a regular series of speeches and festivities both to give thanks for statewide emancipation and to inspire and agitate for the same on a national level. The fact that the British Empire had ended slavery the previous July only brought greater optimism and urgency to this year's plans.

The society had officially come into being in Philadelphia in December of 1833, when a large number of men, for the most part from New York, Philadelphia, and Boston, drew up and signed a constitution of the American Anti-Slavery Society. The Tappan brothers, Lewis and Arthur, had put some of their dry-goods fortune to work a few years earlier with the launching of an abolitionist newspaper, *The Emancipator*, in New York City, while William Lloyd Garrison was bringing out its more famous Boston equivalent, *The Liberator*. Now the Tappans and Garrison had joined forces with Theodore Dwight Weld and others to form a national antislavery organization, and they had gathered a racially mixed group to bring it into being. Among the signers of the constitution of the new society, in addition to philanthropists and activists like Gerrit Smith and Washington Irving, were St. Philip's parishioner Philip Bell and the Rev. Peter Williams.[1]

The organization's fond hopes for a few days of services of thanksgiving and speeches of exhortation to continued labor, however, were thwarted by what was the worst eruption of violence the city had ever seen.[2] The antiabolitionist riots of 1834 were ten days of wanton brutality and destruction. Incited by newspaper accounts that listed the where and when of every upcoming abolitionist meeting, mobs drove the Anti-Slavery Society out the back door of the Chatham Street Chapel and disrupted the society's every effort to gather for celebration. Yet these disruptions turned out to be only a prelude. More brazenly, the mobs assaulted and beat every African American and Englishman (because of their recent abolition of slavery, apparently) they encountered, caused great damage to the homes and stores of the Tappans, and literally tore apart the houses and businesses of African Americans in the vicinity of the Five Points slum district, shattering windows and furniture and ripping apart roofs and walls. This district was notorious for its poverty, overcrowded tenements, and multiracial population, and was to achieve dubious fame a few years later in the appalled account of these conditions by Charles Dickens.

The violence was at its most vicious and widespread on July 11. Mobs surged all evening in and around the Five Points, causing massive damage. Around 11:00 P.M., one group attacked St. Philip's, which was only a block from the intersection that gave the slum its name. The mob broke into the church and went berserk. They shattered the stained-glass windows, pulled down the reredos, destroyed the organ, candlesticks, and curtains, and broke the altar in pieces; they then hauled pews into the street and set them on fire. The Sunday services two days later had to be canceled.[3]

According to one report, rumors spread among the crowd that Williams had officiated at the marriage of a black man and a white woman. While there is no evidence that such an event ever took place, it is certain that such a rumor would have inflamed passions. It is also possible that his position on the board of the American Anti-Slavery Society was known, and the church suffered the consequences. But it is apparent from an analysis of the targets that the mobs were particularly focused on attacking symbols of African American economic self-sufficiency: while many of the worst tenements housing African Americans were ignored, businesses and homes owned by black New Yorkers were ransacked and vandalized.[4] Thus the attack on St. Philip's may have been motivated only by its convenient proximity and by the fact that it was an independent black institution. Surely the most visceral message of the days of terror was that white New Yorkers did not want black New Yorkers to feel they had any right to believe they belonged in the city, let alone any right to self-determination and autonomy.

The tenuous position of African Americans in antebellum New York and in the nation as a whole could hardly have been made more violently explicit. Yet it was not a new message, nor was it one that had been ignored. For the previous three decades, the struggle to end slavery had been entwined with the struggle by African Americans to assert the fact of their Americanness. The legality of slavery (in the state of New York, until 1827, and in the South, throughout the first half of the century) meant that African Americans were first and foremost defined by their status—slave or free—yet that definition blurred in the eyes of white Americans so that all black Americans were viewed in the same light. For regardless of their current status, free black Americans *could* be slaves, while white Americans could never be; and if one could be a slave, in the eyes of those who could not it mattered little whether or not one actually was.

This was what William Hamilton was hoping emancipation would change when he spoke from the pulpit of Zion Church on the day slavery ended in New York State. The president and a cofounder of the New York African Society for Mutual Relief, Hamilton was rumored to be the son of former Secretary of the Treasury Alexander Hamilton. "We stand redeemed from a bitter thralldom," he proclaimed, for "no more shall *negro* and *slave* be synonymous."[5] Though slavery was almost gone from the city by 1827 (less than five percent of the African American population was enslaved), the mere fact of its legality in the state had meant that all African Americans were perceived through its lens. Hamilton's hope that such perceptions would alter, however, was dashed by the persistence of legal slavery elsewhere in the nation. These perceptions played out in a variety of ways during the first three decades of the nineteenth century, and Peter Williams was developing a reputation as someone who was willing to speak out on their implications.

Williams first publicly addressed the issue of slavery in his speech at Zion Church, at a celebration of the federal legislation abolishing the importation of slaves (a proscription more honored in the breach). In the British Empire, the slave trade had ended the year before, and the two events were thought to signal a new era. James Varick was the featured speaker, preaching a "Sermon of Thanksgiving on the Abolition of the African Slave Trade" in the afternoon of an all-day event on January 1, 1808, the day the legislation was to take effect. William Hamilton composed special hymns for the day, and Peter Williams spoke in the morning. In the grandiloquent prose of the time, he condemned the "unnatural monster" that was the slave trade and particularly noted its pernicious effects on his naive view of the "simplicity, innocence and contentment" that marked African culture: "Oh, Africa, Africa! . . . thy shores, which were once the garden of the world, the seal of almost paradisiacal joys, have been transformed into regions of woe; thy sons, who were once the happiest of mortals, are reduced to slavery, and bound in weighty shackles, now fill the trader's ship." His naïveté regarding Africa did not prevent him, however, from acknowledging that the foulest effect of the slave trade had been to reduce Africans to trading in one another for their own benefit.

Williams also asserted that this occasion and each subsequent advance, however minor or unenforced, would engender hopefulness in the lives of African Americans: "Thus, evincing to the world that our garments are unpolluted by the stains of ingratitude, we shall reap increasing advantages from the favors conferred; the spirits of our departed ancestors shall smile with complacency on the change of our state; and posterity shall exult in the pleasing remembrance." Having named the various figures, from early Quaker antislavery activists to Samuel Wilberforce, Britain's antislavery leader, who had been so instrumental in what little activism regarding slavery had occurred so far in the United States, Williams called not for agitation on the part of his fellow African Americans but for the energetic pursuit of "knowledge and virtue" as the keys to continued advancement. This would remain the primary theme for him throughout his future ministry: he understood that the pursuit of education and virtuous conduct would not only be beneficial to individual development, but would also help to ameliorate the image of black Americans in the eyes of white Americans.[6]

This was the speech that provoked a public challenge regarding whether Williams was truly the author, and he had to take the step of having it published with certifications of his authorship provided by, among others, Bishop Moore. At the same celebration a year later, in 1809, William Hamilton took to the podium brandishing a copy of Williams's speech and, referring to the controversy, declaimed, "If we continue to produce specimens like these, we shall soon put our enemies to the blush; abashed and confounded they shall quit the field, and no longer urge their superiority of souls."[7]

But while white New Yorkers were hard put to imagine that their black compatriots could produce an actual oration, the real problem for any progress toward the abolition of slavery was to get white Americans to imagine a biracial nation—to imagine accepting black Americans as members of the same society. For most of the white population, in the North as much as the South, the thought was not just odious, but impossible. While slaves were simply treated as less than human, free African Americans were generally regarded with some mixture of rage, contempt, and fear. Henry Clay famously pronounced, "Of all classes of our population, the most vicious is that of the free coloured."[8] One prominent effect of this in the early nineteenth century was the bizarre amalgamation of motives behind the emigration of African Americans and the colonization movement. The former involved the free choice made by free blacks to leave this country for settings with greater potential for justice and equality, while the latter was envisioned as the (for some, forced) repatriation of free blacks to their supposed native continent.

The emigration ideal found its inspiration with the creation of Sierra Leone on the western African coast by the British government, and its use for the repatriation of freed Canadian and West Indian slaves. Paul Cuffe, a free African American from New Bedford, Massachusetts, had developed his own shipping business with a fleet of various vessels, after an early career as a sailor. He decided that emigration was a worthy option for his African American brethren, and connected with British and American authorities, as well as the Sierra Leone settlement, in 1811. At his own expense, he launched his first expedition in 1815, transporting thirty-eight people (nine families) to the northwestern coast of Africa. He envisioned making himself available for annual transports, but unfortunately died the next year. In October of 1817, Peter Williams eulogized him in an address delivered before the New York African Institution, which had supported Cuffe's expedition. There he spoke of his personal friendship with Cuffe and of his support for the efforts of those who felt it impossible to continue to live under the racial inequality of this nation.[9]

Williams subsequently helped found the Haytien Emigration Society in 1824 in an effort to keep the emigration option available. The black revolution in Haiti was much admired among New York City's African American community. Williams was joined in this effort by, among others, parishioners Boston Crummell (father of Alexander Crummell) and Samuel Ennals, and hundreds of black Americans were sent to Haiti over a two-year period.[10] Williams even accompanied one expedition as an observer, but, as a historian has noted, "his trip . . . was tarnished because more than fifty blacks who had gone earlier to Haiti returned on the same boat."[11]

Unfortunately, a direct result of Cuffe's successful expedition was the creation in 1816 of the American Colonization Society. James Weldon Johnson referred to this organization as "the only instance in American history in which groups holding conflicting opinions on the polymorphous Negro question united for a common end; and, stranger still, each group felt that it was realizing its intention."[12] It was indeed a tangled web of white hopes and fears: those who were antislavery proposed to purchase slaves from their owners and return them to Africa, those who were proslavery felt that removing free blacks from the country would make them less disruptive to the continuation of slavery, and those of either persuasion who simply feared African Americans believed that they could (or should) never live in equality in American society, so they would be better off going "home." The more pious motive offered was that free blacks would bring Christianity to Africa.

The American Colonization Society, dedicated to sending free African Americans to Africa by one means or another, was the result of simultaneous efforts by a variety of people, including the Rev. Robert Finley, a Presbyterian minister from Basking Ridge, New Jersey. He gathered an illustrious group of politicians for a meeting in Washington on December 21, 1816. Henry Clay was persuaded to preside over the meeting, and James Monroe, Daniel Webster, Francis Scott Key, and George Washington's nephew, Bushrod Washington, were among those in attendance. They launched the society with a constitution after meeting again the following week, and elected Washington the first president. The aim was to secure government funds for a nationwide program. That funding was approved in 1819, and the society's first ship sailed in January of the following year, establishing the colony that soon became Liberia.[13]

The reality, of course, was that Africa was not "home" anymore. The vast majority of free blacks in America were a generation or more removed from Africa, had no interest in going there, and were insulted to be considered less than American. As to those who gave up in despair of ever living in this country with justice and equality, their individual desires to leave could be either understood and supported or condemned as bad choices, but the notion that African Americans as an entire people were not and never really could be American was appalling. One response by African Americans during this period was to begin referring to themselves as "colored" rather than "African," as the latter term, formerly the norm, was seen as abetting the American Colonization Society's desire to portray them as non-American.[14]

The problem then, as it is for historians today, was that the term "antislavery" meant such a wide range of ideas and approaches. The basis was a developing religious conviction that slavery was a sin, and that its presence tainted the nation as sinful. Everyone from gradualists, who believed that slavery should be ended by a gradual and organic process, generally with some government incentives for freeing slaves, to abolitionists, who believed that slavery should simply be abolished no matter the consequences, and every reasonable or wild idea in between all came under the same "antislavery" rubric. There were no organizations in the first two decades of the nineteenth century that approached the issue on a national level; the New York Manumission Society, for example, was focused only on slavery and its aftereffects in the state. Even the Quakers, who were the first to publicly take an antislavery stand, were not in any sense organized or even in agreement. Thus the American Colonization Society's opportunity to step into the vacuum and gather not only the entire range of antislavery sentiments under its wing, but proslavery advocates as well.

The more publicity the American Colonization Society received for its scheme, however, the more African Americans felt called to oppose it, and emigration began to be seen as an individual choice that put an entire people at greater jeopardy. Williams's efforts to walk the fine line of supporting emigration while despising colonization became a source of difficulty. John B. Russwurm, the first black graduate of an American college (Bowdoin College, in Maine), launched the first black newspaper in the country, *Freedom's Journal*, in New York City in 1827. Samuel Cornish served as its other editor, and Peter Williams and Boston Crummell were part of the founding group. The primary purpose was to encourage African Americans to plead their cause and work for self-improvement, and thereby contradict the assumptions of their unfitness for citizenship fostered by the American Colonization Society. Yet when Russwurm gave up the fight in 1929, began advocating emigration, and finally sailed for Liberia late that year, he was roundly condemned by Cornish and most other black leaders. The support that Williams offered, as he had offered to Cuffe and the Haitian expeditions, led many to see him as vacillating on the issue.

What some saw as vacillation, however, could also be seen as the development of a sensitive position on a difficult issue: was it not possible to understand those who chose to leave a nation they saw as full of prejudice and hatred without suggesting that all African Americans should leave? Was it not possible to support what seemed to be exciting experiments in black self-determination in both Haiti and Liberia, and yet still believe that African Americans were American? In a sermon given the year after Russwurm left and subsequently published in pamphlet form, Williams used the rhetoric of understatement most eloquently to articulate what he felt the nation owed African Americans:

> We are natives of this country, we ask only to be treated as well as foreigners. Not a few of our fathers suffered and bled to purchase its independence; we ask only to be treated as well as those who fought against it. We have toiled to cultivate it, and to raise it to its present prosperous condition; we ask only to share equal privileges with those who come from distant lands to enjoy the fruits of our labour. . . . We cannot but doubt the purity of the motives of those persons who deny us these requests, and would send us to Africa to gain what they might give us at home.[15]

The riots of 1834, then, can be seen as the violent culmination of a struggle that had been going on for decades. The struggle for African Americans was to assert their right to belong to the new nation—to be American—in the face of white America's powerful belief that the races were never to mix. In this context, every advance by the city's black population—legal, economic, and even religious—was taken as a threat to the established social order. Those who felt most threatened, then, were not just the Irish and other European immigrants who were competing with African Americans for jobs and room to move up the socioeconomic ladder. It was also the middle and upper classes, who felt the social order and their own place therein challenged. It is perhaps not as shocking as it first seems, then, to discover that there is ample evidence that many of those who made up the mobs that behaved so viciously in those days of rioting were "gentlemen of property and standing."[16] Slavery may have left New York City, but a bitter thralldom of racism remained pervasive.

Whatever immediate reasons lay behind the mob's attack on St. Philip's Church, the damage served to remind the parish that its desire for religious self-determination would be bound up with the efforts of all African Americans to claim their right to America. The aftermath of the attack would make this conjunction all the more clear, and all the more problematic.

CHAPTER 7

A Godly Admonition

John Henry Hobart died in 1830, at the relatively early age of fifty-five, bringing to an end one of the most productive bishoprics of the early Episcopal Church. The first few years had been awkward, with two living bishops still nominally with authority over him, but he had shown bold leadership nonetheless, and came completely into his own with the deaths of Provoost in 1815 (which technically made Moore the diocesan, though he was still disabled by his stroke) and Moore in 1816. Hobart had expanded his diocese, launched the first Episcopal seminary (the General Theological Seminary, in New York City), and laid the groundwork for the theology that would provide his denomination with its distinctiveness during a century dominated by evangelicalism. He had traveled extensively in Europe, and had connected with (and significantly influenced) the English divines whose ideas and writings came to be called "the Oxford Movement," from their home base, or "Tractarianism," from the numbered "Tracts for the Times" they published, in which they promoted their theological crusades. He had founded the Protestant Episcopal Theological Society, the New York Bible and Common Prayer Book Society, the Missionary Society, and the New York Sunday School Society, all designed to compete directly with their evangelical and more ecumenical counterparts. And he had raised up a black congregation, consecrated its church, and ordained its priest—at Hobart's death, one of only two black Episcopal clergymen in the country. Hobart had been a busy man.[1]

His hand-picked and easily elected successor was Benjamin Tredwell Onderdonk, an assistant at Trinity Church and teacher at the seminary. Onderdonk had grown up in New York City, where his father had been a vestryman at Trinity; his brother Henry had gone from the rectorship of St. Ann's Church in Brooklyn to become assistant bishop to William White in Pennsylvania. Trained under Hobart, Onderdonk was a staunch upholder of High Church theology. He was also renowned for stubbornness, taciturnity, an inability to gauge how others responded to him, and an absolute dearth of tact. These qualities seem to have provided him with a forceful leadership style, but they were eventually to be his downfall.[2]

On July 12, 1834, the morning after the attack on St. Philip's, Williams notified Bishop Onderdonk of the events and that he would be forced to cancel services. Later the same day, he received a letter of condolence by messenger from his bishop. "I am sure I need not assure you of the sincere sympathy which I feel for you and your people," the bishop wrote, and he stated that he had enclosed a letter to the congregation to be read to them as soon as possible. That letter has unfortunately been lost; it would be intriguing to see how he put to the parish the sympathy he felt no need to elaborate to Williams personally. For in his letter to Williams he immediately proceeded to a more practical response, which, incredibly, he seemed to think the priest would find helpful: "Let me advise you to resign, at once, your connexion, in every department, with the Anti-Slavery Society, and to make public your resignation."[3] From the perspective of the twenty-first century, it is hard to imagine a more thoughtless response coming at a more difficult time. Where is the offer to assist with the repairs to the church? To speak to the frightened congregation? To demonstrate Christian compassion and concern in some concrete manner? The implication of this demand is that the suffering the parish had endured was the rector's fault.

Even more surprising is that Williams agreed to the demand with no apparent hesitation. His resignation was published in several newspapers two days later. "My Bishop, without giving his opinions on the subject of Abolition, has now advised me . . . to resign connexion with the Anti-Slavery Society," he wrote. "There has been no instance hitherto, in which I have not sought his advice in matters of importance to the Church, and endeavored to follow it when given; and I have no wish that the present should be an exception."[4] The tone of submissiveness and self-effacement sounded as obsequious to his peers as it does today. Why did Williams not challenge his bishop to place the blame where it belonged, with the racist mobs? Why did he not argue that his work with the Anti-Slavery Society was essential to his ministry to his people? Why did he not stand up for himself, and stand against racism and violence? His acquiescence has all the hallmarks of a man more interested in retaining the limited status granted him by a white power elite than in taking a moral position whatever the consequences.

That acquiescence damaged Williams severely, both with his contemporaries and in the eyes of history. Alexander Crummell—who grew up in the parish, owed his educational opportunities to his rector, and deemed him a mentor in his own pursuit of ordination—nonetheless in his later years lambasted Williams as "a timid man" who felt all his life "the extreme pressure of Episcopal power." The rector's public prestige suffered enormously: an editorial in the *Liberator*, while calling Williams "one of our dearest friends," nonetheless concluded that he was "culpably submissive" when his duty was "as a minister of the gospel, and especially as a man of color, to cry aloud and spare not—and lift up his voice like a trumpet, and plead for his enslaved brethren." The judgment of historians is best summed up in the dismissal offered by Carter Woodson, the dean of black church history: "It does not appear that he had that moral stamina to impel him to renounce his connection with a church seeking to muzzle a man praying for the deliverance of his people." Woodson goes on to suggest that advanced age was a factor in this meekness. Such judgments, however, are unfair, for they betray significant misunderstandings of both the polity of the Episcopal Church and the fierce loyalty and faith Williams and his parishioners felt toward their denomination.[5]

The first misinterpretation lies in believing that Williams was simply cowed by his bishop and could not stand up for what he believed. At his ordination to the diaconate and again at his ordination to the priesthood, Williams was required to answer affirmatively to the question: "Will you reverently obey your Bishop, and other chief Ministers, who, according to the Canons of the Church, may have the charge and government over you; following with a glad mind and will their godly admonitions, and submitting yourself to their godly judgments?"[6] This was no rhetorical question; it went to the heart of the theology of the apostolic succession and therefore of the polity and identity of the denomination. Disobedience could be cause for removal from a position or even from the priesthood itself. Bishops, in this denomination, were the embodiment of the continuity of Christian teaching from the time of Jesus and his apostles to the present day, and it was from that assurance of continuity that they drew their authority of pastoral and canonical oversight of their congregations and their clergy. Williams had been nurtured by Hobart's High Church perspective, so in his eyes the episcopacy was also the very embodiment of the Christian Church as a whole. Disobedience to one's bishop, then, would be breaking not just with the denomination, but with the church itself. Knowing how long and hard his parishioners had struggled to create a church that was validated by his ordination, it is not hard to see why Williams would find acquiescence to his bishop, however disappointing or painful, infinitely preferable to abandoning his flock, his denomination, and his church. The *Liberator* either did not know what price they were asking

Williams to pay, or if they did, they apparently felt that the antislavery cause should have outweighed the ecclesiastical attachment.

Williams clearly disagreed. He opened his public letter of resignation by referring to his vow of obedience—"when I received Holy orders, I promised 'reverently to obey my Bishop'"—and then outlined the circumstances that led to his call to ministry and the sense of duty that impelled him to "live upon the scanty pittance which a colored minister must expect to receive for his labors, and to endure the numerous severe trials peculiar to his situation." Williams also attempted to clarify his positions on colonization and emigration, the need for education and thereby the cultural improvement of the lives of African Americans, and the work of the Anti-Slavery Society. He argued that he opposed the American Colonization Society's "idea, that a colored man . . . can never enjoy the privileges of a citizen of the United States," believing that "the principles of the Declaration of Independence, and of the Gospel of Christ" were sufficient to raise any man "to that rank." Yet, he went on, "whenever any man of color, after having carefully considered the subject, has thought it best to emigrate to Africa . . . I have felt it my duty to aid him, in all my power, on his way. . . . " Williams then linked his hopes for emancipation to his hopes for educational advancement, noting that it was through their support of his efforts to create a college or school that he first came into contact with "Anti-Slavery men":

> I joined with them in this work heartily, and wished them all success, as I still do in their endeavors, by all means sanctioned by law, humanity and religion, to obtain freedom for my brethren, and to elevate them to the enjoyment of equal rights with the other citizens of the community; but I insisted that while they were laboring to restore us to our rights, it was exclusively our duty to labor to qualify our people for the enjoyment of those rights.[7]

The letter reveals how nuanced his approach to these issues was and how carefully he attempted to remain consistent in his own beliefs and goals despite the inability to fit them neatly into broader corporate stands or more popular slogans.

Williams resigned from the board of the Anti-Slavery Society, but he maintained his membership in it and served as a delegate to its next two conventions. He detailed in his resignation letter his activism in abolitionism, describing his colleagues as "good men, and good Christians, and true lovers of their country, and of all mankind." But he also noted that he felt his primary role in the society to have been a moderating one. In a tone that sounds to our ears suspiciously like groveling, Williams explained his perspective:

> I would have offered my resignation long before this, had I not thought that there might be occasions, when by having the privilege of addressing the Board, I might exercise a restraining influence upon measures calculated to advance our people faster than they were prepared to be advanced, and the public feeling would bear.

While this statement seems humiliating by twenty-first-century standards, it can be taken seriously within the context of the antislavery movement. Abolitionists tended toward a range of radical reforms—including, eventually, women's rights and, for many, a disavowal of organized religion—which were widely seen as threatening to the social order. Williams, having no interest in such radicalism, may well have felt that many of his colleagues were placing the cause of antislavery in a detrimental context.

It is also true that most of the major abolitionist figures, and certainly those of whom the public were most aware, were white, and actually knew very little about the lives and needs of their black compatriots. Williams's statement can be understood, then, as the expression of a pragmatic African American ruing the more idealistic—and to his mind naïve—flights of his European American colleagues. As has been noted, Williams was most deeply committed to including education and cultural advancement in the antislavery program as necessary both to prepare black Americans for American life and to convince white Americans of their worthiness of the same. "It was my anxiety to promote the object of the Phoenix Society, which is the improvement of the people of color in this city, in morals, literature, and the mechanic arts," he wrote in his letter. He goes on to discuss the various efforts with which he was involved to create high schools and girls' schools for black New Yorkers. Immediate abolition without any provisions for education or economic opportunity, Williams felt, could only result in the kind of poverty and prejudice with which he was already too closely acquainted.

The resignation letter also reveals an apologetic ambivalence on Williams's part about the public nature of his role in the church and the wider society, from the opening sentence ("It has always been painful to me to appear before the public") to the last ("I hope that . . . the public generally will judge charitably of this hastily drawn communication"). He asserts that he had little to say in the meetings of the Anti-Slavery Society, and that he normally sat in the gallery of the Chatham Street Chapel during those meetings, effacing himself to the chagrin of his black colleagues. Yet as the few speeches of his that survive amply demonstrate, he was not afraid to take strong and difficult stands, ones consistent with his own principles rather than popular opinion. Williams here makes manifest the lack of unanimity, and resulting controversy, among antebellum black leaders over methods of enhancing the status of African Americans: "They did as they thought best, and I did as I thought best; but I have learned that it is a most difficult matter to avoid extremes on subjects of great public excitement, without being more censured than those who go to all lengths with either party." His efforts to steer a middle course, on antislavery or colonization and emigration, proved costly. They were, however, to have a significant and long-lasting effect on his parishioners and their leadership styles, including even Crummell.

Williams did not make his letter public himself. He sent it to Bishop Onderdonk, who published it together with his own. It would seem that the bishop did a bit of editing before sending the letters out to the newspapers, or so Williams assured his fellow board member, the white antislavery activist and philanthropist Gerrit Smith. Williams had been in correspondence with Smith regarding some young parishioners he wished to send to the Oneida Institute, an interracial college that Smith had been instrumental in launching. In the middle of a letter written later that month, on July 26, to recommend to Smith's attentions two young men, Robert Banks and George Simms, Williams felt it important to assure the activist of his position regarding the antislavery cause:

> You have probably seen my letter announcing my resignation of office in the Anti-Slavery Society. The letter was not published as I wrote it. My strongest anti-slavery sentiments were omitted. I consider myself still a member of the Society, and consider its principles to be those of the Gospel of Christ, and of the declaration of American independence, and can never renounce them, though some have so construed my letter.

In a letter written two months later, Williams expressed his gratitude for Smith's support of his position, stating that "I had been persecuted so much on the charge of having abandoned the principles of Anti-Slavery that it was quite serviceable to me to shew that a gentleman of your standing saw nothing in my letter to warrant such a charge."[8]

This version of events is corroborated by Arthur Tappan's son, Louis, in his biography of his father. He may have been the only contemporary who truly understood the issues Williams faced. Tappan explained:

[Williams's apology] expressed his opinions, modestly but firmly, of the anti-slavery cause. This apology he left with his ecclesiastical superior, who undertook to alter it by expunging several sentences and then causing it to be published without consulting Mr. Williams! The aggrieved man of God keenly felt the outrage, but deemed himself bound by his ordination vows to submit in silence.[9]

It would seem that Onderdonk's humiliation of his priest was not complete with the forced public resignation, but required that he shape the resignation itself, to Williams's everlasting detriment.

The second misinterpretation of this incident, by contemporaries and historians alike, is the assumption that Onderdonk demanded this resignation because he felt that Williams's membership in the Anti-Slavery Society was the cause of the riot and the ensuing vandalism. This was nowhere stated in Onderdonk's letter, nor did Williams understand that to be the implication. The bishop did not make this demand because he thought his priest's anti-slavery views had incited the mob, but because Onderdonk saw Williams's public involvement with the American Anti-Slavery Society as a threat to church unity.

Contemporary Episcopal commentators understood this exchange of letters not as a bishop disciplining one of his clergy (or of a white superior putting his black subordinate in his proper place), but as a denominational triumph of "church unity over misplaced individualism." This is how the High Church journal, the *Churchman*, saw it: "We aim as Episcopalians to direct the current of Christian feeling in the channels marked out for it by collective wisdom and guard against its being diverted by wayward impulse and wasted on worldly and ephemeral projects."[10] This is typical of attitudes of the time, for the Episcopal Church was strongly opposed to the involvement of any of its clergy—or laypeople in churchly roles—in the issues and affairs of the world. The church was meant to be in this world, but not of it. This commentator, therefore, was praising Onderdonk's emphasis on detachment from political ("worldly and ephemeral") debates, not his ability to silence an upstart priest.

Onderdonk outlined the importance of this stance more concretely and broadly three years later, when at the 1837 diocesan convention he admonished both clergy and laity not to permit their church buildings to be used for anything other than religious purposes. When the convention journal was printed, he took the opportunity to clarify his views even further, and appended a lengthy footnote to the printed account of his speech. He began by asserting that "there are important differences of opinion among the best members of the community" regarding a range of issues: temperance, anti-slavery, and other moral reform movements. Such issues therefore promote divisiveness, which is a threat to the church and must be avoided: "Whatever views her ministers and members may entertain in the matter, should be confined to them as citizens and members of society, and not be brought to bear upon them *as belonging to the Church*. All ecclesiastical bodies, therefore, should be kept free from discussion or committal respecting them." These movements are in fact extraecclesial and are not sponsored by the church's commitment to its gospel, and so "her organized bodies, vestries, conventions, and societies, should not engage in them."[11] Onderdonk's problem, then, with Williams and the riots was that the violence and vandalism had made a public issue of the priest's commitment to a divisive, worldly, secular organization.

Thus the bishop's letter to Williams, in what to modern eyes can only seem an extraordinarily ironic approach, admonished him to place Christian detachment above moral rectitude, and Christian unity above even a struggle for justice: "Let it be seen that on whichsoever side right may be, St. Philip's Church will be found on the Christian side of meekness, order, and self-sacrifice to common good, and the peace of the community." Hence Williams's assertion that the bishop had not given "his opinions on the subject of Abolition"; Onderdonk apparently could not have cared less about the issue of slavery, for what mattered to him was maintaining unity and peace. "You will be no losers by it," he promised, regarding detaching the parish from its work against slavery, "for the God of peace will be to you also a God of all consolation."[12]

The aftermath of the destruction of St. Philip's, then, pointed to the attitudes that were to mark the rest of the parish's struggle for acceptance by its denomination. During Onderdonk's time and the rest of the years leading up to the Civil War, the Episcopal Church, both locally and nationally, would exert itself mightily to dodge taking a stand on slavery. Ten years after this incident, the Methodist and Baptist national organizations would split into Northern and Southern denominations over the issue, demonstrating precisely what the Episcopalians, High and Low, feared most: the sin of schism. Better unity through apathy than that. Episcopalians therefore avoided the issue of slavery, and since any discussion that involved race was understood to touch on slavery, it was avoided as well. This would make it difficult for St. Philip's to get diocesan conventions to address its petition for admission.

The exchange between bishop and priest, and the subsequent diminution of Williams's reputation, also made it clear that there were differences of opinion among African Americans about how best to address slavery and prejudice. There were ways those issues were intertwined with religious beliefs and practices that were difficult to anticipate and even harder to articulate. Abolitionism must have seemed to many to be a simple stand to take—of course slavery should end—but Williams asserted that emancipation could not be a simple goal, but needed to be addressed in concert with issues of education and economic opportunity. He was not the only black leader, and certainly not the first, to insist on this approach, but combining this perspective with his attachment to a formal, white denomination opened him to condemnation as being more interested in cozying up to white "culture" than in fighting for the needs of his people. Such a charge contained a degree of truth: in a period when Victorian (that is, white Anglo-Saxon) culture was beginning to be believed by those proto-Victorians to be the pinnacle of human achievement, Williams's belief that black Americans could and should measure up to the same standard was neither uncommon nor unjustified. Such a belief, however, could be seen in two ways: either as reflecting an unbounded optimism about what African Americans could be, or as an unflattering envy of all things white.

What is most clearly revealed in these dealings with his bishop and his fellow New Yorkers is the extent to which Williams was trapped in the "double-consciousness" that W. E. B. Du Bois so famously outlined as the condition of all African Americans.[13] Williams was, in every setting, both black and Episcopalian, black and a New Yorker, black and American. Race—his own awareness of it, and his awareness of the awareness of his bishop, his fellow Episcopalians, and even the mob—was inextricably entwined with every choice and action that Williams took, even as other elements and motives impinged on those choices and actions as well. This is hardly surprising for an African American of almost any period or setting in American history, and it was certainly a fact of life in the first third of the nineteenth century. Yet race was not a simple or straightforward factor in these choices and actions; his faith, his denominational loyalty, and his understanding of the church were enormously important to Williams's decisions. He and his congregation had chosen to identify themselves with a denomination whose polity was hierarchical and focused on unity, and this choice, above all others, mandated a constant interaction with a white bishop and a body of white leaders. Such a choice bound Williams and the people of St. Philip's to a complicated path. His efforts, in this incident as in all others, to work out the best course for himself, his congregation, and his people were hampered by conflicts and tensions among these factors that others have too eagerly attempted to resolve or dismiss.

What is striking, however, is the extent to which this "double-conscious-ness" would appear also to have been an condition for Onderdonk. Du Bois felt that white Americans escaped this self-consciousness, seeing themselves solely as American and without needing to be constantly aware of their race, but the bishop's interactions with Williams and St. Philip's reveal that Onder-donk was also trapped in and by racial assumptions. The bishop's actions may have been motivated primarily by ecclesiology and by an understanding of High Church theology that overruled all other considerations, but his sense of himself as distinctly different in nature from this particular congregation and its priest is manifest in every aspect of his response to this attack on one of his churches. Had it been a white congregation that was attacked, he would have been outraged, not formulaic, in his sympathy. Had he admonished a white priest for antislavery activities, he would have surely have expected an argument: it was a most contentious diocese in these years, and few white priests would have felt as beholden as Williams did. But because the priest and congregation were black, he could not truly sympathize with what had happened to them, he was totally unaware of (and indifferent to) the impli-cations for Williams of his patronizing "admonition," and he had no sense that slavery or race were issues that should matter to him or his church. That very indifference, lack of sympathy and understanding, and patronizing at-titude, however, came not from separation or isolation from black Americans, but rather from his sense of himself as so completely "other" in his frequent interactions with them. For even if he was incapable of understanding this parish, polity and theology prevented Onderdonk from ignoring a black con-gregation under his jurisdiction. St. Philip's was one of his churches, and Peter Williams was one of his priests. Race and religion were thereby as entangled for Onderdonk as they were for Williams.

In addition to the public and publicized negotiations between Williams and his bishop, there was a more indirect interaction that was to be impor-tant in the history of St. Philip's. John Jay, grandson of the first chief justice of the Supreme Court and former governor of New York, made his first contact with the parish in the course of these riots. Born in 1817 to William and Augusta McVickar Jay, John had gone to Columbia College at the age of fifteen and graduated second in his class in 1836. His was a lineage of both Episcopalianism and antislavery activism: Jay's grandfather had been one of the founders of the New York Manumission Society, had attempted to have emancipation written into the state's first constitution (of which he was the principal author), and as governor, had enacted the bill for the gradual elimi-nation of slavery in New York. William Jay was an active abolitionist who served as judge for Westchester County until the 1840s, when his opponents on the slavery issue managed to have him removed. John Jay II (so called to distinguish him from his illustrious grandfather) acted early on this abolitionist heritage: in the spring of 1834, his sophomore year, he became manager of the New York Young Men's Anti-Slavery Society, an auxiliary wing of the state organization.[14] During the riots that summer, he "rallied with his associates to defend the dwelling of Dr. Abraham L. Cox, and the warehouse of Arthur Tappan, against threatened attack by the lawless mob which had already sacked the premises of other prominent anti-slavery citizens," according to one of his contemporaries.[15] While no direct contact occurred between Jay and St. Philip's during those terrible days, he was soon to become quite involved in the parish's struggles.

Jay's father also weighed in publicly at this point, completing in February of the following year a work entitled, *An Inquiry into the Character and Tendency of the American Colonization Society and the American Anti-Slavery Societies.* This argument in favor of immediate emancipation was at least partially in response to the riots, with the elder Jay noting the responsibility of the colonizationists themselves for several inflammatory newspaper articles just prior to the violence.[16] Soon father and son, less circumspect in their approach to their denomination than Peter Williams, would become ardent spokesmen for the parish's cause and harsh critics of their denomination's avoidance of the slavery issue, with no fear of episcopal admonition.

CHAPTER 8

Peculiar Circumstances

The riots violently illustrated a constant fact of life for the city's African Americans: they could not escape interacting (however balefully) with the city's white population, no matter how "independent" their institutions and organizations and no matter how much that same population wished to segregate and isolate them. The riots made the corollary of that situation obvious as well: such interactions between the races in New York City were always about power. White New Yorkers had the power to determine to what extent and under what conditions black New Yorkers were permitted to belong to the American society. For the people of St. Philip's, the interaction between their rector and their bishop in the aftermath of the riots was a conjunction of that basic power with the religious power built into their denomination's institutional structure. Accommodating oneself to power—learning how to operate within it, around it, and despite it—was a constant necessity for black New Yorkers if they wished to find a way to belong.

Few were as successful at such accommodation, and paid as straightforward a cost, as restaurateur and parishioner Thomas Downing.[1] Tall and dignified, he had arrived in the city in 1819, from Chincoteague, Virginia, with a knowledge of oysters. Working the harbor waters in a flat-bottomed skiff, manipulating the long-handled tongs used for harvesting, and returning to sell his catch from his residence on Pell Street, Downing built up a business. By 1825, he had opened his own oyster "refectory" in the basement of 5 Broad Street, just around the corner from Wall Street. Ten years later he had achieved such success and fame that he leased the adjoining basements to expand his restaurant, decorating it in high style: one contemporary described it as "the very model of comfort and prosperity, with its mirrored arcades, damask curtains, fine carpet, and chandelier."[2] He became enormously wealthy, his oyster bar patronized by the city's elite politicians and businessmen. Downing was renowned for catering all the finest affairs, such as a ball at which Mayor

Philip Hone introduced Charles Dickens to 2,500 select New Yorkers. He even shipped oysters abroad, once sending a choice batch to Queen Victoria, who dispatched him a gold watch in thanks. His success meant that Downing was able to offer employment to a large number of African Americans—but he was not able to offer them a table: it had been made clear to him at the outset of his enterprise that he could serve either black or white in his restaurant, but not both.[3]

It is impossible to know how Downing or his fellow African Americans felt about the price he paid for his wealth. He may have felt guilty about making his fortune by refusing to cater to black New Yorkers, and they may well have thought of him as having sold out to white power brokers for personal gain. On the other hand, he may have felt proud of the job opportunities his business had created for those he could not serve. Such negotiations between black and white could be either crude or delicate in the antebellum period, and modern readers need particularly to avoid making hasty assumptions. Downing served on the vestry of St. Philip's for ten years in the 1840s and 1850s, and was an important figure in the antislavery and black suffrage movements; such leadership roles would indicate that the black community held him in the highest esteem.

Downing's eldest son, George, born the same year Thomas arrived in New York, started out with him in the business; he would eventually go on to establish his own catering firm, which would take him to Newport, Rhode Island, where he opened a hotel, and Washington, D.C., where he ran the mess at the House of Representatives. Like his father, he would spend his career serving white clientele, would become quite wealthy, and would also publicly serve the antislavery and suffrage causes. In 1841, George married Serena Leanora DeGrasse, uniting his family with an even more remarkable St. Philip's clan.

George DeGrasse, Serena's father, had come to New York at the turn of the century. In 1804, he became a naturalized citizen, with no reference made to his racial heritage. According to one biographer, he was originally a native of Calcutta, India, and was adopted as a boy by Count DeGrasse, a Frenchman.[4] George apparently arrived in this country already wealthy, as he immediately began amassing property. He married Maria Van Surley, whose parents were German, in 1808. They had at least two sons, Isaiah and John, and two daughters, who were both famous for their beauty. What was this cosmopolitan family, whose heritage betrayed no evidence of African origin, doing at St. Philip's Church?

Here the difficulty of pinpointing any technical definition of race asserts itself. How much African background or blood determined one's racial placement? Who made such determinations? As has been noted, "colored" and "African" were interchangeable designations used by white and black Americans alike until the American Colonization Society attached "non-American" connotations to the latter term. But what exactly did either term designate? In published works on slavery and race issues, both William and John Jay referred to issues of hierarchy and economic status with the term "caste," while others spoke of "complexion."[5] "Race" was bandied about in many contexts without any greater specificity or any of today's sociological or anthropological technicalities. In a part of the country that by this time lacked the enforced boundaries of "slave" and "free," it seems to have been generally clear to all involved who belonged on which side of the racial divide, yet locating the divide itself—both then and looking back now—remains obscure. This paradox was likely a cause of the vehemence with which the divide was defended by those who considered themselves white.

How, then, or why, did the DeGrasse family arrive at St. Philip's Church? Did someone at a white Episcopal church remark upon the color of the father's skin and suggest that they would be more comfortable at the "colored" parish? Or did the DeGrasses understand themselves to be "colored" because George was Indian—or because he actually did have some African heritage as well? In an 1834 letter to Gerrit Smith describing the eldest DeGrasse son, Isaiah, Peter Williams stated that he was "a mixture of Asiatic and European with African blood"—but whence this African blood? And how did Williams know? In 1831, an article in Garrison's antislavery newspaper the *Liberator* agreed with the father's later biographer by asserting that Isaiah had "no African blood in his veins."[6] Who is correct here? The historical record cannot answer these questions with certainty, but the fact that these sources disagree on the family's ethnic makeup points to the fluidity and confusions inherent in what some devoutly wished were rigid categories.

The issue is of course further obscured by the agendas of those involved. While designations of color were for white New Yorkers primarily about establishing and maintaining social, political, and economic power, the very desire of black activists to overcome racial oppression required identifying—and identifying with—the commonality of those oppressed. For those who wished to demonstrate the equality of their people with those who were oppressing them, they first had to accept an oppressive designation of what made them distinctive. Thus it was as important to African Americans as to European Americans to determine who was what.

The letter from Williams to Smith that detailed his understanding of the

DeGrasse family background illustrates this paradox perfectly. Williams was again recommending to Smith a student for the Oneida Institute—not DeGrasse. But he did so as part of a broader educational plan he was putting together:"I have been for a long time particularly interested about his education—he being of pure African descent, and I wishing him to have a liberal education, that he might prove, that all that has been said about the inferiority of African intellect is false." This student was the young Alexander Crummell, whose father was descended from the Temne chiefs of West Africa. Williams went on to describe his agenda further to Smith:

> I selected three lads with this view [of disproving assertions of African intellectual inferiority], one of whom has such a mixture of Asiatic and European, with African blood, that he was readily received in Geneva College, and has been there two years, and given great satisfaction to the professors. The second is a mulatto, and has been two years in the University of Glasgow, Scotland. He is a superior scholar for his opportunities.

These two would be Isaiah DeGrasse and a young parishioner named James McCune Smith, respectively. "I have not been able to obtain means as yet for Alexander, who is the third, to give him as good an opportunity as the others but am in hopes that he may be able to do very well in your school, as he is very ambitious of learning."[7] The racial composition of each of these young men was as important to Williams as their educational opportunities, as their differing admixtures of African background—the cause of their oppression—created a sliding scale for the proof of equality their rector sought. Could he have attributed a portion of African heritage to DeGrasse because it furthered his agenda? But again, why would this family be attending St. Philip's if none of them were of African descent to any degree?

DeGrasse, with the least reason to be categorized as "colored," was the first of Williams's experiments to encounter severe obstacles over his racial status.[8] Contemporaries described him as so light-skinned as to be indistinguishable from a white man, which surely (and paradoxically, given Williams's agenda) was a factor in his success in gaining admission to Geneva College.[9] Under his rector's tutelage, he decided to enter the Episcopal ministry, and in 1836, he was accepted by the bishop and Standing Committee as a candidate. The General Theological Seminary, founded in Manhattan under Hobart's leadership almost twenty years earlier, proclaimed that "every person producing to the faculty satisfactory evidence of his having been admitted a candidate for Holy Orders, with full qualifications according to the customs of the Protestant Episcopal Church in the United States, shall be received as a Student of the Seminary."[10] DeGrasse accordingly applied, was admitted after examination by the faculty, selected a dormitory room, and began attending classes. The issue of his race or color apparently did not come up.

On October 11, 1836, Bishop Onderdonk met with DeGrasse and told him that he could not continue at the seminary. According to DeGrasse's diary, the bishop said that "there were fears that my presence there as a regular inmate, and especially my eating in common with the pious students, would give rise to much dissatisfaction and bad feeling among them." But DeGrasse's actual experience had been rather different: "Thus far I have met with no difficulty from the students, but have been kindly treated."[11] Nonetheless, Onderdonk ironically argued that DeGrasse was too strongly identified with people of color, and would give offence. The bishop suggested that he could continue to attend lectures and consult with professors, but he was not to be formally enrolled nor live at the seminary. DeGrasse found this offer repugnant, and instead chose to pursue private studies on his own. Two years later he was ordained to the diaconate, and Onderdonk reported him to the convention that year as "a young man of African extraction, whose examinations had evinced ample literary and theological attainment."[12] The bishop managed to sound proud of the educational achievements of a man he had barred from the standard process for receiving that education.

This was a stunning course of events. How could DeGrasse have been accepted as a candidate for the ministry without the bishop and the Standing Committee being aware of his heritage? He could not have been attempting to "pass" for white, as his parish allegiance would have been part of the application process, and Williams's recommendation would have been the necessary first step. What was Onderdonk thinking? Did he accept DeGrasse as a candidate hoping he could pass at the seminary, but then change his mind? Or had he just assumed that DeGrasse would not attempt to attend the seminary? DeGrasse's diary does not fully explain the bishop's motives or agenda. Nor does it indicate whether the bishop ever really understood DeGrasse's ethnic makeup.

What the diary does make plain is the basic racism of Bishop Onderdonk. The only factor on which he seems to have been clear was DeGrasse's membership at St. Philip's, which meant to the bishop that he was "colored" and "African." This racism was then coupled with the bishop's fear of alienating slaveholders in the denomination: Onderdonk, DeGrasse wrote, "thinks that the South, from whence they receive much support, will object to my entering" the seminary.[13] Yet DeGrasse had caused no stir on his arrival at the seminary, so it is just as likely that the bishop was simply looking for a reason to validate his own discomfort. Whatever the perceived mistake made in the process of accepting the young man as a candidate, Onderdonk felt no compunction about correcting it as instantly and bluntly as possible. On the other hand, he certainly had a use for DeGrasse, sending him off to serve as "missionary" to "the colored Episcopalians" of Jamaica, Newtown, and Flushing (all now part of the borough of Queens).[14]

DeGrasse died only three years later, in 1841, in the West Indies. He had attempted to start a second black parish in Manhattan, St. Matthew's Free Church, after a year in Queens County, but the project never got off the ground, and he then went to the Caribbean (possibly Jamaica) in an futile effort to improve his health. Onderdonk eulogized him at the diocesan convention as "a young man of African extraction, who had entered the ministry, and prosecuted its duties with talents and acquirements of a superior order."[15] Still focused on the least visible yet most volatile aspect of DeGrasse's ethnicity, Onderdonk was nonetheless thrilled with what the new priest was able to accomplish once he knew his place.

This bizarre interaction between a "colored" man and his bishop, however, might well have disappeared quietly from view were it not for its repetition three years later. The "pure African" of Williams's experiment, young Alexander Crummell, completed his studies at Oneida in 1838 and was approved as a candidate for holy orders that November. He then applied to attend the seminary the following year, despite Bishop Onderdonk's objections. According to Crummell's autobiography, he was inspired to this course by "the catechising of my pastor, Rev. Peter Williams . . . and kindled, as I well remember, by a sermon of Doctor Whittingham."[16] As to the influence of the rector whose acquiescence to the bishop he had so severely criticized, Crummell recalled that Williams had "charged me never to allow myself to be abused and insulted, as he [had] suffered himself to be, and expressed the hope that the rising young men of intelligence among his people, especially those in the ministry, should stand erect in their position as men and not allow themselves to be cowed by any power or authority."[17] This is powerful advice, and captures Williams's paradoxical combination of striving and submission. Crummell spent the rest of his life attempting to put this approach into practice, and it cost him dearly.

Crummell was born in 1819 to Boston and Charity Crummell. His father had been brought to this country as a slave at the age of thirteen (around 1780). Charity was free-born and had grown up on Long Island. The elder

Crummell became legendary, however, as a man who "could not be a slave": as his son told the story, after ten years of service, Boston simply announced to his owner, Peter Schermerhorn, that "he would serve him no longer." He moved to another part of town, and refused to return despite "all remonstrations and intimidations."[18] For at least a portion of his son's early life, Boston Crummell worked as an oysterman, like his contemporary and fellow parishioner Thomas Downing.

Alexander Crummell was a classmate of George Downing's at the African Free School; Isaiah DeGrasse and Williams's other project, James McCune Smith, were a few years ahead of them. Other schoolmates included Henry Highland Garnet and Samuel Ringgold Ward, both of whom would also enter the ministry and, like Crummell in the end, emigrate; Patrick Reason, who became a well-known engraver; and his brother Charles, who enjoyed a long career as an educator, becoming one of the first African Americans to teach at the college level. In addition to his two years spent at the Oneida Institute, Crummell worked summers as a delivery boy at the New York office of the Anti-Slavery Society.

From this background of self-assertion in racial interactions, Crummell presented himself to the dean of the General Theological Seminary, William Whittingham, the same man whose sermon had "kindled" the gangly young intellectual's desire for ordination. But in Crummell's (perhaps idealized) re-telling years later, the dean told him, "You have just as much right of admission here as any other man. If it were left to me you should have immediate admission to this seminary; but the matter has been taken out of my hands in DeGrasse's case; and I am sorry to say that I cannot admit you." Crummell immediately appealed to the seminary's board of trustees, which unfortunately included the bishop of New York. During a heated debate, Onderdonk sent for Crummell and verbally attacked him "with a violence and grossness that I have never since encountered save in one instance in Africa," reducing Crummell to tears. The Rt. Rev. George Doane, bishop of New Jersey, was the only trustee to stand up for him, and the board denied the application. Appalled and dismayed, Crummell requested permission to go outside the diocese to pursue his theological studies at Andover Seminary, but Onderdonk refused him this as well, insisting that Crummell study privately in the city. Crummell then requested that his candidacy for orders be terminated. This freed him from Onderdonk's authority, enabling him to pursue ordination elsewhere.[19]

On the advice of supporters, Crummell went to New Haven, studied at Yale under the conditions DeGrasse had rejected (he was allowed to attend lectures, but not to be formally enrolled), and was accepted as a candidate for orders in the Diocese of Massachusetts by Bishop Alexander Griswold. In 1841, he left Yale (without, of course, a degree) and accepted a call to be lay reader at Christ Church, a small black Episcopal congregation in Providence, Rhode Island. He was ordained by Griswold to the diaconate in 1842, but shortly thereafter left for Philadelphia, where his episcopal difficulties recurred: the bishop of Pennsylvania was none other than Henry U. Onderdonk, brother of the New York bishop whose prejudices Crummell had fled. Adding to his troubles was the fact that in the midst of this circuitous road to the priesthood, he had made the acquaintance of the young John Jay.

Shortly after the fiasco at the seminary, Jay had come to call upon Crummell. He had heard of Crummell's difficulties and wanted to offer assistance. While that mostly took the practical form of personal financial support—he provided six dollars a month while Crummell attended Yale—Jay also helped to bring his case before the public. He was the author of a pamphlet, *Thoughts on the Duty of the Episcopal Church in Relation to Slavery*, that took his denomination to task for its failure to oppose slavery and racial prejudice. Originally a speech delivered to the New York Anti-Slavery Society convention, it had just been published. Jay was the perfect companion for controversy, and Crummell had no intention of abandoning his disagreement with Onderdonk: ten years later, he was still producing new publications about it. In a letter late in 1839, he assured Jay that he felt "the entire matter, all the correspondence, should be published—exposed to the public eye, and held up to severe scrutiny; and this too at the risk of blasting every hope and desire I have ever cherished concerning the Gospel Ministry."[20] Crummell was willing to risk all, and Jay was willing to help.

The seminary's board of trustees fired the first salvo, publishing Onderdonk's interpretation of the controversy in the *Churchman*; Jay responded with a lengthy article based on Crummell's version, complete with all the correspondence the bishop and candidate had exchanged. Four years later, Jay published a pamphlet entitled *Caste and Slavery in the American Church*. This not only reprised the Crummell case, but for the first time put before the public the story of Isaiah DeGrasse's seminary rejection as well. Jay, whose family had business dealings with George DeGrasse,[21] managed to get permission to use the excerpts from Isaiah's diary, which remain the only documentation of his dealings with Onderdonk. The pamphlet was widely read, eventually making its way to England, where Samuel Wilberforce used it as a source for his *History of the Protestant Episcopal Church in America*, a polemical look at his perception of the denomination's proslavery stance. (A neat circle was completed when William Jay produced a pamphlet to restore Wilberforce's harshest remarks to public view after the American edition of his work had been mutilated.)[22] Crummell, meanwhile, would continue to develop a reputation for brilliance, intransigence, and insufficient respect for the episcopacy.

Crummell's problems were not only with white bishops; he had left the Rhode Island parish largely because of personality conflicts with his congregants. They found him self-righteous, rigid, and aloof, and finally told him so. It is not hard to imagine, then, how Bishop Henry Onderdonk found the man who was pursuing a public campaign against his brother! And it is therefore hard to imagine why Crummell thought he would be supported by this brother any more than the other.

Henry Onderdonk greeted him by stating that he would only accept his letter dimissory (the document that transfers a priest from one bishop's jurisdiction to another's) if Crummell would agree to never attempt to attend the diocesan convention. Crummell, of course, adamantly refused. He did not at this point have a congregation, but Onderdonk expanded his ban to include "any church you may raise in this city." Crummell sought the advice of Bishop George Doane of New Jersey, the only man to support his original effort to attend the General Seminary, and Doane insisted that Onderdonk was wrong to impose such conditions and Crummell was right to refuse them. Onderdonk had another move ready, however: he accepted Crummell's letter dimissory (to have refused the letter would have placed him in an awkward position with its writer, Bishop Griswold of Massachusetts), but persuaded the diocesan convention to do the dirty work. Referring to the first black Episcopal congregation in their diocese and in the nation, the convention resolved that "No Church in this diocese in like peculiar circumstances with the African Church of St. Thomas, shall be entitled to send a clergyman or deputies to the Convention, or to interfere with the general government of the Church." In 1844, though he was finally ordained to the priesthood in St. Paul's Church, Philadelphia, by Bishop Lee of Delaware, Crummell was frustrated on the other counts: he failed to raise a church of his own and he failed to overcome the limitations his denomination was still placing on black clergy.[23]

The "peculiar circumstances" of the convention's resolution was only a euphemism for the color of the skin of the priest and his potential congregation. Yet for Crummell, as for the DeGrasses and the Downings and so many others, the real "peculiar circumstances" were the constraints of living in a society that by its very attempts to keep black and white separate forced them continually to have to deal with each other. For these particular African

Americans, being Episcopalian only exacerbated the problem: their religious lives required the approval of white denominational structures at every turn, even as they attempted to find independence within that denomination. The Downings had made their accommodation to white power in business, but would continue to be active in pursuing the parish's self-determination; Isaiah DeGrasse's struggle ended with his death in the West Indies; Crummell would continue his efforts in other venues, reappearing in the St. Philip's story only intermittently, and ultimately leaving for Liberia. In many ways, the person to carry on the battle in and against the peculiar circumstances of racial interaction and prejudice, and to most powerfully articulate its vagaries, was the third young man of Williams's educational experiment, James McCune Smith.

CHAPTER 9

The Chains That Bind

In 1851, James McCune Smith appeared as an expert witness in a legal proceeding to determine whether one John Bolding was a runaway slave or had been illegally kidnapped to be sold into slavery. By this time, Smith was perhaps the most renowned African American in the city: the first African American to earn an M.D., he was a polymath and public intellectual who had helped to start newspapers, cultural societies, and educational institutions in the black community. Smith was a well-known speaker on subjects ranging from antislavery and black suffrage to scientific rebuttals of the inferiorities of African Americans. The novel strategy undertaken by the lawyers from the Anti-Slavery Society was to argue that Bolding had no African heritage, and therefore could not be a fugitive slave. Smith was one of several putative experts called to testify for and against Bolding's assertions regarding his racial composition. A short, thickly set man with bright eyes and a somewhat stuffy demeanor, Smith argued that his study of Bolding's physiology demonstrated that he was "of white and Indian [that is, Native American] blood without any admixture of African blood." This conclusion was based on a knowledge of several contemporary comparative physiological studies, which led him to make the following points: "John's conformation, so far as the skeleton is concerned, is purely Indian. . . . A fair mulatto has crooked hair . . . the curl in his hair is not from African admixture, but different, and the curl at the end now is evidently artificial." Smith bolstered his reasoning by pointing out individuals present in the courtroom as examples of various physiological types.[1]

It would seem that Smith had more than just scientific knowledge of the subject, for on cross-examination he stated his own heritage: "My mother is a mulatto, half white and half African—my father white; I am three-fourths white."[2] This ardent spokesman for the cause of racial equality was the illegitimate son of a slave from South Carolina and a father unknown to history—perhaps his mother's owner. To the ambiguities of early-nineteenth-century racial identity Smith thus brought his own complicated mix, with its bitter lessons about racial interaction and prejudice. The self-creation of identity, and the defense of that identity against all impositions from others, was a lifelong project for Smith, and it seems likely that his heritage provided some of the motivation. One constant that ran through his extraordinarily diverse and impressive career was the importance of education for the advancement of individuals and thereby a people, particularly as a means of self-definition.

Lavenia Smith was brought to New York City around 1805 by her owner, and her son James McCune was born on April 18, 1813.[3] Early in life he was a star at the African Free School No. 2, with his work displayed on occasions of public inspection of the schools. For an 1824 visit of the Marquis de Lafayette (the Manumission Society had made him an honorary member of the school board in 1788), the eleven-year-old Smith was chosen to deliver the greeting. While the speech may well have been prepared either by Charles C. Andrews, the white superintendent of the African Free Schools, or by Smith's teacher, Ransom Wake (a St. Philip's member), it is plausible that Smith wrote it himself at their direction. In any case, his graceful delivery was complimented in the newspaper account of the event. The close of the brief speech wonderfully combined the themes that would mark the rest of the young boy's life—education, color, and freedom:

> Here, Sir, you behold hundreds of the poor children of Africa, sharing with those of a lighter hue in the blessings of education; and, while it will be our pleasure to remember the great deeds you have done for America, it will be our delight also to cherish the memory of General Lafayette as a friend to African Emancipation, and as a member of this Institution.[4]

There were still three more years until New York State law would free Smith from slavery.

While details of Smith's early life are sketchy at best, it is known that at the tender age of sixteen he was a founding member of the city's first African American cultural organization, the Philomathian Society. And while it is unclear how or when he first became connected with St. Philip's, Peter Williams undertook to further his education, as has been noted, as part of an effort to demonstrate the intellectual capabilities of those of African descent. After finishing at the African Free School, Smith continued his studies—either with Williams himself, or, through arrangements that would have to have been made through Williams, at Trinity School, a charity school founded by Trinity Church. One report asserts that he studied with a Mr. Curtis, "a tutor in Trinity School, probably as a private student"; another source claims that Smith was attending "an Episcopal collegiate school . . . one of the high schools in the city" (which would have to be Trinity School). At the very least, he developed a solid grasp of Latin during this period. After Smith was turned down by both Columbia College and Geneva College, it was Williams who arranged funding for him to go abroad to pursue medical studies.[5]

Arriving at the University of Glasgow in 1832, Smith was almost immediately the toast of Scotland's abolitionists. He was a charter member of and frequent speaker for the Glasgow Emancipation Society, whose members confronted the American captain of the ship on which Smith was to sail home and demanded that he be permitted to travel as a cabin passenger rather than in steerage. Having mastered classical languages, natural and moral philosophy, mathematics, and medicine and surgery, Smith received a B.A. with full honors in 1835, an M.A. in 1836, and an M.D. the following year. He graduated first in his class, spent a few leisurely months in Paris, and returned to New York City in triumph that September.[6]

His return was an occasion to both celebrate his achievements and remind Smith of the burden of expectation he now bore. Several gatherings were held, including one hosted by his old teacher Ransom Wake. It was advertised in the *Colored American*, the newspaper founded earlier that year by Philip Bell (briefly known as *The Weekly Advocate*). In addition to Bell, other luminaries who signed on to cosponsor the celebration included the teacher at the other African Free School, John Peterson; Smith's classmate Patrick Reason and his brother Charles; and several others, most of them members of St. Philip's also. Wake took the opportunity to suggest that Smith was not only an "ornament to [his] country," but needed to be an "advocate for the oppressed." At another gathering the next month, a letter from the Mental and Moral Improvement Society of Troy, New York, was read, lauding the "respect and admiration of the enlightened world" Smith had now garnered, which they hoped he would soon use "in advocating our rights and pleading our righteous cause."[7]

Smith did not disappoint. He established a medical practice and pharmacy that endured for the rest of his life; for years he ran an advertisement in whatever black newspaper was in existence, stating simply, "Dr. James McCune Smith may be consulted at his Office, 93 West Broadway, from 7 till

10 A.M., from 2 till 3, and from 8 till 10 P.M." He also signed on as associate editor at the *Colored American*, and began speaking out for racial equality (which speeches the newspaper frequently and considerately published in full). In his first public discourse after his return, he drew upon his scientific and medical knowledge to attack "the fallacy of phrenology" and efforts to use that pseudoscience to demonstrate the superior brain capacity of the white race. By the next year, Smith was also addressing the political dimensions of oppression as one of the keynote speakers at the annual convention of the American Anti-Slavery Society. In both of these careers—as doctor and as "advocate for the oppressed"—he was immediately and continually successful. This caused occasional conflicts: years later, he would have to beg off attending a convention in Buffalo because of, as he put it, "the utter impossibility of arranging one week's absence from my patients, unless I intend to give them up entirely: I have repeatedly found two days and a half of absence inflict an injury upon my medical (punctual) reputation which months could not remove."[8]

Smith's speech at the Anti-Slavery Society's 1838 convention celebrated the abolition of slavery in the French and British colonies on the latter's effective date that year, and of that abolition's influence on his own country: "One moral victory gained raises the mind to an eminence whence it perceives others that must be achieved, and inspires it with new energies for the struggle." Another speaker on this occasion was Gerrit Smith, whose activism and financial support were crucial to the abolitionist cause.[9] This was the first encounter between two men who were to be close friends for the next two decades, despite the racial divide between them. One result of this encounter was Gerrit Smith's appointment in 1846 of McCune Smith, along with his friends Henry Highland Garnet and Charles Ray, as agents to recruit families for an ill-fated scheme to create a free black settlement on land Gerrit Smith donated in northern New York State.[10]

Another result of their meeting was that the next year, McCune Smith sent Gerrit Smith a letter requesting financial assistance for Alexander Crummell, who had just undergone his tumultuous rejection from the General Theological Seminary. Smith asserted that Crummell wanted to go to either the British West Indies or Canada to pursue theological studies, since Onderdonk had also rejected his desire to go to Andover, and such costs would be beyond his means.[11]

This is a remarkable letter, written with tact and boldness, given that it was a request by a near-stranger for money. It demonstrates Smith's confidence in himself and his ability to communicate in writing, and it displays a complete mastery of the rhetorical style of nineteenth-century correspondence. Smith's opening salutation, "Respected dear sir, I beg that you will forgive the liberty I take in soliciting your sympathy and aid . . . " is echoed in the closing: "Respected and dear Sir, yours, with the strongest sentiments of respect and gratitude, James McCune Smith." There is nothing obsequious here, nor any sense of presumption, but rather a tone of an equal making a request with the professions of gratitude and respect that were standard for the time. As the one was an enormously wealthy white man and the other a black man dependent on the funds of others for his education, the latter's tone is impressive. Smith couched his appeal in the story of Crummell's encounter with racial prejudice, comparing this rejection with the past glories of African Christianity: "Rejected, on account of his complexion, from a Religious School, in which St. Athanasius, St. Ambrose, Augustine and Chrysostom are looked up to as Fathers in God!" He assured Gerrit Smith that Crummell's various petitions and requests to the seminary and the bishop were "respectful and well argued," and that he was a longtime member of the denomination "in which he felt that it had pleased God to call him to minister in holy things." Smith also alluded to Crummell's history of graduating from the Oneida Institute, and cited Beriah Green, the Institute's president, and Peter Williams, who had written Gerrit Smith about helping Crummell to attend Oneida, as support for his assessment of Crummell's character and abilities. In this manner, he placed his request in a continuum of familiarity, so it was not just something arriving out of the blue.[12]

McCune Smith had followed Gerrit Smith on the speaking platform the year before, and he had clearly taken note of what he had heard. Gerrit Smith had spoken of prejudice in the Northeast, and had urged his audience, largely composed of white men, to become "colored" themselves. Thus McCune Smith knew that he could appeal to Gerrit Smith with a story of prejudice and issues of "complexion," and the latter's duty would be clear. Gerrit Smith sent twenty dollars in return, despite a clear policy, as McCune Smith had noted in the letter, against "aid to an individual in preference to the mass, or to an institution."[13]

In these early years, Smith can be seen successfully exploring approaches to articulating the themes of racial identity, equality, and prejudice that would dominate his work as perhaps the first African American public intellectual. Whether approaching these themes in scientific, historical, political, or personal settings, he was equally at home and equally in command of a high-toned, concise, and yet imagistic style of writing. In a letter to the *Colored American* in 1840, Smith sounded the broad humanistic note that would come to dominate these public stands: the sense that racial equality was at heart an issue of human equality, and as such was of concern to all humanity. He argued that though he regularly attended the black conventions that were agitating for suffrage, he actually disagreed with their separatist basis:

> I am not at all opposed to all action on the part of the colored people—but am opposed to action based upon complexional distinction; believing that whilst a movement based on principle will effect our enfranchisement, that, on the other hand, a movement based on the complexion of the skin will end in riveting still more firmly the chains which bind us.[14]

The price he felt African Americans paid for identifying themselves as a people in order to combat their enforced separation from the rest of society was to further separate themselves, and that price was too high.

Yet Smith was not a man to stand too rigidly on principle. Having registered his objection, he nonetheless attended the conventions: his principles reflected an idealism about humanity that was balanced by a strong pragmatic sense.[15] The humanistic approach would dominate his intellectual perspective, but his pragmatism rested on an awareness that freedom for African Americans without opportunities and qualifications for improvement could prove meaningless. Thus in the area of "separation" on the basis of "complexion," he was a staunch advocate of furthering the educational possibilities for black New Yorkers. As he put it in a later letter to Gerrit Smith: "I will devote myself to the improvement of colored *children*. . . . A generation must be raised up who can recognize the work, and who under God will have the mental and moral discipline to essay and do it."[16] For Smith, a primary benefit of attending the black conventions was to push for the establishment of schools for African Americans.

Yet even in this area he felt himself trapped by the paradox between his broader humanistic principle and the need for schools for black students taught by black teachers. In 1849, he wrote:

> It has ever been my solemn conviction, that separate organizations of all kinds, based upon the color of the skin, keep alive prejudice against color, and that no organizations do this more effectually than colored schools. All arguments in favor of the especial appropriateness of colored teachers for colored children must cease when colored children are freely and equally admitted into white schools.

Yet despite this vision of a future hope, Smith was a founding member of the New York Society for the Promotion of Education Among Colored Children only two years earlier, and he served as its treasurer until his death. He gave a benefit speech in 1841 for the Association for the Benefit of Colored Orphans, founded three years earlier, and donated the proceeds of $201.50 to the association. In 1844, he became the attending physician for the Colored Orphan Asylum, which the association had opened the year before, and he served in that capacity for the rest of his life.[17]

Smith's self-perception regarding this commitment to the future of his people, and his efforts in organization and support of it, was quite amusingly put in a letter to Gerrit Smith:

> This kind of work suits me because it is very hard, and somewhat noise-less: in the series of metempsychoses, I must have had a coral insect for a millio-millio-grandfather, loving to work beneath the tide in a super-structure that someday when the labourer is long dead and forgotten, may rear itself above the waves and afford rest and habitation for the creatures of the Good, Good Father of all.[18]

It is intriguing to see the same paradoxical combination of personal shyness and public outspokenness that was noted in Smith's mentor, Peter Williams. For despite his "beneath the tide" protestation, there was no mistaking the public nature of his life outside his medical practice. The public realm served his work on the self-creation of identity as well, for the apotheosis of his public persona was probably reached when, in 1855, he served as the chairman of the founding convention of the fully integrated Radical Abolitionist Party. He was the first African American to chair a national political convention, and he received much public praise for the graciousness and diligence with which he handled both the speaking and administrative aspects of that role.[19]

It was through the power of his intellectual perceptions and his ability to articulate them that Smith established his influence. The absence of any great body of published work (the speeches published in pamphlet form that survive are terribly few) has left him obscure to history, but his acuity of thought when it came to issues of identity, oppression, and the relations between black and white and oppressed and oppressor, remains impressive. In a letter to Frederick Douglass, published in the latter's eponymous newspaper in 1854—they too had become close friends—Smith gave voice to his grasp of why the movement to end slavery and improve the condition of African Americans seemed so hard to sustain among African Americans themselves:

> We are not united as a people, and the main reason why we are not united is that we are not equally oppressed. . . . You cannot pick out five hundred free colored men in the free States who equally labor under the same species of oppression. In each of the free States, and often in different parts of the same State, the laws, or public opinion, mete out to the colored man a different measure of oppression.

Because differing conditions of suffrage, property ownership, intermarriage, and even residential requirements caused differing senses of how one was oppressed, it was difficult for individuals to perceive their condition as shared.

> The result is that each man feels his peculiar wrong, but no hundred men together feel precisely the same oppression; and while each would do fair work to remove his own, he feels differently in regard to his neighbor's oppression. . . . When earnest men are thus rent apart by impulses they cannot control, [how can they] in good and hearty faith earnestly unite in a common resistance to their diverse oppressions?

The problem for Smith was that from any perspective, black and white defined each other at least as much as they defined themselves, and were thus bound to each other in ways both more and less obvious.[20]

It is striking that the extant sources to Smith's public and private lives—his speeches and published writings on the one hand, and his letters to Gerrit Smith on the other—make no mention at all of his connection to St. Philip's Church. At no point, either in those first days back from Scotland or in all the later years when he became so instrumental to its battle for acceptance by the diocese, did Smith speak about, write letters to the newspapers about, or otherwise publicly communicate his thoughts on his parish's oppression and segregation. Nor at any point did he even mention in passing to Gerrit Smith the church he happened to attend, let alone the fact that by the mid-1840s he was serving as secretary to the vestry and was clearly one of its most important lay leaders.[21] Perhaps his commitment to a particular church was something he felt to be part of his private life. Whatever the reason for his reticence on this subject, his Christian faith itself was not kept hidden in either public or private settings. In the speech for the benefit of the Colored

Orphans Asylum, for example, he lauded the women who had founded the institution with a Biblical paraphrase:

> Their zeal in this cause is infinitely beyond all praise of mine, for their deeds of mercy are smiled on by Him who has declared that "whosoever shall give to drink unto one of these little ones a cup of cold water, shall in no wise lose her reward."

In his keynote address to the American Anti-Slavery Society convention in 1838, Smith concluded:

> The citizens of the Church Catholic of the Redeemer may be spread through many climes and subject to various forms of political government, but no difference in clime, no diversity in form of political creed can break the links which make them fellow-citizens in Christ, or free them from obedience to the precepts of the Saviour.

Such formal pronouncements of faith were, of course, fairly standard for the time, but they manifest a dimension of Smith's life that has been largely ignored.[22]

Smith's faith is revealed most touchingly in passages about his family life in letters to Gerrit Smith. By the mid-1840s, McCune Smith was addressing Gerrit Smith with the salutation "Dear friend," and while their correspondence conducted much business, there was also room for intimacy. Smith had married Malvina Barnet sometime shortly after his return to New York. Details of this marriage are either missing or muddled. One source asserts that Barnet was "the daughter of one of the most esteemed black families in the city," while a city census entry on Smith noted cryptically, "(wife—white)," and a third source claims the marriage was against her parents' wishes. Whatever the case, the marriage lasted for his lifetime and resulted in at least eleven children, only five of whom survived to adulthood.[23] It was in describing these joys and tragedies to his friend that Smith revealed the importance of his faith.

In a letter from 1848, explaining to Gerrit Smith that his obligations to his practice was the reason he could not attend a convention in Buffalo, McCune Smith described his sense of responsibility to his family:

> My wife is a fruitful vine through God's blessing, and three little souls look up to me for support and discipline and guidance: what a holy trust! It is

my prayer to be spared to train them aright and then fling them on the tide of progress dependent upon their own well-developed resources.

Sadly, he would quickly outlive all three of these children. The eldest, Amy, was also the first to die, just shy of her sixth birthday in 1849. Only the faith he shared with his wife helped Smith to cope with the loss, as he commiserated with Gerrit Smith:

> After a year of ailment ... which she bore with child-like patience, it pleased God to take her home to the Company of Cherubs who continually do Praise Him. You have been afflicted in like manner and know the bitterness of it. For one thing I am deeply grateful, her mind was serene to the last, and intelligently hopeful of a Blessed Immortality.

Amy's faith in eternal life was clearly learned from her parents, as Smith elaborated:

> My dear wife was sorely afflicted ... she is growing more cheerful, however, and we both live in the hope of meeting our dear little one where there will be no more sickness, nor pain nor parting forevermore.[24]

By 1854, the other two children had died, but three more had been born: a daughter, Anna Gertrude, and two sons, Peter Williams Smith and Frederick Douglass Smith. All three died that year, however, within the span of a month; most likely it was the cholera epidemic that was sweeping the city, though no cause is given in the sources.[25] Smith once again sought his friend's solace, writing to Gerrit Smith in March of 1855:

> My heart yearned to you in the midst of our deep affliction: and now, when the first strong bitterness is past, there is no one I would rather commune with among men than you. I seem suddenly to have leaped over a long period of life: and oh it is sad to have no children playing round the hearthstone. I try, and may God give me the Grace to succeed, to look into other little glad eyes and listen to other little glad voices; and I try to reason myself out of the selfishness that they are not mine. Oh that meeting hereafter![26]

Another daughter was born that October, and more children in the ensuing years who did survive Smith and gave him great joy, but by then his friendship with Gerrit Smith had foundered in the latter's breakdown over his role in support of John Brown's attack on Harper's Ferry, and the intimate letters had ceased.

These Christian expressions of hope and faith in God's mercy and eternal life appear fairly rote on the surface, but under circumstances of personal tragedy they are more than mere Victorian flourishes. It is clear that Smith's faith sustained him through his family sorrows. It is also clear that he turned to that faith when discouraged by the often futile battle against oppression. He was subject to bouts of melancholy that sapped his desire to continue the fight, as he expressed to Gerrit Smith in a letter from 1846:

> Each succeeding day, that terrible majority falls sadder, heavier, more crushingly on my soul. At times I am so weaned from life, that I could lay me down and die, with the prayer that the very memory of this existence should be blotted from my soul. There is in that majority a hate deeper than I had imagined.

Smith saw faith as his only recourse: "I must strive humbly to draw near unto God, for renewed faith and hope and encouragement. He Reigneth over the 'raging of the waves and the madness of the people.'"[27] It is important to note that unlike the expectations of so many white Christians, such faith did not make Smith more accepting of his "condition" as an oppressed member of an oppressed people; rather, it was a galvanizing source for the ongoing struggle against that oppression.

This shy man with the very public life, normally quite formal but capable of eloquent intimacy, was to become a driving force in the life of his parish and its struggle for self-definition after the death in 1840 of his mentor, Peter Williams. Yet even in the 1830s, at the very beginning of his successes as a public intellectual for the cause of the African American people, James McCune Smith's most powerful dichotomies—race and identity, faith and political action, and specific concern for his people and commitment to the broad humanistic principle of equality—were already in creative tension. While bound in chains forged by the white majority, he was also bound by these tensions created by his heritage and his intellectual insight. Perhaps the idiosyncrasy of an oppressed people choosing to be part of a white-dominated, hierarchical denomination seems less odd given the "peculiar circumstances" and idiosyncrasies that permeated the life and personality of James McCune Smith. For in the light of his faith and his hope, how odd could one more paradox held in tension or one more set of chains binding him to his oppressors truly have been?

CHAPTER 10

Promoting Improvement

The state of New York enacted legislation in 1810 that permitted African Americans to legally incorporate. The first organization to record its certificate was the New York African Society for Mutual Relief, which had been created informally two years earlier. Its object was the collection of dues to assist its members with burial costs when they died, and to provide for their widows and orphans. The founders included George DeGrasse and fellow St. Philip's members Alexander Elston and Isaac Gosiah, both bootmakers, and Henry Scott, when he was a sailor and not yet a businessman. Peter Williams, at this early stage only a licensed layreader, was one of the primary forces behind the society's formation. It became instantly successful, and by 1820 had erected African Society Hall on Orange Street to serve as its headquarters and as a meeting place for other black associations. In the 1830s and 1840s, the society was a significant force in the antislavery and black suffrage movements, and it had a trapdoor installed in the hall to facilitate its use as a stop on the Underground Railroad. For more than a century, the society boasted both prominent and ordinary black New Yorkers as members. It was the first of what was to become an entire array of organizations and associations created by African Americans for African Americans, in areas where there would be little if any white support or interest.[1]

The interaction of race, or color or "complexion" as Smith and others preferred to style it, was ever more evident and complicated in the lives of individual parishioners, and therefore in the life of St. Philip's Church itself, throughout the 1830s. Yet the congregation's difficulties were different only in kind from those of their fellow black New Yorkers. All African Americans, by virtue of their color, were in constant contact with the white culture that held sway over them—and all were subject to the irony that the constraints imposed upon them by white culture, meant to isolate them, actually required such interracial contacts for their enforcement and negotiation.

A direct result of this constant interaction was the creation of political, social, and cultural institutions by black New Yorkers that paralleled their white counterparts. Such organizations, though embodying Smith's paradox of promoting racial uplift while furthering the segregation of the races, were nonetheless essential methods for the growing free black population of the city to improve both their immediate lot and their hopes for the future. They were also the institutions that helped to bring into being the perception, if not also the reality, of a black community. The congregation of St. Philip's Church was integral to all of these institutions.

Caution must be exercised in considering the idea of a "black community," however, as there was never a time (nor could there be) in which the African American population of the city could be construed as a monolithic group, one with easily shared goals and a universal understanding of how to achieve them. Certainly an end to slavery, an amelioration of prejudice, and the rights to equal economic, social, and political opportunities were all seen as a common agenda, and were pursued with vigor by St. Philip's parishioners as much as anyone else. But within the umbrella of those large ideals, there were widely divergent views on goals, means and priorities, and even how those goals, means, and priorities should be defined. To speak of a "black community," then, is to speak of a set of individuals whose primary and sometimes only commonality was the possession of the physical characteristics of the black race, a race whose attributes and qualifications for membership were defined by a different group—a group that exclusively held that power of definition. The diverse involvements of individual members of this parish in pursuing common ideals, then, should be seen first and foremost as particular examples rather than as representative of some general mindset.[2]

On the other hand, it is also possible to misinterpret such involvements from the opposite perspective, as being exclusive to this specific set of individuals for the betterment of their own peer group irrespective of the wider black population. Oppression creates at least the shared condition of being oppressed, and any individual's attempt to improve his or her circumstances under that oppression, or any effort to ameliorate or remove it, is necessarily directed to some degree to that common cause, whether other individuals agree with that effort or not. Many of the members of St. Philip's, such as Downing and Smith, saw themselves as—and could therefore be dismissed as—participating in the rise of the city's black middle class. Their cultural aspirations, coupled with their financial successes, could be labeled signs of bourgeois elitism. The parish as a whole, then, especially in its Episcopalian desires, would be open to the same charge. But such a view would require seeing these parishioners as isolated from those whose oppression they shared, despite the relative successes they had achieved.

There is, of course, a modicum of truth in both of these errant perspectives, in both the charge of self-interest and the assumption of a grand commonality. Many St. Philip's parishioners did have middle-class aspirations, and did deplore what they saw as egregiously lower-class behaviors and attitudes among black New Yorkers. Williams, Crummell, and Smith, for example, all understood European culture to be the epitome of civilization (as did most white Americans of the time), and aspired to its attainment for themselves and for their people. They were proud of their own achievements, and believed that they had found the best ways to improve their own lives under oppressive circumstances. But they understood their aspirations to be for all African Americans, not just themselves or their peers, and they therefore pushed publicly and hard for education and moral improvement as a means to raise black culture to the same standard. Thus these men saw their work as directed at a "black community"—at the entire range of humanity that constituted such a concept—and hoped that unified action and common goals were achievable and would bring their ideals to pass.

The most realistic perspective, then, is the union of the two: to see the efforts of specific individuals to improve themselves and their peers as a mixture of self-interest and broader hopes. Such a mix of motives is simply human, and such a perspective neither objectifies a group of people whose group definition was provided by their oppressors nor dismisses the common hopes and dreams conferred by that common condition. This is a particularly helpful vantage point for considering the array of individuals and activities that composed the life of St. Philip's Church as an institution of the black community under the leadership of Peter Williams.

The actual church membership in the late 1830s represented the full range of black New York employment possibilities. The new bourgeoisie was well represented not only by Thomas Downing and George DeGrasse, but also by the now hugely successful pickler Henry Scott, the tobacco factory supervisor Peter Ray, and the shipper Peter Vogelsang (whom James McCune Smith was later to call "one of the five important black businessmen in New York").[3] But St. Philip's was not simply an upscale gathering place: one longtime member, John Marander, was listed for thirty years in the city directories as "porter." Such a job involved knocking on doors offering to cart items around the city; it was poorly paid, and the licensing of horse-drawn carts (which made more money and eased the job) was severely biased against African Americans. Others with the same occupation were Thomas Hoffman, Henry Williams, and

John Berrian. The parish included barbers, whitewashers, cigarmakers, and those who simply listed their occupation as "laborer." There were teachers, musicians, grocers (often a euphemism for purveyors of cheap liquor), carpenters, bootblacks, coachmen, jewelers, tailors, and waiters. It is hard to suggest, therefore, that this was an elitist or exclusive congregation.[4]

Judging church statistics for this period is difficult. Then as now, church membership categories and the numbers that accompanied them were not always clearly defined or agreed upon. By any reckoning, though, St. Philip's grew significantly under Williams's stewardship. The category of membership reported to the diocese each year, that of "communicants," went from ninety-three in 1820 to 160 in 1830, and then to 227 in 1838. This category, however, represented only a small (though important) portion of those actually attached to the church, for a communicant was a person who had been confirmed by the bishop and was receiving communion regularly over the course of the year. Communicants made up the voting membership of the parish as well. Not included, therefore, were women (who could not vote), children under fourteen (the normal age for confirmation then), probably children under eighteen (the age of majority), and anyone who had not had the time or inclination to be part of a confirmation class or participate in the rite. A much larger number of people would therefore have considered themselves to be "members" of St. Philip's by virtue of nothing more than regular attendance there. In the 1850s, the parish began reporting that while there were roughly 200 "communicants," the parish consisted of some "700 souls"; this would not be an unreasonable estimate for the Peter Williams period as well. Comparable figures—from Zion Church (1,200 members in 1839), Bethel AME (410 in 1837), Abyssinian Baptist (400 members in 1850), and Shiloh (originally First Colored) Presbyterian (453 in 1853)—show St. Philip's to have occupied an at least equivalent position in the religious community.[5]

What is missing from any available data—since they were not voting members—is the role of women. It is an historical truism that women have always made up the majority of any American congregation, and there is no reason to believe anything different about St. Philip's. By the 1830s, women at the parish had formed the Female Assistance Society to care for the indigent and the sick. Who they were is almost impossible to say (though John Marander's wife, Elizabeth, reported at one point on the society's finances to the vestry), as the organization's records have vanished. Clearly these women were financially astute: they once loaned the vestry money to cover its budget.[6] It is unfortunate that the historical perspective on the church is so deeply skewed by this lack of information.

Little can be said about the children of the parish either, though here too impressive growth occurred under Williams's oversight. He reported to the diocesan convention in 1819 that there were about eighty students in the Sunday School, which institution he felt would be beneficial "to the cause of literature, morality, and religion." The number of pupils remained steady in the following decade, but by 1838, Williams could report that it had increased to 195, with fifteen teachers.[7] Such an increase points to growth in young families, which is most conducive to a lively and stable parish. Things under Williams were going well.

The vital importance of education was of primary interest to Williams and many other parishioners. They had graduated from the African Free School themselves and understood only too well the importance of education for personal improvement and advancement. This school and its partner, African Free School No. 2, were opened in 1787 and 1820 respectively by the Manumission Society, whose white members believed that educating African Americans was the surest method of combating the prejudice against them. By 1820, the first school had moved to Williams Street, and its teacher was Ransom Wake, while John Peterson was the teacher at the second, located on Mulberry Street. The schools were transferred to the New York Public School Society in 1833 (when enrollment peaked at almost 1,500), and then to the newly created Board of Education in 1853. Wake and Peterson were still teaching, and by then were drawing the highest salary of any black teacher: $800 per year. White teachers averaged $1,200. The white principal of these schools for much of their early years was Charles C. Andrews, who was pushed out in 1832 when it became clear that he supported colonization. He was also known to have caned a student for referring to someone as a "black gentleman," as Andrews argued that no black man could bear such an appellation.[8]

Williams and his parishioners wanted to make educational opportunities as widely available as possible. The African Free Schools were under the auspices of white-run organizations, but various parishioners, in union with other members of the community, sought to establish black-run schools as well. Most of these efforts were either short lived or never came to fruition, but they nonetheless indicate how important it was to African Americans to take charge of their educational visions. The basement room at St. Philip's was the site of the first of these attempts, the B. F. Hughes School for Coloured Children, in 1828. John Russwurm was its head, and his emigration the cause of its demise the next year. Three years later, Boston Crummell, Thomas Downing, and others joined with Peter Williams in creating the

Canal Street High School; it lasted less than two years. In 1836, the Phoenix Society launched a high school that again functioned for only two years. St. Philip's basement was used one more time in 1839 to house the New York Select Academy, an evening high school under the leadership of Alexander Crummell and his good friend (and Oneida Institute classmate) Thomas Sidney, but it closed the same year for lack of funds and students.[9]

In addition, an effort to create a manual labor college in New Haven in 1831 was brought firmly to a close when the city's mayor issued a prohibitive order and the citizenry rioted in front of the homes of the college's supporters. Williams, Boston Crummell, Philip Bell, Thomas Downing, and Peter Vogelsang were appointed to the fundraising committee for New York (another was created in Boston) to support this ill-fated venture, at which Alexander Crummell had hoped to be a student.[10]

This project grew out of the black convention movement, which managed to have its fingers in several pies: anticolonizationism, emigrationism, antislavery, black suffrage, and education and moral improvement. These conventions, which became annual (generally) affairs with elected delegates, were begun as intentionally ongoing efforts in 1830.[11] They brought together African American leaders to debate such occasionally conflicting issues and to create organizations for action. Vogelsang and parishioner John Zuille were particularly active in these events, and helped to bring the convention to New York City in 1834. The conventions were least successful in the areas of education and suffrage (most school plans fell through and all petitions for easier access to the vote were ignored), but they had the virtue of bringing black leaders into contact and debate with one another on the wider slavery-related issues.

Two black literary (and more) societies have been mentioned in passing: the Philomathian Society and the Phoenix Society. Both were deeply entwined with parish leaders, and both sought to provide another avenue for the improvement of education and culture in the black community. The former was founded in 1829 by, among others, the youthful James McCune Smith and Philip Bell. The Philomathians met weekly for lectures, readings, and debates; over the years, Isaiah DeGrasse, Ransom Wake, Thomas and George Downing, John Zuille, and John Peterson were all involved. The society was founded with a circulating library, and eventually had a reading room and lecture hall. It later metamorphosed into a lodge of the Order of Odd Fellows.[12]

Though the Phoenix Society existed only from 1833 to 1839, it was a dynamo of activity. Anyone who contributed in any amount was considered a member, and it created ward associations whose agents were to visit and register every family of color and attempt to get them to join the society. It was thus the first real effort to create an institutional structure throughout the city's entire African American population. Though its purpose was ostensibly the same as the Philomathian—"to promote the improvement of the coloured people in Morals, Literature, and the Mechanic Arts"—it soon became a prime means of organizing for abolition and suffrage instead. This society also included white members, most notably the abolitionist Arthur Tappan, who was a major financial supporter. The familiar names from St. Philip's—Downing, Bell, Zuille, Boston Crummell, Peter Vogelsang—were all involved in leading the society, while George Downing and Charles Reason, as young men, read prize-winning essays to the society in 1837.[13]

Two black newspapers enjoyed brief yet important lives in New York City. *Freedom's Journal*, the first black-published newspaper in the country, was begun in 1827 by John Russwurm. It folded as a result of his emigration in 1829 to Liberia. The Rev. Samuel Cornish, who had coedited *Freedom's Journal*, launched *The Weekly Advocate* with Philip Bell in February 1837, and then changed its name to *The Colored American* the next month. Smith's return to the country that fall became an occasion for him to help out with writing and editing for a brief period, and then their mutual friend Charles Ray took it over. This paper lasted only slightly longer, folding in 1842 for lack of funds. Efforts in the 1840s to create a local edition of *The Frederick Douglass Paper*, published in Rochester, also languished for lack of financial support.[14]

Along with the black churches, these sorts of institutional structures provided the means of gathering a community together for the mutual support of its members in their personal, social, political, and religious lives. Yet as noble as these projects and their aims may have been, they clearly did not enjoy universal support. Whether speedy or eventual, the collapse of schools, newspapers, and societies was as much an indication of disagreement over priorities as their existence was of loftier goals shared by "leading" citizens. Even at their peak, the African Free Schools never enrolled more than a quarter of the eligible population, for example; too many parents felt that their children needed to earn more than learn. The constant editorializing and moralizing on this subject in the similarly neglected newspapers and societies did little to increase the number of those who understood education or cultural "improvement" to be of great importance.[15]

The black community, in other words, was united by larger goals but not specific approaches, programs, or organizations. Slavery was universally seen to be the primary evil oppressing individual lives both directly and indirectly, and prejudice the primary obstacle toward self-improvement, but how best to address either was not so easily or agreeably determined. The promotion of middle-class values and the denigration of lower-class behaviors were not obvious routes to better lives for those who had not already invested themselves in that agenda. The presence of members of St. Philip's in leadership roles in all of these efforts, however, suggests the centrality of this parish to both the strivings of an oppressed community to overcome its oppression and the debates over those strivings themselves.

CHAPTER II

Partaking of the Heavenly Gift

The ironies that abounded in the interactions between white and black New Yorkers were hardly lost on the parishioners of St. Philip's Church. It is hard for the modern mind to credit the possibility that they were not equally visible to white New Yorkers as well, yet that was overwhelmingly the case. An awareness of such ironies would imply a perspective that granted full humanity to African Americans and attained full self-consciousness regarding the behaviors and social structures that suggested otherwise. Such a perspective was impossible for most Americans of the early nineteenth century; those for whom it was possible, to any degree, were the minority that became antislavery activists and their supporters. Hence the anger and sarcasm that pervaded the writings of the Jays, father and son, on the blindness of their fellow Episcopalians to the ironies of their treatment of St. Philip's. It reflected, to some degree, their helplessness before such willful disinterest.

The vehemence of the Jays on this subject reached its zenith over the funeral that was celebrated for the Rev. Peter Williams. Williams died rather suddenly at the age of fifty-four, on October 18, 1840. He had contracted some sort of influenza, and had been sick for three days when he failed to awaken on that Sunday morning. The elaborate service and public praise then offered by the diocesan leaders for a man they had isolated, ignored, and treated as of a different order than themselves was simply more than either Jay could believe or bear. William Jay wrote a long letter to his daughter Anna, detailing the occasion and its outrages, and John Jay left an unfinished manuscript description clearly intended for publication, though that does not appear to have come to pass.[1] Williams himself left only his wife Sarah, his adopted sister Mary (who shortly after, moved in with Sarah, the two living together until Mary's death), and a daughter, Amy Matilda, who had married the first world-famous African American antislavery speaker, Charles Remond.[2]

The account of the funeral in the *Colored American* passed over the ironies and instead focused on the honor finally being paid to a man the paper and its community had long esteemed. Forty of the fifty Episcopal clergy in the city and immediate environs attended; sixteen of the twenty clergy invited from other denominations were also present. Such an Episcopal clergy turn-out was usual for funerals for white priests, but was rather unexpected in Williams's case. The Rt. Rev. Benjamin Onderdonk, as bishop, preached and presided; the Rev. William Berrian, as rector of Trinity, led the opening parts of the service; and the Rev. Thomas Lyell of Christ Church, as Williams's first teacher and supporter, offered the readings. The procession from his home to the church was led by the clergy, with the three officiants at the end followed by the casket. The pallbearers included two professors from the seminary and one from Columbia College, prominent New York priests, and the Rev. Evan M. Johnson of St. John's Church, Brooklyn. He would prove to be a most important ally to the parish in the years ahead, though no specific connection had been established by this time. After the casket, the procession continued with "the male relatives, then the vestry of St. Philip's Church, next students of the Theological Seminary, next the Phoenixonion, and other literary so-cieties, then the public, and [was] closed by the scholars from the colored public schools, in charge of Messrs. R. F. Wake and John Peterson." After the service, the vestry took over as pallbearers and conducted Williams's body to a walled tomb in the parish's cemetery on Chrystie Street, about a dozen blocks northeast of the church.[3]

Two weeks later, the *Colored American* had obtained a copy of the bishop's sermon, and published it with this comment: "The solemnity of the scene was much enhanced by the impressiveness of the discourse, and particularly by the application which the Right Reverend Bishop Onderdonk made to the particularities of the occasion. The text was from I Cor. xv:52—'We shall be changed. . . . '" The paper editorialized further inside: "That part [of the sermon] found on our first page, is the application of [the text] to the life, character, and death of the reverend and deceased brother, and which, in the delivery of it, mostly affected us, and would doubtless, most interest our readers; we ask for it a careful reading." Williams's good friend Charles Ray, editor of the newspaper, chose to dwell on the positive aspects of the occa-sion without reference to the past relationship of the priest to his bishop or his diocese.[4]

The Jays, however, found the ironies of the situation impossible to ignore. William Jay wrote to his daughter, who was married to the Episcopal priest Lewis Balch, his belief that the honors paid to Williams were evidence of a "triumph of abolition principles and influence," hopeful that he and his son and their supporters were finally getting through to the diocesan leadership. On this judgment he would prove to be sorely mistaken, but it does temper the sarcasm of his account of the funeral with some measure of glee.

> So Peter Williams the *Negro* minister has had a grand funeral. Bishops honored his obsequies—Doctors of Divinity and even *Trustees and Professors of the Theological Seminary* (!!) held the pall over the Coffin; and the Right Reverend Preacher of the funeral sermon declared Peter Williams to have been "a good and faithful Christian pastor—a holy minister of Jesus—a good man and full of the Holy Ghost and of faith—*a partaker of the heavenly gift of ministerial commission;*" and the Man of the Churchman [the Rev. Samuel Seabury, editor of the Episcopal journal, *The Churchman*], who sometime since maintained in his columns that the laws prohibiting 2 millions of Negroes from reading the Bible "did not touch upon the law of God" now reports all their posthumous honors to a Negro without one malignant sneer or one insolent taunt!

Jay pointed out to his daughter that to truly understand the situation, "you should know how Peter Williams was treated by his fellow partakers 'of the heavenly gift of ministerial commission' during his life."[5]

For herein lie the true ironies. Representatives of the Episcopal seminary that would not accept the two people Williams sponsored for ordination were among his pallbearers, and the student body from which DeGrasse and Crummell were excluded marched in the procession. The bishop who had publicly humiliated Williams over his membership in the American Anti-Slavery Society and who never included him in any clergy gathering now praised him as an upstanding fellow priest. As the elder Jay put it:

> This "good and faithful Christian pastor . . . this good man full of the Holy Ghost and of faith" was not numbered among the "clergy entitled to seats in the convention." God had given him a black skin and therefore St. Philip's Church has never been received into union with the convention. . . . I have known [Williams] attend as a spectator but not as a member.[6]

Under such "peculiar circumstances" Jay could not countenance the honors these supposed colleagues were paying Williams in death.

The younger John Jay's description, as it was meant for public rather than private consumption, is rather more melodramatic in tone—and, if possible, even more self-righteous and angry. He began with the snide remark that "not a little surprise was excited in this city a week or two since by the somewhat pompous funeral of the Rev'd Peter Williams," and went on to comment on Onderdonk's sermon "praising him to the skies and placing him in heaven." Jay's vivid portrait of how Williams felt about his fellow "partakers of the heavenly gift" is probably idealized, but was most likely based on personal contacts with both Williams and Crummell:

> The poor old man mourned in secret the treatment he received except when he poured his sorrows into the bosom of some sympathizing friend, and spoke with deep feeling of the cutting neglect, the contemptuous treatment, and careless apathy of his Episcopal brethren, amid the insults and oppression to which himself and his people were constantly exposed. He well knew that both he and they were coldly regarded by the high dignitaries of the Holy Church in whose courts he ministered, because God had given them a coloured skin.[7]

This portrait makes quite a contrast with the one offered by Onderdonk in his funeral sermon:

> It was my privilege, as I know it was of reverend brethren before me, to be often the depository of the cares and anxieties, the longing desires and earnest endeavors, the watchful solicitudes, the cheering hopes, the affectionate fears, and withal, the humble faith, and practical dependence on God's grace, with which [Williams] gave himself . . . to his pastoral charge.[8]

It is hard to imagine that Williams would ever have confided in his bishop in such manner, as both Jays well knew.

It is difficult for the modern reader to disagree with the Jays' outrage at the ironies of this funeral. Onderdonk's blissful ignorance of the implications of his sermon was, even for him, truly extraordinary. He had the audacity to ask his fellow clergy to compare themselves with Williams:

> I have often said, and would now say, in conscious sincerity and integrity of heart, that in all the wide range of my observation, I never knew a pastor whose whole soul seemed more engaged in the great work to which he has been set apart. . . . But wherefore say this here? O, not

to eulogize the dead; but that we, dear brethren of the clergy, may lay these things to heart, and ask if we could thus appear before our great Lord and Master, if now our summons should come; if we go with a conscience as purely washed as we may trust his was, in the blood of the atonement.

It is simply bizarre for a bishop to suggest that a gathering of priests compare the state of their souls with that of a priest who was not thought worthy to attend their gatherings.[9]

Reporting Williams's death to the following year's diocesan convention, Onderdonk compounded the ironies once again by praising the departed priest and his congregation to the very assembly from which they had been barred: "This excellent brother, as you well know, being one of themselves, had been for many years the faithful, devoted, and eminently useful pastor of a parish formed of Africans and their descendants. A better ordered parish the Diocese does not possess." He went on to laud Williams's faith, learning, and pastoral abilities without, apparently, ever noticing the contrast between such praise and the fact that he would not actually associate with the man except as his superior. What comes through this brief mention as of lasting importance to the bishop and to the assembled delegates is that Williams was "one of themselves," one of the "Africans and their descendants."[10]

And yet, despite the sarcasm of the Jays, the desire for honor of the *Colored American*, and Onderdonk's more than usual tactlessness, the bishop actually had it right. Peter Williams was "a good and faithful Christian pastor." He had tended his congregation as best he could, earning their trust and admiration along the way. He had taught their children, baptized their babies, buried their dead, performed their marriages, and led their regular worship. He had adhered to the strict order of the Book of Common Prayer and obeyed his bishop in all things, doing what he could to solidify the congregation's identity as Episcopalian. And he had served his community, willingly being one of the people who could be counted on to help create or support whatever organization was needed to address whatever need had been identified. Perhaps the final irony for Peter Williams was that only in death could his denomination acknowledge the man and priest they had chosen to ignore in life.

Within his own community, however, Williams's life and achievements were mourned and celebrated without irony. In the *Colored American*, Ray reported that "the vast concourse that crowded in and about the church where his remains were taken showed that Mr. Williams was loved and esteemed by every class among us." Ray then summarized the paradoxical nature of his friend's life and ministry by quoting the passage from the sermon Williams preached against colonization, cited earlier, which begins, "We are natives of this country; we ask only to be treated as well as foreigners." Ray noted, "The sentiment is cutting, but the spirit, peculiar to him, is kind." The mixing of intentions found in this passage, combining a desire to call white America to account with a desire to yet be part of America, is emblematic of Williams's effort (like that of so many of his contemporaries) to hold in tension the paradoxes that marked his life and career. His most passionate stands were always tempered by his willingness to understand other views. He would be remembered not as a firebrand leader, but as a pastor who "had deeply at heart the interests of our whole people."[11]

Beyond the loss of a beloved minister, Williams's death brought about an enormous change for the parish. During his rectorship, the congregation could point to Williams as the embodiment of their identity as Episcopalians: one of their own, one of their own color, properly ordained and serving in a properly consecrated building. No amount of isolation or segregation could take away such recognitions of his fundamental denominational status, and that status made the denomination tangible for the congregation. Who would fulfill that role for St. Philip's now that Williams was gone?

Arrangements were made immediately for the congregation to again be served by a rotation of white clergy, but it was thought by all that this was only to be temporary. Little did the parish know that it would be thirty-two years before they would again have a rector, for it would be that long before they had a black priest to lead them. None of the white clergy who served in the meantime would ever receive a title beyond "officiating minister," and the vestry was forced to fill the void in leadership. In the absence of a priest who could embody their identity, it should not have surprised anyone that the congregation would seek other ways to establish their denominational authenticity. While both Jays in their accounts of the funeral spoke of the conditions imposed upon Williams's ordination as if they were public knowledge, the parish leadership would always deny that any such conditions had ever been accepted. Yet it is true that only after his death did those leaders feel the urgent need to secure their right to attend the diocesan convention just as any other parish could. It is yet another irony of racial interaction that this final step in establishing the religious identity of the congregation of St. Philip's Church required the death of their religious leader.

CHAPTER 12

To Employ a Colored Clergyman

From the beginning, the people of St. Philip's had wanted first and fore-most "one of their own colour" to be their spiritual and pastoral leader, and this desire remained strong after their rector's death. During the Williams years, the congregation had managed with difficulty to raise up two black priests. Unfortunately, DeGrasse died young and Crummell's battles with Onderdonk had apparently poisoned the diocese for him, so neither priest was available when Williams died and a new leader was needed. But while the campaign for admission to convention was to become central to the parish in the 1840s, the search for an appropriate priest of color continued to be of enormous importance to the parish's sense of identity.

In the immediate aftermath of Williams's death, St. Philip's was supplied by a rotation of clergy from around the diocese. Thomas Lyell of Christ Church took the first Sunday after the funeral and Bishop Onderdonk celebrated communion the following Sunday.[1] According to the bishop's report to the convention the next year, at some point in 1841 the Rev. Benjamin Evans, who had been appointed city missionary-at-large, became the regular offici-ant. Evans was initially assisted by the Rev. Donald Frazer, who was ordained deacon that April, but he lasted only a few months. The Rev. Alexander Frazer (no relation) became Evans's assistant at some point in the fall, begin-ning a productive association that ended only with his death in 1848.[2]

Frazer's ministry in the Diocese of New York began sometime in the 1830s, with the Mission Church of the Holy Evangelists, one of the projects administered by the New York Protestant Episcopal Mission Society (later the Episcopal City Mission Society), which was started in 1832 under On-derdonk's direction.[3] Originally a nonpartisan organization, it was quickly accused of being another venue in which the bishop could push his High Church agenda (which says something about Frazer's liturgical and theo-logical leanings). In 1837, Frazer was appointed missionary-at-large, which position he held until 1840, when he combined teaching (perhaps at Trinity School) with being chaplain of the Sailors' Snug Harbor, a home for retired and indigent mariners on Staten Island. He continued to hold this latter position throughout his time with St. Philip's Church, taking one service at each place on Sundays.[4]

In February of 1842, Evans left St. Philip's and Frazer took over as officiating minister on his own. The next year, he was assisted with services in Lent by the Rev. Charles H. Williamson, and then by the Rev. Ralph Hoyt, who had been ordained deacon that fall. Hoyt was made priest the next year, and continued to assist at St. Philip's on alternate Sundays until the fall of 1846, when the Rev. Thomas Clark took over as assistant. Another confusing period took place after Frazer's death in May 1848, until the Rev. William Morris, rector of Trinity School, was hired as "officiating minister" in August 1849, in which position he continued until 1860.[5]

The point of this summary is that all of these men were white. Clearly, several of them saw their ministries as dedicated to the poor and marginalized of the city, and it must have felt rather odd for the parish to understand that they were perceived as such by these mission-oriented men. Nonetheless, Frazer and Morris in particular were dedicated to St. Philip's and enormously helpful to the parish both as pastors and as allies in the effort to gain admission to convention. But they were white, they were part-time, they were never named "rector," and they did not administer the life of the parish. The vestry hired them, passed on requests to them, and occasionally invited them to attend a meeting to discuss an issue of importance. Normally, the rector of a parish presides over vestry meetings; during this period at St. Philip's, the vestry was in charge of the life of the parish and the clergy were there to help.

This was not the situation the parish or its vestry desired. They wanted a black priest. The pool of available men was quite small, and as the negotiations among the vestry show, they were not going to settle for just anyone. They took the enterprising step of creating a society for "assisting pious young men in preparing for the Christian ministry" in 1842,[6] yet it was a lack of support from the parish that caused one young man, Charles Reason, to abandon his hopes for the priesthood entirely. He instead went on to a long and successful career as a teacher and eventually college professor.

The historical record for this period is spotty, but it indicates that Reason had determined to pursue the ordained ministry and the vestry had agreed to support that pursuit in the fall of 1842; he began studying with a "Rev. Mr. Mead" that December. The next September, Reason sent a note to the vestry complaining of "the unexpected position taken by the Venerable Diocesan [Onderdonk]" and "of the vestry and the remissness of the same in not endeavoring to secure (to him) at the appropriate time the rights of Studentship as enjoyed by other candidates in the General Theological Seminary." After the experiences of DeGrasse and Crummell, it is hard to imagine that either Reason or the vestry could have expected the bishop to allow him to attend the seminary. Reason, however, went on to say that he was determined "to make the matter known to the Bishop immediately," and then threatened that if he were "denied the rights of the church institution," he would "resign his candidateship." With Jay's pamphlet about the Crummell affair just published, the merits of being confrontational with the bishop would seem obscure at best. The members of the vestry were appalled by his entire tone and his threat to go to the bishop, and they hastened to form a subcommittee to "inform the Bishop that Mr. Reason has taken this step to the surprise of and without the consent of this vestry."[7]

The vestry, at this point, was composed of such figures as warden Peter Ray, secretary James McCune Smith, Ransom Wake, Thomas Zabriskie (a member of the parish's first vestry), and others. This was an impressive group of men who knew all about the history between their ordinands and the bishop, yet their immediate response to Reason's problem was to affirm the bishop's prerogative of denying Reason a place in the seminary. They summoned Reason to a special vestry meeting two days later. After hearing him out, Smith asked simply, "Did the committee [of the vestry that had evaluated his desire for ordination] promise that you should have the *rights* of other students in entering the Seminary?" Since Smith himself was part of that subcommittee, Reason could only reply, "I cannot say that they did distinctly promise me the rights as enjoyed by other students." As far as the vestry were concerned, case dismissed. Smith and Alexander Elston then went to call on the bishop, and they reported back to the next vestry meeting that "the Bishop had expressed his thankfulness to the Vestry for their confidence in him."[8]

Reason next sent a note to the vestry stating that he had decided to remain a candidate despite the fact that he would have to continue private study rather than attend the seminary. The vestry, by now skeptical of Reason's motivations, required a written statement from him detailing his reasons for wishing to be ordained. They also decided to inquire of the bishop as to the state of Reason's studies during the previous year. Reason responded by saying that he had an "earnest desire to enter the Christian Ministry" and had given up his "former determination" to study at a seminary or resign, and instead wished to continue as a candidate. The vestry resolved that "taking all the facts of the case into consideration, this vestry, whilst their confidence in Mr. Reason has been greatly shaken, yet hope that, with his present views of duty, he will, by diligently pursuing his studies, and a peaceful demeanor, succeed in restoring that confidence."[9]

At the November meeting, the group that had spoken with the bishop and Reason's teacher about the candidate's studies reported that there had been a few interruptions in that area: "on two occasions Rev. Mr. Mead had been absent when waited on by Mr. Reason; and . . . Mr. Reason had been prevented by family afflictions from pursuing his studies with vigor." Before any course of action could be decided upon, however, "two notes were received from Mr. Reason: the first . . . requesting to know why the confidence of the vestry in him had been shaken; the second . . . containing an announcement of his 'resignation . . . as a candidate for holy orders.' " As far as the vestry was concerned, the matter was now closed.[10]

This was an extraordinary series of exchanges, all carefully recorded in the minutes of the vestry meetings. The complex nature of the relationship between this parish and its bishop is here fully at play. The vestry clearly did not want to become involved in a confrontation with the bishop over the seminary: that battle had been fought and lost twice, as Jay's pamphlet was only too recently reminding them and everyone else. The priority of the parish's leadership was to get one of their own color ordained, despite the indignities that lay along the way. Alongside this priority may well have been the vestry's desire to begin trying to gain admission to convention, for which they would need the bishop's support and assistance, not his animosity. The conflict between being Episcopalian, and therefore working with the institution and its bishop and leadership, and being African American, and therefore demanding equal rights as enjoyed by other Americans, is starkly outlined here. As Peter Williams had decided, so the vestry agreed: the parish's needs took precedence over individual needs.

This conflict returned four years later, when Alexander Crummell appeared to be the next viable option for a black priest. Crummell had returned to New York City in 1845 to take charge of the Church of the Messiah, a second black Episcopal congregation. Isaiah DeGrasse's church, St. Matthew's, had largely collapsed by the end of 1840 (ironically, Alexander Frazer was the last priest to be in charge of it, taking over in June of that year while still under the auspices of the City Mission Society).[11] DeGrasse himself had left that year for the West Indies, where he was soon to die. Crummell attempted to recreate the parish under its new name, with only mixed success. He was still rigid and self-righteous, and after his experiences in Rhode Island and Philadelphia, he was feeling unappreciated as well. And now he was back in the diocese with whose bishop he was waging an ever more public war.[12]

The relationship of this second congregation with St. Philip's was always a tangled one. Several men who served on the vestry at St. Philip's were at various times vestry members at St. Matthew's/Messiah, including John Peterson, Samuel Rankin, and William Tyson. At the end of 1845, the St. Philip's vestry reported that "a communication was received from the Church of the Messiah," but the minutes are silent about its contents beyond noting that they resolved to give it consideration. The January 1846 meeting "broke up in discord" over "the subject matter of the letter from the Church of the Messiah," but the cause of the controversy and its specifics are again left out. The matter is ignored the next month, and then settled in March:

> This vestry, having respectfully considered the said communication, are of the opinion that the plan contemplated therein (for the organisation and special union of Colored Episcopal Churches) would be of no advantage to either church, and would not tend to the Spread of Episcopacy; and is therefore declined by this vestry.

Messiah was in dire financial straits, and had lost its worship space that fall when the room it rented had burned; their desire for a merger would have been sensible. But one of the burdens St. Philip's would have had to take on in such a merger would have been Crummell himself, and, as became clear the next year, this apparently gave some of the vestrymen pause.[13]

The departure of Ralph Hoyt as assistant in the fall of 1846 created a conflict with Alexander Frazer. At the January meeting that year, the vestry had appointed James McCune Smith and George Jamieson to be a committee "to select a young man for the ministry, for this church." No further progress, however, was ever reported. That summer, Hoyt sent a communication to the vestry about some aspect of his contract, which the vestry resolved was not their concern, as they had "left the arrangements in question with Rev. Alexander Frazer"—which would indicate that jurisdiction over assisting ministers belonged to the officiating minister. Nonetheless, the vestry in October requested that Frazer hire "the Rev. Mr. Sweetser" (another white priest) to assist. Frazer responded by stating that he wished to hire Thomas Clark instead. The December meeting resolved that "while this Vestry have the highest esteem for Mr. Clark as a *Christian* and as a *gentleman*, yet in compliance with the wish of this congregation, we wish the Rev. Mr. Frazer would call the Rev. Mr. Sweetser or some other that the congregation would be pleased with for assistant." In other words, anyone but Clark would do— and Frazer went ahead and hired Clark.[14]

At the March vestry meeting in 1847, vestryman George Lawrence proposed that they hire a "Rev. Gary," another white priest, "to fill the pulpit of St. Philip's church." Whether this was over the Clark matter or something else, Lawrence apparently was not enamored of Frazer, and sought to replace him. The resolution was rejected. Smith proposed instead that Frazer "be requested to request the Rev. Alexander Crummell occasionally to occupy the pulpit of St. Philip's Church," and this motion passed. This was a fairly diplomatic maneuver: Smith did not suggest that Crummell replace Clark, only that he preach from time to time. Crummell grew up in the parish, so having him preach on occasion was an easy way to retain that historic connection and to have a black clergyman visible in St. Philip's once again, all without implying anything about Frazer's adequacy. It also, however, allowed Smith to dangle before the congregation the tantalizing prospect of Messiah failing and Crummell being more available, and thus appears to have been a move preparatory to trying to hire Crummell to either assist or replace Frazer.[15]

The vestry minutes marked this motion as "agreed," the term used to indicate a unanimous decision. Yet there was disagreement nonetheless, as the April meeting minutes include the following entry: "Moved that the Secretary do notify the Rev. Alexander Frazer of the resolution passed at last meeting. Lost." Why had Smith not already requested that Frazer invite Crummell to preach, as the vestry had agreed? One or more vestrymen must have had misgivings about Crummell's public attacks on the bishop and conveyed them to Smith. Or perhaps, with vestry elections coming up before the April meeting, Smith felt he should delay until seeing whether the new group would continue to support the invitation, yet only two of the previous year's vestry were not returned to office. Whatever the reason, the new vestry rescinded the invitation by deciding not to communicate their previous desire to Frazer, and the matter was put to rest.[16]

In November, the matter returned with greater force. The vestry that month agreed to hire Frazer as "officiating minister of this church" for another year, at a stipend of $500, and then resolved "that this vestry do invite the Rev. Alexander Crummell to be assistant officiating minister of this church, to preach therein on the alternate Sundays" for a stipend of $300. This resolution was "carried," indicating that the vote was split, and Thomas Downing, George Jamieson, and Samuel Rankin asked that their opposition be recorded in the minutes.[17]

Frazer's reaction was swift. Three days later the vestry held a special meeting to address the priest's objection: "I presume that no vestry did ever yet invite anyone to assist their minister, knowing that such an one would not be agreeable to him." Yet beyond his concerns that the vestry had not consulted him, overstepped their bounds, and acted precipitately, Frazer continued: "Permit me to say that I cannot receive any one to assist me in whom I have not the fullest confidence, whom I cannot control, and who would not be acceptable to at least a fair majority of the congregation; I therefore cannot accept of the Rev. Alexander Crummell to assist me."[18] Crummell's independence and controversial nature were clearly more than Frazer would endure, and he felt this was true of the congregation as well.

The vestry had also already received a reply from Crummell accepting their appointment, so now things were in a fine fix. Zabriskie, Smith, and Ray were appointed to confer with Frazer about his objections, and the vestry turned to a discussion of what to do about Crummell. It was moved that, Crummell having been offered and accepted a position, and the vestry "regarding him as every way fitted for the office," the agreement be honored. To this motion was added the deliberately provocative challenge that Crummell be accepted "until, before some regularly constituted ecclesiastical court, he shall be proved guilty of what unfits him for exercising the office and functions of the Christian ministry." In addition to the argument about Crummell and his difficulties with the bishop, this challenge also manifested the vestry's struggle for power: the motion was essentially asserting that the vestry had the right to hire and fire ministers, and since Frazer served at their pleasure, he had no grounds for refusing their choice.

The vote on this motion was split evenly: Smith, Zabriskie, Ransom Wake, and George Lawrence agreed, while Scott, Downing, Rankin, and George Jamieson dissented. Peter Ray, as warden, then cast the deciding vote against the resolution. The appointment of the committee to confer with Frazer was reconsidered, and it was decided to meet as a body with him four days hence.[19]

Frazer arrived at that meeting willing to compromise, and after stating his objections to Crummell, proposed three conditions for employing him:

First, that he (the Rev. Alexander Frazer) was willing to exchange pulpits immediately with the Rev. Mr. Crummell, after a friendly interview; secondly, that as soon as Rev. Mr. Frazer has tangible proof that a majority of the seatholders are in favour of Rev. Mr. Crummell, he will be willing to accept him as an assistant. Thirdly, the Rev. Mr. Frazer requests three months' notice for Rev. Mr. Clark.

The vestry agreed to convey these conditions to Crummell and to attempt to negotiate their fulfillment, and asked Frazer "to discontinue the services of the Rev. Mr. Clark" as of three months later. The vestry made its purpose clear, stating that they "were anxious to employ a colored clergyman," rather than Clark, "to officiate."[20]

The rest of the discussion verges on the comic. Crummell, in high dudgeon, attended the next meeting ten days later and presented his case in a letter. He lambasted Frazer for acting as if he, rather than the vestry, had the authority to hire clergy, and for placing "a Presbyter of good standing and unimpeached, in the position of a probationer before the church." After three years as a candidate for orders and more than two as a deacon (and all of it under circumstances by now well known to all), Crummell said, "my time of trial has passed" and "I am unwilling to subject myself to an ordeal to which no other clergyman in our church has ever been brought." He then complained that Frazer would not permit him to be accompanied by his warden John Peterson and the two St. Philip's wardens Ray and Zabriskie for his "friendly interview," with Frazer instead demanding that their conversation be "strictly private." Crummell concluded by praying this all might end in "peace, quietness, and blessing," but that such peace and quiet be not "divorced from right, justice, and equity." He then spoke to the vestry of "his relations with the Rev. Mr. Alexander Frazer," though the minutes of the meeting do not elaborate on what he had to say.[21]

Crummell left the meeting, and Thomas Downing attempted to present "a letter containing a professional opinion and a Protest." The letter was returned to him, apparently unread, and the meeting adjourned. When the vestry reconvened two weeks later in December, the entire affair ended with a whimper rather than a bang. Crummell sent a letter announcing his intention to go to England to raise funds for his church (he would, in addition, stay there long enough to receive a degree from Queens College, Cambridge), and the vestry sent him off with a letter of recommendation. They voted to remove from the resolution of the previous month, regarding the termination of Clark's tenure as assistant, the phrase "as this vestry is anxious to employ a colored clergyman to officiate in his place." A motion was then made to "call Rev. Mr. S. V. Berry as assistant minister, after the congregation is in his favour, if the Rev. Alexander Frazer assent," thus imposing on another man the conditions Frazer had imposed on Crummell; this motion was voted down. Then a committee of three was established "to enquire concerning the appointment of an assistant officiating minister," but a resolution to insert the word "colored" into the charge of the committee was defeated. Downing, Lawrence, and Jamieson were appointed to the committee, and the vestry went home.[22]

The dispute over Crummell, with his cantankerous and self-righteous style, threw the entire vestry into disarray. They ended up taking no stand whatsoever, and poor Mr. Berry got himself tangled up in it as well. Samuel Vreeland Berry had grown up at St. Philip's and been supported by them for ordination; it may well have been he the vestry had in mind with their resolution of January 1846 to seek "a young man for the ministry." He was ordained at St. Philip's on December 10, 1847,[23] but four days later the vestry could not be satisfied that Berry would do as an assistant. In January, the vestry committee reported back that Berry would accept the position if called, so they offered it to him for six months "at a salary of $200." He and Clark apparently served together for the rest of the year, as Frazer died in May and the vestry decided to keep both men in place until something more permanent was worked out. That took longer than expected, and Berry and Clark were asked to continue well into 1849. In May of that year, it was proposed that Berry become "Pastor of this Parish," but the motion was voted down. In August, the vestry hired William Morris to be "officiating minister," and Berry resigned, insulted that he had been passed over for a white clergyman. He subsequently served parishes in Buffalo and New Haven, but otherwise disappears from the historical record.[24]

The disputes over Reason, Crummell, and Berry point to the conflict for this congregation between the desire for a black priest and the desire for proper Episcopal leadership—once again, between racial pride and denominational identity. Reason and Crummell both embodied the risk of alienating the parish from the bishop and diocesan leaders, as they did not seem to understand the proper relationship between priest and bishop and why that would matter to a congregation. Berry seems to have been simply inadequate—whether as preacher, worship leader, or pastor is unclear—and being the right color could not make up for that. The issue of being Episcopalian, and being seen as such by the rest of the denomination, was all the more pressing during the parish's campaign for acceptance by the diocese. They needed a "colored clergyman"—but they needed a clergyman who could provide the proper kind of leadership more.

The conflict over Crummell is the most intriguing. His reputation as a controversial figure in the diocese was, by this time, being matched by his growing renown as a brilliant and thoughtful figure in religious and moral philosophy and as a fiery speaker against racial inequalities. His sermons and speeches were widely praised, and his keenest desire was to find some venue from which to become a public intellectual and man of letters. Crummell and Smith were thus in many ways kindred spirits. They shared as well the convictions that self-improvement through education should be their people's highest priority and that their best hope lay in the divinely ordered progress of history.[25] A few years apart at the African Free School as children, both interested in classical languages and philosophy, they were the embodiment and legacy of Peter Williams's hope to demonstrate the intellectual capacities of their race. It is easy to see why Smith would have been excited about bringing Crummell to St. Philip's, even if he was hard on Reason for threatening to embroil himself in the same controversies that so occupied Crummell. It is also not hard to imagine that Thomas Downing, a man who had not the educational advantages of Smith and Crummell (or even of his own son George), and for whom adjustment to white expectations and constraints was a daily aspect of doing successful business, would find Crummell so objectionable.

The search for another "one of their own color" to serve as their religious leader highlighted the interaction of identities for this parish: they were people of faith and people of color. This doubleness required constant negotiation among themselves as they strove to reconcile these two sides, for there was no clear path to resolution. The conflict over white and black clergy was an internal one, and the external conflict over this double identity in their exclusion from the convention was occurring simultaneously. No clear path to resolution awaited the congregation there either, but the developments of the mid-1840s would at least point to new possibilities.

CHAPTER 13

A State of Schism

The opening salvo of the campaign to admit St. Philip's to the diocesan convention was fired by John Jay in 1844, when he asked the convention to appoint a committee to investigate why St. Philip's "continued in a state of schism."[1] The parish's vestry minutes prior to 1843 have been lost, but there is no mention in the meetings of 1843 or 1844 that they had made any decision to pursue this question.[2] It would appear that Jay simply acted on his own, thus launching a campaign that would involve a great number of people over the next ten years. It would also appear that he had been working toward this point for several years and for a variety of reasons.

Jay, as has been noted, came from a renowned family of antislavery activists, beginning with his famous grandfather. He also came from a notably humorless family, which even the keepers of the family's flame have been willing to acknowledge. The family sketch produced by the Friends of the John Jay Homestead notes that the elder John Jay was "not known for his humor," while the younger John Jay is said to have been "less stern and self-righteous than his father," which is a backhanded compliment at best.[3] Jay's mother was the daughter of the Rev. John McVickar, who for almost fifty years held the grandiloquent title at Columbia College of Professor of Moral Philosophy, Political Economy, Belles Lettres, Rhetoric and Logic, and Evidences of Religion, Natural and Revealed, and was one of his grandson's teachers.[4] This was not a background destined to bring about lightheartedness.

The younger Jay's pamphlet castigating his denomination for failing to oppose slavery, *Thoughts on the Duty of the Episcopal Church in Relation to Slavery*, was published in 1840 and established his reputation in the diocese. This was furthered by his publication in 1843 of the full details of the DeGrasse and Crummell disputes with Bishop Onderdonk as *Caste and Slavery in the American Church*. Here he made the connection between the particularities of individual cases and the generalities of the slavery issues, a connection that would persist in his dealings with St. Philip's and the diocese. Jay would also fail a second time to endear himself to his bishop and diocesan leaders with this supposedly anonymous publication challenging their prejudice and accusing them of being beholden to Southern cotton interests.[5]

Jay had come under more private fire earlier in his career when the famous diarist George Templeton Strong, who was two years behind him at Columbia, sneered to his diary about the graduation ceremony of 1836, "Next came the super-super-fine Mr. John Jay with an English Salutatory remarkable only for the quantity of blarney it contained." Strong's writing was never intended for publication, so he really let himself go sometimes, as when he wrote the same year: "Met Mr. John Jay and his intended walking up Broadway. She's as ugly as sin; I think he's made a bad bargain." (Eleanor Kingsfield, who the Jay Homestead biographer termed "lovely," was the daughter of a wealthy real estate speculator and merchant in the China trade; she and Jay were married in 1837.)[6] By the time Jay published *Caste and Slavery*, Strong had worked himself into full lather:

> John Jay has been writing some very flippant and foolish articles in the *New World* about church matters and abolitionism. As he is possessed of but one idea himself, he thinks it queer that the church is not equally limited in its range and can't understand that it should have other objects in view besides that of educating gentlemen of color. Well, if a man has a penchant for niggers, he has a perfect right to indulge it.[7]

As Strong eventually declared himself (to his diary, at least) to be antislavery despite his casual and caustic use of racial epithets, it would appear that it was Jay's singlemindedness and self-righteousness that put Strong and many others off.

A more positive response to Jay's publication came in the form of a letter from the Rev. Evan Malbone Johnson, rector of St. John's Church in Brooklyn and earlier noted as one of Peter Williams's pallbearers. Johnson declared himself enlightened by the experience of reading Jay's pamphlet:

> I have reason to thank God, that whatever may have been my opinions formerly on the subject of which it treats, I have been brought truly to *believe* that "God hath made of one blood" the whole race of man. I think the more we can realise the great truths, *that every member of the Catholic Church is also a member of the body of Christ*—and that *in him*

we are all one—the more shall we disregard the wicked notion, that the colour of the skin ought to make any difference whatever in our inter-course, as Christians, with those who, with us, are buried "with him by baptism in his death."[8]

This is a remarkable foreshadowing of the role Johnson would play only a few years hence, as the one who would provide the diocese with the theologi-cal understanding that those who are baptized and confirmed by a church cannot then be kept out of that church. On a more immediate level, this connection with Jay led to an acquaintance with Crummell, whom Johnson eventually invited to share both his pulpit and his dinner table. Crummell's biographer noted that despite Jay's moral and financial support of Crummell and their mutual affection, "neither of them even seemed to consider it a pos-sibility that Crummell might be welcome in Jay's home and family life at any time."[9] While Jay was adept at using particulars as the basis for expounding general principles, Johnson was apparently more willing to follow his general principles with regard to the treatment of particular cases.

One broader context that added to the difficult reception of Jay's work, and especially his request to the 1844 convention, was the developing per-ception of the antislavery and abolitionist movement as radical and scandal-ous. The 1840 annual convention of the American Anti-Slavery Society was the occasion for internecine warfare among the both liberal and evangelical church leaders who had been its foundation and the more discouraged and openly radical followers of William Lloyd Garrison. The conflict had been building for some time, as Garrison became more insistently perfectionist in his approach, demanding that the organization attack all sinful behav-ior and refuse to cooperate with sinful institutions. This led to his call to cease voting, as a government that allowed slavery was sinful; to embrace feminism, as discrimination against women was sinful; and to either force churches to take antislavery stands or leave them as sinful themselves. None of these ideas were popular with the churchmen who were part of the so-ciety, but the last one particularly struck them as wrongheaded. The 1840 convention, then, saw the Garrisonians gain the upper hand in radicalizing the society, so the church leaders left to form the American and Foreign Anti-Slavery Society. The true fallout, in terms of public relations, was the branding of the antislavery movement as antigovernment, socially radi-cal, and antichurch. It is easy to imagine, then, the reaction of New York's Episcopal elite, especially the High Churchmen, to the antislavery calls of John Jay.

The fears the movement was engendering in church leaders were brought to fulfillment with the 1844 split between Northern and Southern Methodists. This had been in the works for at least two years, and finally occurred when Southern adherents agitated for the national General Conference to take a proslavery stand and confirm a slaveholder as bishop. The conference refused, the Southerners took this as a statement that slavery was sinful, and the denomination separated into regional organizations. This schism was replicated the next year by the Baptists, as mission groups decided that they could not appoint slaveholders as missionaries and the denomination separated. It is clear that both schisms were caused not by increased antislavery pressure from the North, but from the refusal of Northerners to acquiesce to Southern proslavery agitation. Whatever else denominational leaders, especially Episcopalians, may have been asked to call sinful, there was no doubt in their mind that schism was a sin. They did not need Jay's motion to remind them of that terrible possibility.[10]

The other broad issue that affected the reception of Jay's motion in the 1844 diocesan convention was the state of the Episcopal Church in general and the Diocese of New York in particular. The old High Church–Low Church division had continued after the death of Hobart, exacerbated by Onderdonk's constant tactless pronouncements to his clergy fostering High Church principles and practices, but by the turn of the 1840s it had intensified significantly. The primary impetus was the arrival in this country of the series of *Tracts of the Times*, the manifestoes of the Oxford Movement in the English church, written from 1833 to 1839. These writings, from the primary figures of John Keble, E. B. Pusey, Hurrell Froude, and John Henry Newman, caused theological tumult in their own country by calling for the renewal of their church by restoring the importance of dogmatic tradition and placing a greater emphasis on piety. The Tractarians wanted to continue the Hobartian focus on the apostolic succession not just for its historic connection to the earliest church, but also for its symbolic embodiment of the true teachings of Christ being passed on through the theological traditions of the church. This was a more dynamic and incarnational view of the church, which led to an understanding of the sacraments as not just visible means of grace available to all, but also as the ground for acting on hope and seeking greater holiness of life. To evangelicals, this all sounded rather Romish. Their greatest fears were realized when Newman converted to Roman Catholicism in 1845, becoming John Cardinal Newman in 1879.

As their writings became available in America, the storm stirred up by the Tractarians in the Episcopal Church was largely symbolic (thereby excusing to some degree this radical oversimplification of their work). Even their greatest supporters admitted they had read very little of the tracts, and the work most revered by Hobartian leaders was not a tract at all, but Pusey's *Letter to the Lord Bishop of Oxford*, a piece largely obscured and superseded by Newman's writings. Nonetheless, the Oxford Movement became the touchstone for the greater interest in ritual that was developing in High Churchmen, who saw in the movement's approach to tradition and the sacraments the opportunity to elevate the importance of the church through its rituals. And the movement served usefully as the *bête noire* of Low Churchmen, who saw Roman Catholicism creeping in through that very ritualism and its accompanying theological deemphasis of Calvin and the other reformers. As Charles McIlvaine, bishop of Ohio, thundered in 1840, Tractarianism was "the systematic abandonment of the vital and distinguishing principles of the Protestant faith, and a systematic adoption of the very root and heart of Romanism, whence has issued the life of all its ramified corruptions and deformities."[11] This fear was made more concrete by the increased visibility of Roman Catholicism in the 1830s, due to massive immigration, and the delight several Roman Catholic journals seemed to be taking in attacking Anglican and Episcopal theology.

Some of the specific results of this controversy in New York City will be taken up shortly; suffice to say at this point that the Hobartian High Church emphasis on the unity of the church was by the 1840s under assault from too many quarters for denominational leaders of any stripe to be comfortable. The detachment from worldly issues that characterized Bishop Onderdonk's admonition to Williams after the 1834 riots had become the standard Episcopalian response to social concerns and radical reforms ten years later, precisely to avoid the kinds of schisms and assaults on the unique nature of the church that were now all too real. And the battle for the definition of the Episcopal Church itself was now threatening its unity as well, as could be seen in the investigation of the teachings of that High Church bastion, the General Theological Seminary, by the House of Bishops in the summer of 1844. Accusations of heresy began to be tossed about by and against bishops of both parties, and it was widely acknowledged that Onderdonk's brother, Henry U. Onderdonk, was forced to resign as bishop of Pennsylvania and was suspended from ministerial duties that same year not only because of problems with alcohol and women, but because of the extreme High Church–Low Church factionalism in his diocese.

Into this atmosphere John Jay lobbed his grenade at the New York convention that September. He was serving as a delegate from his home parish of St. Matthew's, Bedford, and it was the morning of the first day of business. One of each convention's first duties was to hear the report of the Committee on the Incorporation of Churches, a small panel empowered to inspect the credentials of any new parish applying for admission to convention and rule on whether they had been properly established by denominational canons. The convention had just voted, as was pro forma, to admit the delegations of those parishes approved by the committee when Jay took the floor to submit his resolution: "Resolved, that the Committee on the Incorporation of Churches be instructed to inquire and report to this Convention, the reasons why the Church of St. Philip in this city has for more than twenty years continued in a state of schism." The resolution was immediately ruled out of order by the chair of the convention, Bishop Onderdonk.[12]

The wording of the resolution could not have been more provocative. Jay did not simply ask that the convention consider rectifying the parish's separation from the diocese, he invoked the dread term "schism" and implied thereby that the diocese was in a state of sin. And there was patently little need for the committee to inquire about the reasons for the separation, as everyone there knew and had known for years exactly why: the journals for the conventions had been listing St. Philip's as "(colored)" since 1820. Requesting that a standing committee of the diocese investigate was just an opportunity to hammer home how long they had all been nodding and winking at the situation.

Being ruled out of order did not daunt Jay, though when he resubmitted his resolution the next day he had replaced "schism" with "separation." This did not mollify anyone, and his resolution was tabled.[13] This convention was not going to even think about having African Americans in its midst, and it certainly was not going to put it to a vote. Parliamentary procedure would be the convention's standard dodge for most of the years to come.

Jay's launching of the campaign to gain St. Philip's admission to the convention may have ended with a fizzle, but it is striking that he took the lead in this effort without any official consultation with members of the parish. Surely he was in private conversation with some, at least through his connections with Crummell and George DeGrasse, but there is no indication that the members of the vestry were aware of his plans. Jay must have been emboldened by the historic event of the previous year, when the delegation from Christ Church, the black congregation in Providence that Crummell had raised up and then left, were seated at the convention of the Diocese of Rhode Island.[14] They were the first African Americans granted this right in the Episcopal Church. Surely the people of St. Philip's, as well as Jay, had heard the news; surely if Rhode Island could do it New York could as well. Perhaps it was decided informally to have Jay make the first move and see how the convention would react; perhaps it was simply his ongoing support of Crummell and his excitement over the achievement of Crummell's old parish. Whatever the details, the battle was now joined.

CHAPTER 14

A Bishop's Trials

By all accounts, Benjamin Onderdonk never knew just how much trouble he was in, or just how angry he had made the Low Church leaders of his diocese. When Jay presented his resolution in the 1844 convention, he probably had a better idea than the bishop did of how provocative he could afford to be toward him. Jay was aggrieved by Onderdonk's racial attitudes, but he was also one of the Low Church agitators, and he knew of the movements afoot to bring the bishop down.

Onderdonk's bishopric had been extremely successful on many levels. In 1838, he reminded the convention that he had thus far ordained 148 deacons and 112 priests, consecrated ninety-six new churches, and confirmed almost 9,000 Episcopalians in his eight years as bishop. He had managed the delicate business of leaving the rectorship of Trinity Church to become bishop full-time in 1837; as there were no provisions for the diocese to pay a bishop's salary, he had to create the Episcopal Fund (largely endowed by Trinity) to free himself and future bishops from having to hold two positions to make a living. And he presided over the division of the Diocese of New York in 1838, breaking off the western half as the Diocese of Western New York, as the increase in population and the number of churches in the state made it impossible for him, despite his extensive travels, to oversee the entire geographic region. This was a tricky piece of work, both within the diocese and at the national level, as no such division had been effected before. It went off relatively smoothly, and Onderdonk felt a measure of personal triumph.[1]

Such accomplishments notwithstanding, the bishop's style and obvious High Church sympathies were throughout the 1830s accruing him enemies and difficulties of which he too often seemed blissfully unaware. Even his good friend and admirer Bishop Doane of New Jersey admitted that Onderdonk "suffers solely from faults of manner, the impulses of a kind and loving nature uncontrolled by sound judgement."[2] Hence his convention addresses regularly turned into lectures on matters liturgical or architectural, to the exasperation of clergy who either were certain they knew how to conduct worship properly or were too financially pressed in the years after the 1837 Panic to afford the costs, for instance, of raising the chancel to the minimum of two feet above the nave that he desired. Onderdonk's penchant for Gothic arches and cross-tipped steeples enraged the evangelical clergy and laity and caused a snicker or two among the High Churchmen who knew that the bishop had never traveled to Europe and thus had never actually seen the buildings he wished his churches to imitate. But whatever the topic or the hearers' ritual and theological leanings, none of the clergy appreciated being instructed in such dry detail and made to look less than competent in front of their parish leaders, who were serving as convention delegates.

Amid this atmosphere of ill will, the controversies over the Oxford Movement embroiled Onderdonk in the incident that was likely the last straw: the ordination of Arthur Carey in July of 1843. Onderdonk had been teaching at General Seminary throughout his ministry, and his attachment to it was well known: he had instituted the practice of designating graduates of the seminary in the clergy list published in each diocesan convention journal, which did not endear him to those clergy who had not been so fortunate or who found the seminary's leanings more than a little suspect. Carey was a student at General and a Tractarian enthusiast, but he was too young to be ordained when he graduated. He spent a year as a lay assistant at St. Peter's in Chelsea, where his ritual tendencies ran him afoul of the Low Church rector, Hugh Smith. The rector of St. Mark's-in-the-Bouwerie, Henry Anthon, was one of the major forces in the Low Church party, and Smith kept him apprised of his concerns that Carey was more Roman than Anglican. When Carey was to be approved for ordination, Smith refused to sign the endorsement, and he and Anthon were appointed to a committee of eight to examine the young man's beliefs as a result. The others, a reasonably representative crew, outvoted the two Low Churchmen and approved Carey for ordination as being Tractarian but not Roman Catholic. Smith and Anthon refused to accept this decision, however, and were widely supported by their fellow evangelical clergy. Tensions were high at the ordination service, and when the customary question was asked as to whether anyone present knew of any impediment to proceed,[3] Smith and Anthon read lengthy protests, but Onderdonk dismissed their complaints as already heard and satisfied by the committee. The service continued as Smith and Anthon, infuriated, walked out.

Carey, a sickly young man, died the next year, but the argument continued by pamphlet. It was felt by evangelicals that Onderdonk's actions legitimated the most controversial tendencies of the Oxford Movement. It was this controversy that led to the investigation of the seminary by the House of Bishops, after a lengthy and cantankerous debate over Carey and Tractarianism at the General Convention of 1844. And it led to a hardening of the animosity toward Onderdonk, which he did little to ameliorate. When John Duer, a noted judge and scholar from one of the state's oldest families, rose to address the diocesan convention in September of 1844, Onderdonk knew of his antipathy and refused to give him the floor. When Duer insisted, the bishop shouted at him to "sit down," and another enemy was convinced that Onderdonk's highhandedness could no longer be borne.[4]

What Onderdonk did not know was that the same General Convention debating the Carey ordination—and accepting the resignation of Onderdonk's brother—was gathering tales about the New York bishop as well. There had long been concerns among Onderdonk's friends of his unconscious habit of touching those with whom he was speaking; but there had also long been stories among his detractors of the bishop, in his cups, being rather more consciously tactile with women. It is said that a standing joke in New York City parlors whenever the gaslights went out was for someone to intone in the darkness, "Ladies need not fear; the bishop is not present."[5] Such jokes and accusations were embarrassing to all, and were sufficiently persuasive to his fellow bishops that three were dispatched to investigate after the national and diocesan conventions had ended. The mix of moral disgust and theological outrage proved combustible, a presentment was issued, and Onderdonk was tried by the House of Bishops. He refused to attend the proceedings, sending in only a broad denial, and was rapidly found guilty of "immorality and impurity" on January 2, 1845. His supporters, anxious to ward off the punishment of deposition from the ministry, agreed to a sentence of "indefinite suspension," thereby dooming him to futility and frustration for the remainder of his life. It also created chaos in the diocese: Onderdonk could no longer function as bishop, yet he could not be replaced until General Convention said so, for he was still a bishop.

The trial was sufficiently sordid that even Onderdonk's supporters could not deny there was truth in the accusations, though they remained forever convinced that it was church politics that had done him in. George T. Strong mentioned his disappointment over the entire affair in his diary in February of 1845, having just read John Jay's pamphlet, *Facts Connected with the Presentment of Bishop Onderdonk*: "Confound that most miserable business." But he had also noted the previous fall that "the Rev. Henry Anthon, I can't doubt after what

I've heard, is the real mover in the matter, and with him [Thomas J.] Oakley, [John] Duer, John Jay!!! and I fear the whole of that unhappy minority."[6] If Jay's role was already known by the time he made his resolution on St. Philip's at the 1844 diocesan convention, it must have sounded to many as if he had simply found another way to bait the bishop.

It would be logical to assume that the people of St. Philip's would be among those celebrating the downfall of a man who had oppressed two members of their race and congregation who had wanted to become priests, who had publicly humiliated their late beloved rector, and whom their supporter John Jay was busily taking to task. Yet this was not the case. The relationship between this parish and its bishop did not fall into such neat lines of either racial divide or even church politics, but was rather more complicated. And with a suspended bishop, the question of who was in charge of the diocese added even more complexity.

Rather than celebrate his defeat, then, the vestry chose to send Onderdonk a letter of commiseration and support. The missive was unwavering in stating that body's loyalty to the bishop and sorrow for his misfortune:

> We do not know aught of the truth of the charges that have been preferred against you, although too painfully aware of the feelings to-you-ward of a portion of those who in this matter have judged you. We only know that for a season we are deprived of the public services of our shepherd in spiritual things—and this knowledge brings with it profound and overwhelming grief.[7]

There may have been others in the congregation equally adept at such tactful and somewhat flowery language, but since James McCune Smith was currently secretary of the vestry, it was surely his hand at work here.

This was certainly more than mere flattery. Despite its difficulties with Onderdonk, the parish had always appreciated the office and function of bishop, and they remembered with pride that theirs was the first congregation to which Onderdonk preached after his consecration. And despite the perceptions of both William and John Jay, the parish was flattered that the bishop had presided at Williams's funeral, which Smith also saw fit to mention in the letter:

> When it pleased God suddenly to take unto himself the humble and devoted presbyter (the Rev. Peter Williams) whom our souls loved, in that hour of painful bereavement, you came and ministered unto us

comfortable things in the Lord, and taught us to bow in submission
to the dread will of the Almighty. From these and other circumstances,
whatever may be the judgment of men—one cannot believe that they
are the acts of a prelate with an evil heart.

So they reminded the bishop to "be of good cheer," that "our confidence in
you is unshaken," and that they would await his return to office. Smith and
Peter Ray, the senior warden, delivered the letter by hand.[8]

Onderdonk responded immediately with gratitude, and his letter was read
into the minutes of the February vestry meeting. There is, as usual, a touch
of the imperial to his tone: "That in these ways, you, my dear children in the
Lord, have shewn your friendly and filial feelings towards me, is a great allevi-
ation of my sufferings, and a source of cordial gratitude to you, and especially
to the God of grace and consolation by whom your hearts were moved." In
such straits as his, who would not have been touched by a letter such as St.
Philip's had sent? The bishop went on: "That parish has always been near my
heart. I have respected it and loved it and most sincerely respect it and love it
still." Now this may be stretching it, given an historical perspective, but again,
the vestry itself was proud of its letter and proud of the bishop's response.
They recorded both in full in the minutes, receiving the bishop's letter as
sincerely as he had received theirs.[9]

For despite Onderdonk's treatment of DeGrasse and Crummell, it is possible that he was not actually opposed to the parish's admission to convention. Or it is possible that the parish itself was not sure where he stood on
the issue. There is no record of any public statement by Onderdonk for or
against the admission of St. Philip's, he was not the bishop who had imposed
conditions on the ordination of Peter Williams, and there is no record of him
imposing any such conditions on Isaiah DeGrasse, the only African American
he ordained. In such a state of uncertainty, then, there would have been no
reason for the vestry to do otherwise than support the man they still expected
to be the bishop.

In this St. Philip's was no different than any other church in the diocese,
for no one really understood how things would work out with their bishop.
He was suspended "indefinitely," but how long would that actually be? Onderdonk himself clearly expected it to be a few short weeks or months, and
his supporters hoped the same. His opponents had thought he would be
deposed completely, and they too had no idea how long the suspension was
meant to be. The reality was a terrible middle ground: though he could not
function as such, Onderdonk remained consecrated a bishop and thus, he

claimed, the bishop of New York. For the moment, he was still the one everyone had to deal with for any diocesan business, St. Philip's included.

Thus the vestry decided that they should find out what the lay of the land was. In May they resolved "that a committee of two be appointed to wait on Bishop Onderdonk and state that this vestry is anxious to have the parish represented in the next Diocesan Convention; and to enquire what are the necessary steps for that purpose." This is the first mention on the parish's part that they were ready to pursue this goal, and it is a tad ingenuous. They knew well what those steps were: the presentation of the certificates of the parish's legal incorporation and its consecration. The same resolution called on the same committee to place "the necessary documents" in the hands of the Rev. Alexander Fraser, since as a white priest he could attend convention and present the credentials on their behalf. Clearly what the vestry was looking for was some sense of how the bishop himself would view their efforts. Smith and Henry Scott were appointed to make these inquiries.[10]

The next month they reported back to the vestry that "the Rev. Alexander Frazer had furnished the requisite information, and they had therefore not waited on the Bishop." Again, if the vestry already knew what the procedure was, what information had their officiating minister given them? Certainly one piece of information would be his own willingness to present their documents to the Committee on the Incorporation of Churches. It seems highly likely that the other piece of information he would by now have had for them was the fact that Bishop Onderdonk would not be attending convention, so his opinions on the subject of St. Philip's were immaterial and not worth Smith and Scott making the visit.[11]

The vestry went ahead with its preparations. Smith himself paid eighty cents for a legal copy of the certificate of incorporation of the parish, now twenty-five years old, and at that month's vestry meeting they resolved to place it and the certificate of consecration in Frazer's hands for presentation at convention. Then they took the momentous and optimistic step of electing convention delegates for the first time. Ray and Smith were chosen to represent the parish should Frazer's mission succeed.[12] All was in place.

A special vestry meeting was called two weeks later by Ray to work out a problem: he and Smith did not agree about how to vote should an important question come up at convention. Assuming that they were admitted to convention two days later, if a resolution was submitted asking Onderdonk to resign as bishop (and thus clear the way for electing a replacement), they would need to vote as a delegation, not as individual delegates. The vestry resolved "that Bishop Onderdonk should not resign the Episcopacy of this

Diocese under present circumstances." Only Thomas Downing voted against the resolution (thus arguing that the bishop should resign), while Smith and the rest voted in favor. Ray, who tended to cast his vote only when needed as either tiebreaker or to make it unanimous, did not vote but obviously agreed with Downing (since he disagreed with Smith). The vestry had spoken, however, and the delegation now had its instructions. They also decided to augment the delegation by adding Henry Scott.[13]

This brief dispute points to the difficulty of narrating this tale as if "the parish" or even "the vestry" were an entity one could treat as a protagonist. The parish was, of course, a collection of individuals with their own opinions and perspectives, and the vestry clearly reflected that fact in this disagreement. Why did Downing and Ray feel Onderdonk should resign, while Smith, Scott and others did not? Did Smith still believe they could work with Onderdonk on this issue, or did he think that a disabled bishop would be less trouble than a new bishop whose thinking on race and slavery could not be foretold? Were Downing and Ray still mad at Onderdonk about the DeGrasse and Crummell incidents, or did they anticipate that a new bishop might smile upon their enterprise while Onderdonk was no longer of any use to them? It is impossible to say, but this disagreement does point to the negotiations that had to occur within a group of individuals attempting to reach a common goal.

The dispute also removes the simple picture of a bigoted bishop, a righteous young lawyer (Jay) riding to the rescue, and a united, patient, and heroic parish claiming their Christian rights. The evidence for the virulence of the bishop's racial attitudes comes from the pens of Crummell and Jay, both of whom despised Onderdonk and had their own motives for portraying him in the worst possible light—and both of whom were considered by their peers to be rigid and unforgiving personalities. Certainly Onderdonk was as racist as the average Victorian New Yorker, which is to say rather racist indeed. But there is no sign (beyond the testimony of Crummell and Jay) that he had any more particular animus against either African Americans as a whole or this specific parish; rather, his anger appears to have been focused primarily on Crummell's insolence in challenging him. Jay's motives are also shown to have been quite mixed, as advocating for St. Philip's was tied to his dislike of the bishop and his antislavery agenda as much as (if not more than) his desire to help a specific parish dealing with a specific problem. And the parish itself would continue to have disagreements over their own best course of action.

These entanglements of motives, goals, and methods are wonderfully made manifest in the only documented correspondence between members of St. Philip's—purporting to speak on behalf of the parish—and John Jay. Published with a reply from Jay in the *National Anti-Slavery Standard* on May 29, 1845,[14] the letters are in response to a pamphlet published by an anonymous "Looker On" regarding Jay's relationship with the parish. "Looker On" apparently asserted that the vestry's letter of commiseration to the bishop indicated that while Jay was claiming that the bishop and diocese were mistreating "colored Episcopalians," those same Episcopalians did not agree. The letter from the parishioners to Jay begged to differ:

> The letter of St. Philip's Church vestry, however indicative of thankfulness for favors received from their late Diocesan, must not be wrested into an expression of the opinion of the people of that Parish, in regard to the Bishop's treatment of colored Clergymen, and colored candidates for orders on the one hand—or, of your animadversions upon the same, on the other.

The parishioners went on to assert:

> Between "Looker On" and ourselves, there is a broad and impassable issue.... We can allow *no man* to place *us*—colored men—the proscribed class—crushed race—in opposition to our friends. We do appreciate your efforts on our behalf. We do honor your exertions for the freedom and enfranchisement of our people.

Significantly, however, there was no concrete mention of Jay's motion at the last convention or of any other aspect of the parish's desire to be admitted to convention. The only specific reference to the parish was to the cases of DeGrasse and Crummell.[15]

It is therefore important to note by whom the letter was sent. It did not purport to be from the vestry; indeed, the style of writing and the arguments used did not reflect Smith's thinking at all, and Smith would certainly have been the author had it been an official communication of that body. The letter was dated March 8, some six weeks after the vestry's letter to the bishop, and the only vestrypersons at that time to sign were John Peterson and Ransom Wake. Neither was returned to the vestry in the May election, so they did not vote on whether the parish delegation was to urge Onderdonk's resignation, and thus their opinions of the bishop cannot be stated with any certainty. Thomas Downing did sign; he was elected to the vestry in May, and then voted for the bishop's resignation. Thirty-two parishioners signed the letter, at the head of which list (apparently randomly ordered otherwise) are George DeGrasse and Boston Crummell, the fathers of the two candidates so mistreated by Onderdonk. Jay's reply is labeled "Messrs. George DeGrasse, Charles L. Reason, and others," which brings the third seminary candidate into prominence.[16]

Why did these particular people, including George Downing, John Zuille, Samuel Rankin, and William Tyson, feel a need to address this anonymous pamphlet and defend Jay's efforts? Why were the issues addressed so carefully circumscribed, so that the broad concerns of slavery and prejudice and the specific history of the bishop's dealings with the potential seminarians were included, but the problem of the convention was not? These questions, though irresolvable, point to a lack of agreement among the parishioners about just how helpful Jay really was to them, and in what ways and areas. The letter's delicate wording about the bishop reinforces the sense of uncertainty among parishioners about how much of an obstacle Onderdonk was or could be. Above all, the letter demonstrates that Jay was in contact with and perhaps acting on behalf of a number of parishioners, but he was not cast in any role that the vestry itself wished to acknowledge either publicly or in its meeting minutes.

Jay's lengthy response touched only once on the concrete details of the parish's relationship to its denomination, noting that "her Seminary has been closed to your candidates, her Conventions have been barred against your Clergy." The thrust of the letter was an eloquent diatribe against prejudice and oppression, with Jay strongly encouraging the people of St. Philip's to continue their struggle against such forces:

> Be true to yourselves. Acquiesce not in one single act of injustice. Encourage not its repetition by your silence. Repel aggression by lawful means, and where you cannot repel, protest loudly against it; and then, if evil must come, suffer and bear it. The glory of endurance will be yours—the disgrace of the infliction will belong solely to those who cause it; and remembering this, your own consciences being clear, you will feel less disposed to be angry with your persecutors, for their dark treachery, than to pity them for their mean cowardice and their deep dishonor.[17]

This is powerful and moving stuff, revealing the depth of Jay's disgust at racial injustice. It also shows, however, how Jay transformed the concrete struggles of St. Philip's and its parishioners into abstract symbols supporting his argument against the broader issues of prejudice and oppression. Certainly this was a reasonable approach to addressing those issues, but it was not necessarily an approach that helped this congregation achieve its concrete goals.

That fall's diocesan convention was overwhelmed with various moves and countermoves made around and about the suspended bishop, and the issue of St. Philip's admission was largely ignored. Onderdonk's supporters decried the revelation that the bishop had not been paid by the Episcopal Fund trustees since his suspension; his opponents argued that "he can never perform episcopal functions in this diocese with any prospect of usefulness to the Church," and he should resign and forfeit his salary.[18] The convention eventually voted to pay the arrears and to have the Standing Committee invite other bishops to perform any necessary acts for the diocese, but no definitive action was taken nor statement made regarding Onderdonk's status. He was to remain the *eminence grise* of the diocese for another fifteen years.

Frazer and the parish's elected delegates attended the 1845 convention (the latter only as observers, and it is unclear whether they were actually permitted inside), and the application for admission was submitted. No motion for admission was made by Jay this time, however; he was serving as a delegate from a new church in the city, St. Jude's, while his father was a delegate from St. Matthew's, Bedford, and neither brought up the subjects of slavery or St. Philip's at all. The delegation reported back to the vestry that they "had presented their documents to the Standing Committee of the Diocese; that the application had been sanctioned by said Committee; and by the Committee on Incorporations—but had not been laid before the convention by the last committee; which would be the first step to be taken at the next convention."[19] They may not have succeeded, but Smith, Ray, and Scott were hopeful that the process had been initiated, and therefore might well continue to move forward, bishops and Jays notwithstanding.

CHAPTER 15

Exciting the Deepest Feelings

As they approached the diocesan convention of 1846, the vestry of St.
Philip's believed they had cause for optimism. Frazer had reported
the previous year that their application for admission would be placed before the convention this year, and everything that could be was in order.
Hopes were high as the vestry elected its delegates at their own meeting
in September: James McCune Smith, still secretary, and Alexander Elston,
a shoemaker serving his second year as warden.[1] They were sent off with
no further instructions, as the vestry's sentiments on the suspended bishop
had not changed.

The diocesan convention began at ten thirty on the morning of October 2 in St. John's Chapel. This large and impressive edifice was styled
a "chapel" only because it was not an independent congregation but was
administered by Trinity Church and its vestry. It was comfortable for large
gatherings, and pleasantly located on the west side of the city, overlooking an
eponymous park. There were some 150 clergy and a slightly larger number
of parish delegations in official attendance, along with a variety of observers
that included clergy not entitled to vote (such as Frazer). James Watson Webb,
antiabolitionist Episcopalian and editor of the *Morning Courier and New York
Enquirer*, was in attendance as well, to provide vividly detailed accounts of the
proceedings.[2]

The Committee on the Incorporation of Churches reported almost immediately. It was composed of Judge Samuel Jones, of the Church of the
Annunciation in the city; Francis Barretto, of St. Peter's in Westchester; and,
wonderfully, the Rev. Evan M. Johnson, rector of St. John's, Brooklyn. Thirteen churches applied for union with the convention, and the committee
reported twelve of them to be entitled to such union. Only Crummell's
parish, Church of the Messiah, was ruled inadmissible because its certificate
of incorporation "does not appear to have been recorded as required." St.

Philip's was among those the committee recommended for admission. All was proceeding as expected.[3]

Then came the snag. The eleven other parishes "were severally received by the Convention," but an objection was made to admitting St. Philip's. Neither Webb's report nor the journal of the convention record who made the objection, but William Harison, the treasurer of the vestry of Trinity Church, rose to make a motion: "Resolved, that the subject of the admission of St. Philip's Church, New York, and of other congregations of colored people into representation in the Convention of this Diocese, be referred to a special committee to consider, and to report upon, at the present Convention."[4] Now the convention found itself facing the issue of race, with its concomitant implications about slavery, much more directly than it wished.

Johnson immediately objected to Harison's motion. Of Quaker and Episcopal parentage, he had become a beloved figure among the Dutch community of Brooklyn, who referred to him by their title for a Dutch Reformed pastor, "domine." Johnson had founded St. John's by selling a piece of his own property and building the church with the proceeds, and he never accepted a salary from the parish. He was renowned for his willingness to perform marriages under rather liberal conditions. As one contemporary put it, "He would at any time rise at midnight or daylight to marry the humblest couple or do the smallest deed of kindness." An examination of the parish archives shows that there were occasional African Americans who were either confirmed or noted as recipients of the largesse of his discretionary fund, but it is hard to say whether Brooklyn's black community formed a significant part of his ministry. In 1846, however, he was a recent convert to the arguments of John Jay, and that would prove important to St. Philip's.[5]

Speaking of his experience with the Committee on the Incorporation of Churches, Johnson stated that the matter of the admission of this parish had already been "specially considered and reported upon." He could therefore not see what other information the convention needed or a special committee might uncover. Webb reported in his newspaper, "For himself, Mr. Johnson said he saw no objection to the admission of this Church. He did not know why the color of the skin any more than the color of the eyes should determine this House as to the admission of churches to representation in the Convention." Johnson's efforts to overcome prejudice in his own life, as a result of reading Jay's pamphlet, here were offered on an institutional level. Having thus addressed the problem as directly as he could, Johnson urged the admission of St. Philip's.[6]

But this was too much to bear. John Spencer, the Albany judge, High

Churchman, and "among the Bishop's peculiar friends,"[7] was horrified by the prospect of discussing a subject of such potential divisiveness. His response aptly demonstrates how clearly the delegates saw the issue of St. Philip's admission linked to the larger questions of race and slavery.

> This question has been a source of disruption and confusion wherever introduced. It has rent asunder one of the largest denominations of our country—the Methodist Episcopalians. It has disturbed other great denominations. . . . We have agitating questions enough, and this is one that cannot be approached without exciting the deepest feelings.

Spencer therefore moved that the resolution, and the topic of St. Philip's, "be laid upon the table, there to lie where for long years it has laid."[8] Echoing the priorities Onderdonk expressed after the riots of 1834, Spencer argued that the issue of race was itself secondary to its necessary consequence: schism.

John Jay, of course, now leapt in and fanned the flames of this fear. He requested that Spencer's motion be voted on by orders (lay and clergy voting separately), "as the question did involve a most important principle, that of Christian brotherhood and catholic unity."[9] Thus Jay placed the issue in the broadest possible contexts of faith, using "catholic" to signify the universal church, while the opposition offered no theology, just the desire to avoid the issue entirely. Jay's call for a vote by orders forced that distinction to be publicly acknowledged, as the clergymen and lay delegations had to make their stands publicly and by name. The motion would pass only if both orders concurred.

The lay delegates proved more susceptible to such fears and voted for Spencer's motion, but the clergy voted it down and the bid to avoid the topic was lost. Despite Jay's efforts, it is impossible to judge historically any individual votes: those in favor of forming a special committee may have wished either to see it argue to admit St. Philip's or to see the issue addressed and disposed of once and for all, while those against forming such a committee could have been voting either against only the disruptiveness of the issue or against admitting the parish. It is worth noting, however, that most Low Church clergy were in favor of sending the issue to committee, while Spencer's High Church allies tended to support his desire to avoid the discussion. Some intriguing votes: Thomas Lyell, Peter Williams's now aged mentor, voted to table the issue; so did William Morris, who was two years away from becoming officiating minister at St. Philip's; many leading Low Church laymen, including John Duer and Luther Bradish, broke with their clergy and supported Spencer's motion; and Harison's own Trinity delegation voted to table his motion![10] Nonetheless, it was decided that the convention would address the issue of race and admission to convention, whatever feelings it might excite.

The convention returned to Harison's motion, and another effort was made to squelch discussion: the Rev. Hugh Smith suggested that the issue of admitting St. Philip's should be "decided without debate—in order that we might avoid that most dangerous and exciting topic, abolition." Harison responded that he had no problem with the vote on his motion being taken without debate, but not the larger issue itself, "since there were peculiar circumstances connected with this congregation that ought to be known to the Convention before any decision be made, and that a committee only could properly spread those circumstances before it." Jay leapt on this opening, and suggested that Harison himself could explain those "peculiar circumstances" to the assembly. Jay clearly thought that Harison was simply referring to the parish's black members, but Harison's wording strongly suggests that he knew the context in which this phrase had been used in the Diocese of Pennsylvania.[11] There, as has been seen, "peculiar circumstances" referred to the race of Crummell and his congregation in the course of declaring that no such congregation would be granted admission to convention. Certainly there was no need to be oblique about the congregation's composition; the diocesan journals designated St. Philip's as "colored" each year. Harison sounds, instead, like a man who knew something, and wanted everyone else to know it as well: Peter Williams had acceded to the conditions for ordination in New York that Crummell had refused in Pennsylvania.

Before Harison could respond to Jay's request, however, there was a call for the question, and the motion to form a special committee passed without dissent. The Rev. William Creighton of Christ Church, Tarrytown, was the senior priest in the diocese (he had been ordained the longest) and had therefore been pressed into service as chair of the convention in the absence of a bishop. He appointed a committee of five, drawing on the Episcopal tradition of putting the most vocal members to work: Harison, Spencer, and Evan Johnson were all named to the committee, to be joined by the Rev. Reuben Sherwood, rector of St. James's Church in Hyde Park, and John King, delegate from Grace Church, Jamaica, Queens. Jay's absence from the committee, given the appointment of the first three, is conspicuous. The committee was then given special permission to meet during the convention itself.[12]

The next day's proceedings began with the Church of the Messiah presenting evidence of its proper incorporation to the Committee on the In-corporation of Churches. They were judged to be in order, and their admission was immediately referred to the same special committee considering St. Philip's.[13]

That afternoon, the special committee made its report, recommending "that neither St. Philip's, nor any other colored congregation, be admitted into union with this Convention, so as to entitle them to a representation therein."[14] It was signed by a majority of three: Harison, Sherwood, and Spencer. They concluded their report by addressing the long-term implications of such enforced separation, asserting that the result "probably will be, that such churches and congregations will not be responsible to, or under the government or control of this Convention, but will remain subject to the ordinary jurisdiction of their Bishop—and when their members become adequate, may have church councils of their own for their own peculiar government." This was patently absurd, flying in the face of the denomination's very understanding of itself. The willingness of these diocesan leaders to voice such an idea, and the hope that it would be a permanent solution, betrayed the depth of their fear of mingling with these "peculiar" people whose "adequacy" was so disingenuously questioned. While the threat of schism was cause to avoid any discussion of slavery, the reality of racism was sufficient to motivate twisting the denomination into a nearly schismatic pretzel with only a bishop to maintain the fiction of unity—and of course this diocese did not even have such a bishop.

The reasoning offered to support such a tortured vision of denominational polity centered on the assertion of Harison, Sherwood, and Spencer that the question of the admission of St. Philip's had no theological or spiritual implications whatsoever. It was, they argued, an issue "exclusively relating to the temporal government of the Diocese, and ... wholly unconnected with the religious rights or duties of the applicants." It is stunning to see such a statement made by at least two High Churchmen (Harison and Spencer), since High Church theology saw unity as a fundamental duty of the church, and full access to the church and its sacraments as the primary right of any Christian. The key to the majority argument, however, was the term "expediency," in the sense of what is appropriate to and in the best interests of one's purpose: the issue at hand "is one purely of expediency, and not one of Christian privilege or right." In such a view, the diocesan convention was "but a part of what may be called, the civil machinery, instituted by human wisdom," and therefore not subject to considerations of faithfulness to the Gospel. This outrageous opening culminated in the claim that "among the considerations

of expediency which any body of men uniting together for a common purpose would deem the most important, must be that of determining with
whom they would associate, and who should be permitted to participate in
the government of the society." The Episcopal Church has often been accused
of being little more than a social club, but it is disheartening to see such a
view endorsed by some of its leaders in such a public and approving fashion.
Hobart must have been spinning in his grave to hear the community of the
faithful, the Body of Christ, reduced to a "society" that chooses it members
like any other club.

Such an approach allowed the committee majority to argue that the
church had always left a large number of its adherents out of power:

> Thus, for reasons of expediency, females, however worthy, are by our
> canons excluded from being representatives in our Conventions, and are
> by law, incapable of being incorporated as members of churches. . . . If it
> be an incident to church membership to be represented in the councils
> of the church, then have we, in common with all Christian denomina-
> tions, from the time of the apostles, unjustly and tyrannically deprived
> female members of sacred rights.

A twenty-first-century reader can only respond, "Precisely!" Yet the assumption of Harison and the others was that they had not been tyrannical to
women, so they were not being tyrannical to African Americans either. The
inability of those in power to see how unjustly they are wielding that power
is a disappointing truism, and here that failing seems to have granted them an
oddly unassailable logic.

Having established their right to power, the majority members then
moved to the real issue: outright racism coupled with Victorian certitude
about the divine ordering of society's strata.

> When society is unfortunately divided into classes, when some are in-
> telligent, refined, and elevated, in tone and character, and others are ig-
> norant, coarse, and debased, however unjustly, and when such prejudices
> exist between them, as to prevent social intercourse on equal terms, it
> would seem inexpedient to encounter such prejudices, unnecessarily,
> and to endeavor to compel the one class to associate on equal terms in
> the consultations on the affairs of the Diocese, with those whom they
> would not admit to their tables, or into their family circles—nay, whom
> they would not admit into their pews, during public worship.

Instead of acknowledging what they believed about African Americans to be beliefs, they managed to blame God for what they considered a fact: those with darker skin were ignorant, coarse, and debased by nature. The report's authors also assumed—probably correctly, for most of their readers—that the right of one body of Christians to exclude another from worship, let alone from their social lives, was not even to be questioned.

It is clear that Harison, Sherwood, and Spencer, on behalf of most of their contemporaries, simply saw no connection between their Christian faith and their treatment of other human beings. It was inexpedient to alter one's behavior to conform to one's beliefs: "If christian duty require that we should, in all respects, treat equally, all persons, without reference to their social condition, should we not commence the discharge of that duty in our individual and social relations?" Well, yes, one would think so. "And is not the fact that we have never so regarded our duty—or have willfully violated it, sufficient evidence of the existence of a state of society among us that renders an amalgamation of such discordant materials impracticable, if not hazardous to our unity and harmony." The tenet that there can be no distinctions in the community of the faithful, in the Body of Christ—as Paul put it, "There is neither Jew nor Greek, there is neither slave nor free, there is neither male nor female; for you are all one in Christ Jesus"—apparently was either to be dismissed as naive or simply ignored.[15]

The use of the term "amalgamation" was telling, for it was widely recognized as a code word for interracial marriage and sexual relations, acts of class and race blending that were appalling to most white Americans. The charge of favoring such "amalgamation" was regularly thrown at abolitionists to stir up mob emotions. The committee majority deftly united this fear with the denominational one of schism ("hazardous to our unity") and the Victorian fear of social chaos ("hazardous to . . . harmony") for a trifecta of horrors that none of their fellow Episcopalians could be expected to endure.

It was then an easy matter for the three authors to feel sorry for those whom God had made so inferior: "We deeply sympathize with the colored race in our country, we feel acutely their wrongs—and not the least among them, their social degradation." This was something that had happened to African Americans, not something caused by white prejudice and oppression—and certainly not something about which anything could be done. "But this cannot prevent our seeing the fact, that they *are* socially degraded, and are not regarded as proper associates for the class of persons who attend our Convention." It was just too bad, and it was just the way things were. Harison, Sherwood, and Spencer next attempted to disavow their racism:

"We object not to the color of the skin, but we question their possession of those qualities which would render their intercourse with the members of a Church Convention useful, or agreeable, even to themselves." It was as if they thought it coincidental that they considered all persons with black skin to be lacking in the necessary qualities. "We should make the same objections to persons of the same social class, however pure may be their blood, or however transparent their skin." But of course there were by definition no other "persons of the same social class."

Next, the majority report attempted to enlist the creation of black congregations as support for their perspective:

> It is impossible, in the nature of things, that such opposites should commingle with any pleasure or satisfaction to either. The colored people have themselves shown their conviction of this truth, by separating themselves from the whites, and forming distinct congregations where they are not continually humbled by being treated as inferiors.

Here James McCune Smith's fears about black conventions and black schools came to fruition: creating organizations to combat oppression by empowering themselves had come to be seen by white Americans as evidence of a preference for segregation—thus, as he said, "riveting more firmly the chains that bind us." The idea that those against whom prejudicial treatment was constant might seek solace, strength, and the opportunity for betterment beyond the reach of such treatment was impossible for these Episcopalians to entertain, because they did not see their treatment as prejudicial. Thus the three authors asked what for them was a largely rhetorical question: "Why should not the principle on which they have separated themselves be carried out in the other branches of our Church organization?" The need for any kind of change on the part of white Christians was unthinkable. Harison, Sherwood, and Spencer did admit the possibility that someday, "as they advance in intelligence, and refinement," there might be "free and equal communion" of black Episcopalians with white, but that day was so vaguely envisioned as to be meant, clearly, as a mirage.

To add insult to injury, the committee majority then trotted out the conditions imposed on Peter Williams and his congregation for his ordination. They appended the minutes of the Standing Committee's meeting of March 6, 1819, to their report,[16] and then asserted, "It is understood that these conditions were approved by the Bishop, and were assented to by the applicant and the congregation." This could have been no more than an understanding, as there was no record made of any formal assent, but Harison and his cohorts were merely stating what everyone believed to be true. They went on to re-mark, rather snidely, "The present applicants, it is presumed, were not aware of these arrangements, as it is not to be supposed that they would intentionally be guilty of a violation of good faith." The implication, of course, was that the congregation *was* violating good faith—how could they not have been aware of such arrangements playing such a large role in their parish?—thereby re-vealing just what sort of character they possessed. It would seem a bit of a stretch to a modern reader to deem what had been imposed on Williams and the parish as taking place in "good faith," but such distinctions were lost on these writers. Williams and the congregation had made an agreement twenty-seven years earlier, and their successors were expected to abide by it no matter what their interpretation of their faith might be.

The majority members of the committee also made explicit the argument that lurked behind everyone's fears of dealing with this issue at all: the slip-pery slope to abolitionism and schism. Harison, Sherwood, and Spencer had implied it elsewhere, but they state this concern quite baldly at one point:

> Efforts of a similar character, and for the same purpose, have been made to give position in our Churches to colored people, which would com-pel association and intercourse with them. It is obvious that such move-ments are but incipient steps to ulterior objects in relation to the vexed and irritating subject of slavery.

They may as well have mentioned Jay by name, along with this claim that the question of admitting St. Philip's was not driven by the parish's desire to attend convention, but by Jay's search for an issue that would force the con-vention to talk about slavery. Given how little they thought of the "qualities" and "adequacy" of the St. Philip's parishioners, it is small wonder that they assumed the parish was being used for other purposes.

But the three authors continued with a perceptive grasp of how this dialogue could go:

> Beginning with simple and apparently just propositions respecting the abstract rights of this portion of our population, their professed friends and advocates have advanced, step by step, until they have prepared the way to agitate the bold question of the Christian character of those whose sentiments do not accord with their own. The rending asun-der of churches—the disruption of societies—bitter animosities, and all manner of uncharitableness, have been the invariable results.

This is a reasonably accurate summation of the problems encountered by other denominations in discussing the issue of slavery, as Southern slaveholders resented being called sinful and non-Christian by abolitionists and responded by trying to force the denominations to validate slavery as sanctioned by the faith. There is little doubt that Jay was hoping to force such a discussion, and little doubt that it would have been extremely difficult for the denomination to avoid splitting North and South. There is also little doubt, however, that the people of St. Philip's would have preferred such agitation to leaving their rights and their identities as Christians in such an "abstract" state. They were making as much use of Jay's advocacy as he was making of them.

In the end, then, Harison, Sherwood, and Spencer concluded that admitting St. Philip's to the convention "would be attended with the worst consequences to our unity, our harmony, and our efficiency." Their logic was consistent and clear, and had nothing to do with the Christian faith. They nowhere appealed to any Biblical or ecclesiastical authority for their stand; they simply asserted social realities as if they were divinely sanctioned, and carefully limited the concrete people involved to abstract stereotypes. These three men thereby manifested the prevailing attitudes of their time in a manner that is historically illuminating, but it must have been enormously discouraging to the people of St. Philip's. Fortunately, the majority report was not the last word on the subject.

CHAPTER 16

Vouchsafed to All Men

The Rev. Evan M. Johnson and John A. King begged leave to differ with their colleagues on the special committee. As a minority by only one vote, they requested permission to submit their own report on the St. Philip's question for the convention's consideration. While it is impossible to tell whether any one of the three majority members had the greater hand in writing their report, it is fairly clear from Johnson's history that he was the primary author of the minority report. It reflected, in particular, the theological stand to which John Jay's pamphlet had recently exposed him.[1]

The minority report began more delicately, however. Johnson and King apologized for their disagreement with the majority, and assured the convention that "they did not make this report with a view of exciting or encouraging any discussion in this Convention of topics in no way connected with the subject of this application." They thus disavowed any interest in linking the admission of St. Philip's to the issue of slavery or a discussion of abolition, Johnson's allegiance to Jay notwithstanding. Oddly, however, Johnson and King questioned the original formation of St. Philip's as a black congregation: "although at the time of the organizing of this congregation, it was thought to be a wise and salutary measure, yet in their [Johnson's and King's] opinion, subsequent events should lead us to doubt the propriety or expediency of such organization." This approach is historically opaque: did they believe that congregations organized according to race were theologically wrong or just a logistical error? It certainly sounds like they were suggesting that congregations of mixed race membership would not have needed to either ordain a black man or appoint black members to be convention delegates, and thus the issue of admitting African Americans to convention could have been avoided entirely. On the other hand, perhaps Johnson and King were also of a mind with Smith's disapproval of race-based organizations. It is impossible to say, but the use of the term "expediency" is suspicious.

Whatever their meaning, the minority members quickly moved on, stating that they could "see no reason why this application should not be granted, and think there are special reasons why it should." They dismissed the problem of the "arrangements" made with Peter Williams and his congregation as old news:

> We cannot conceive how the present generation belonging to that church can be bound by any stipulation of that kind, made by those who we trust have long since departed hence in the Lord, and been received into communion with the saints in Paradise. The present members of that church do not think as their fathers did on this subject.

The conditions imposed on the ordination of Williams may have been interesting in their time, but Johnson and King found them meaningless now. Note, however, that in their dismissal they have managed to make that original congregation, excluded from the diocese, united with all in Christ and the eternal communion of the faithful. Theological groundwork was clearly being laid.

Johnson and King then discussed what the implications of excluding St. Philip's had for denominational structure and identity. They again approached the problem delicately: "It may be said, that if this church be admitted, others will be organized and apply for admission." This was, of course, already the case: Crummell's parish had made an application at this same convention. They continued the perspective raised at the beginning of their report: "However much this is to be regretted, yet we suppose such will be the fact, and on this very account, this subject merits the very serious consideration of this Convention." There was a stab at realism here, a desire to get their fellow delegates to recognize that it was too late to turn back from what was already true, and too late to escape where it will lead:

> Suppose churches, now to be composed of colored people exclusively, are organized in our principal cities—suppose they are refused equal Christian privileges with other Episcopal Churches—that the Conventions of our Dioceses refuse to take them under their charge, and into their fellowship—will not these churches unite and form a Convention of their own? Will they not choose a Bishop or Bishops of their own? And *under such circumstances*, would they find any difficulty in obtaining Apostolical succession?

The majority report's suggested plan was here considered theologically, and the result became self-evident: "We fear the refusal of our Convention to admit into their fellowship this portion of their Christian brethren will inevitably lead to a schism in the Church, by the establishment of another Episcopal Church in these United States. All must admit this would be a sore evil." Johnson and King here pointed out what the majority had refused to see: the structure they envisioned so as to avoid encountering or discussing race was more likely to lead to schism than such encounters or discussions themselves. Expediency was exposed as shortsightedness.

Again, Johnson slipped in a subtle touch: African American Episcopalians were "their Christian brethren." They were not a separate class, degraded, or inadequate. Any perceptions—right or wrong—of their state or condition in the social sphere were actually immaterial, for they were fellow members of the faith and therefore of the church. This theological language of Johnson's deftly disavowed the distinctions Harison and his colleagues were making, which distinctions were the focus of Jay's condemnation in *Caste and Slavery in the American Church*. Johnson instead harked back to Jay's complaint in the opening conversation of the convention, that the question was one of "Christian brotherhood and catholic unity."[2] Yet it was less abstract than Jay's reference to the large concepts: Johnson specifically linked the congregation under consideration with the individuals gathered in the convention as "their Christian brethren." The diocese was not a club or even a society with divinely ordained strata. It was the church.

This is the point that Johnson went on to develop in thoroughly theological language:

> Can it be that because those who seek admission here are of a different race and complexion from ourselves, that doubts are entertained of the expediency of admitting them to union with this Convention? Have they not the Bible for their guide? Do they read in it that its divine precepts, its universal charity, its promised rewards are limited to any race or nation? Was not the Gospel vouchsafed to all men, to be proclaimed to all nations?

Here Johnson tiptoed right up to the problem first encountered by Episcopalians in the work of Elias Neau: if slaves and free African Americans could be baptized, did they not become fellow Christians? And did they not therefore have souls equal to those of white Christians? And if so, how could any divisions be maintained within the faith without tortured logic? And what did that equality in the faith imply about social equality—could the latter be denied if the former could not? Johnson's approach threatened to relaunch this chain of thinking—and this time, that argument could well prove unstoppable.

Aware of this, he followed up with what seemed to be a careful limiting of his implications but was instead a furthering of his point: "The Minority of your Committee expressly disavow any other motive in thus recommending the admission of this church, than that of promoting peace and harmony, and carrying out into practice the great Catholic doctrine of intercommunion of saints, as taught in the Bible, the word of God." While denying any broad ram-ifications of his argument, Johnson simultaneously reminded the convention that the black Episcopalians were already in the "intercommunion of saints" and dispatched the majority assertion that belief should not shape behavior. If the communion of saints was to have any real meaning, then Johnson (calling on the authority of the Bible itself) was sure that it would require putting that meaning "into practice." His own willingness to act on his newfound understanding of faith and race had led him to change his "practice" quite concretely, by inviting Crummell not only into his pulpit but into his home.

Johnson finished with the unassailable contention that the majority report was trying to deny something that was already real: "These persons who apply for this fellowship, have been made in Holy Baptism, 'members of Christ, chil-dren of God, and inheritors of the kingdom of Heaven'—they 'eat his flesh and drink his blood,' and thus are incorporated into him; with us, they are one with Him, and He is one with them." The use of the present perfect tense ("have been made") expressed his point as something already accomplished, and the use of the present tense ("are incorporated . . . are one . . . is one") to support that point established it as something currently true. Johnson thereby linguistically emphasized his view that black Episcopalians were already united to white Episcopalians through baptism and communion, the sacraments that Hobart had so carefully put at the center of the denominational identity. If this union were already true, then any attempt to claim otherwise was simply delusional. Thus Johnson concluded by once again distinguishing between society and the Christian faithful: "However just and proper distinctions in so-ciety may be in other respects, yet as members of one Holy Catholic Church, there ought to be no other distinctions than that made by superior self-denial, holiness, and virtue." His reiteration of the term "catholic" once again linked the specific Episcopalians present to an historical and worldwide faith.

Johnson and King concluded their report by earnestly repeating their desire to avoid "prolonged or excited discussion of this subject, or the intro-duction of questions not necessarily connected with it." There is no reason to question their sincerity. While the implications for slavery and prejudice of Johnson's theological position reached far, what these two most wanted to address was the concrete issue before them: they wished only to recommend "that this church be admitted into union with this Convention." In their perspective, the question of admitting St. Philip's was not actually about race, but about unity and catholicity.

Sensing that the significance of their argument would require time for thought and reflection, King immediately moved that both majority and minority reports "be laid on the table until the next Convention."[3] This maneuver also reinforced the perception that King and Johnson were not looking to launch a heated debate, but rather wanted only to remind their fellow delegates of the beliefs that they felt should influence their votes in this particular instance. There was no further discussion, and the convention was adjourned.

The vestry of St. Philip's met the next month, and the still-unseated delegates formally presented their report of the convention's actions (and inactions) on their admission. The vestry then voted to convey its thanks to Johnson and King "for their report to the Convention, in favor of admitting this church," and to thank also the Rev. Alexander Frazer "for his zealous efforts in behalf of gaining admission for this church into the Convention."[4] Their gratitude for the committee minority's articulation of their case is understandable, but they must also have felt that Frazer had worked hard to present the parish in less formal ways. Clergy networking and behind-the-scenes politicking were as important to the parish's campaign as public rhetoric. Again, no mention was made of Jay's efforts, public or private.

And thus the convention that the parish had anticipated with such optimism ended with a sincere thanks and a great disappointment. While the vestry did not dignify the majority report with a response in their meeting minutes, it could only have hurt them and their parishioners terribly. To be aware of prejudice, to feel its constant weight and presence, was a painful fact of daily life for the people of St. Philip's. But to have its basis articulated so baldly and boldly, as though it were not only theologically rational but a matter of common knowledge, must have evoked a kind of helpless rage. In the face of such a casual slap, the perspective adopted by Johnson and King was a mixed blessing: while it reminded the parishioners of the basis in faith by which they identified themselves as Christians and Episcopalians, it was also another example of the degree to which this congregation, and all black Americans, were desperately dependent on the goodwill and influence of the few white Americans who could rise above the racism endemic to their culture. The Gospel may have been vouchsafed to all, but the power—even in the Church—had clearly devolved to a few.

CHAPTER 17

The Heart Must Be Changed

As unadmitted delegates to the 1846 convention, were James McCune Smith and Alexander Elston permitted to sit in the balcony with the other observers, or was even that too close an association with the diocese's white leaders for these men of color? If they were allowed to be seated as observers, how their faces must have burned as the majority report was read to the assembly before them. And how measured their pride and gratitude must have been as the minority report was read, with its carefully limited support for their congregation. It is hard to imagine a more vivid and immediate conjunction of the vicissitudes possible in the continual interactions these black men had with the white society in which they lived.

Smith must have felt these vicissitudes even more keenly than his St. Philip's colleague. An eminent physician, speaker, and writer by this time, he had to listen to Harison, Sherwood, and Spencer declare that he was "ignorant, coarse, and debased" and lacked the "qualities" necessary to be a "proper associate" of those conducting the business of the church. He himself would have admitted that many of his fellow African Americans were ignorant, coarse, and debased; he sometimes despaired of the failure of black New Yorkers to fully appreciate the importance of education and culture.[1] But Smith would have charged that the same adjectives could be (and often were) used to describe a rather large number of European Americans as well. More importantly, he must have been appalled to hear an entire people painted with this broad brush and to have his own personal achievements so summarily dismissed under the rubric of such prejudice.

At the end of that year and beginning of the next, in a trio of letters to Gerrit Smith, McCune Smith celebrated a friendship that crossed racial boundaries and affirmed his status as a "proper associate" of at least one very wealthy white family. Addressing his now "dear friend," McCune Smith suggested a visit: "My wife and I look forward with much delight to your return to this city, and feel sure that Mrs. Smith and yourself will honour us with an evening at our home."[2] In light of the assurances of the majority report that whites and blacks could never mix socially, McCune Smith's expectation that Gerrit Smith and his wife would visit his home is remarkable. The following January, the opportunity came for the invitation to be made explicit:

> Being unable to wait until the close of the meeting in the Tabernacle, I write to beg that you will request your Son-in-law and his wife to accompany Mrs. Smith and yourself to tea at our house tomorrow evening . . . at 5 or at 7 P.M., as best suits your convenience. My wife earnestly joins me in this request, and begs to be kindly remembered.[3]

There is no reason to doubt that Gerrit Smith and family accepted the invitation, thereby flouting the assumptions of white society.

McCune Smith could be so bold as to make this invitation because his friend had already entertained him during a trip to the city. Speaking of that visit, McCune Smith wrote of his pleasure in discovering another dimension that cemented their friendship: their religious faith. McCune Smith extolled "that full and abiding confidence in God, that firm reliance on the saving power of the Redeemer's love, which it was my joy to find you express during the short but pleasant hours I spent in your society."[4] Here, again in contrast to his experience with the leaders of his own denomination, McCune Smith could celebrate a faith shared across racial boundaries.

The immediate cause of this warm friendship was McCune Smith's amazed gratitude for and enthusiastic involvement in Gerrit Smith's grand new plan: the creation of an enclave of African American property owners in northern New York State. Gerrit Smith announced on August 1, 1846, that he intended to hand over 120,000 acres of his property to 3,000 black New Yorkers.[5] In doing so, Smith hoped they would be able to live by their own labors and free of the immediate oppression of white society, thus serving as a visible model of black capabilities. He was also granting those 3,000 men the vote, for they would meet the property qualifications for black suffrage—qualifications much more onerous than those for white men. To make this extraordinarily magnanimous gesture, Smith had to sell some $400,000 more of his property, to reduce his debts to a manageable level so that the land he wished to grant would be unencumbered. He appointed McCune Smith and two of his ministerial friends, Theodore Wright and Charles Ray, to be trustees of the project and agents for the recruitment and selection of those to whom it would be donated.

This was an undertaking beyond all imagining, and McCune Smith could hardly conceive of both his friend's generosity and the various prices he would have to pay. Writing Gerrit Smith in mid-December, as the project was getting going, he warned him, "You have borne much and will, for the Truth's sake, and for the sake of your fellow man, but what you contemplate doing will, in the present state of society, subject you to trials more painful than any thing you have endured. You have borne the taint of Fanaticism, you must prepare to be branded as a foolish man." White men who assisted African Americans were generally attacked and ridiculed, but what Gerrit Smith was planning was to severely reduce his personal wealth for the improvement of a derided people, for which he would surely be mocked. McCune Smith was stunned and overwhelmed by the reality and magnitude of it:

> And now that I think of it, there is something even to my mind incomprehensible in your contemplated abandonment of your landed possessions. It is, truly and simply, on your part an obedience to one of the teachings of our Lord and Saviour. How bad must the world be, how wove into it must my soul be, when so simple an act in accordance with one of His principles appears strange to me and incomprehensible![6]

It was most likely the first time McCune Smith had encountered a white American whom he could truly admire, trust, and appreciate. The contrast with those he had encountered at the diocesan convention could not have been more striking.

Gerrit Smith had imposed only three qualifications for receiving deeds: the grantees were to be residents of New York State, they had to be between the ages of twenty-one and sixty, and they could not already own land. The task of serving as agent and trustee gave McCune Smith enormous joy, as he went on to report: "We held a fine meeting on Wednesday night and delivered 60 deeds to a fine set of men. You certainly deprive yourself of a most interesting sight, in declining to see a gathering of the Grantees. Tall, stalwart, hard-fisted, they embody a Hope of the Race."[7] Another 170 deeds were granted by the following March. It was a shaky hope, however, as the land was raw Adirondack wilderness. The grantees would need sufficient tools and animals to clear the land and make it productive, and sufficient capital to sustain themselves until the land could support them. These would prove to be insurmountable obstacles for many of the settlers, who were often forced to take on heavy mortgages or even sell portions of the land outright at deflated prices to wealthier speculators. The project did not ultimately achieve all of its goals, but North Elba (or Timbucto, as it was first called by residents) was soon established sufficiently that it became a major depot of the Underground Railroad and the home of the radical abolitionist John Brown.

McCune Smith himself was given a deed (along with Brown and Frederick Douglass), and he visited North Elba on a couple of occasions. After one such visit in 1850, he wrote to Gerrit Smith of his wish that he could be part of this enterprise:

> I felt myself a "lord indeed" beneath the lofty spruce and maple and birch, and by the trawling brook, which your deed made mine, and would gladly exchange this bustling anxious life for the repose of that majestic country, could I see the way clear for a livelihood for myself and family. I am not afraid of physical labor: but do not think it would be prudent to risk sustenance in my personal labor in the farming line: and the country is yet too sparse to give support to a physician.[8]

This is hardly the dilemma, or the language for expressing it, that would present itself to someone "ignorant, coarse, and debased"; it is instead the very picture of the Victorian bourgeoisie.

Yet despite the hopefulness and enthusiasm brought to McCune Smith's life by both the land-grant project and his friendship with Gerrit Smith, the burdens of being black in America were never far from his mind. McCune Smith's bouts of melancholy were hardly surprising given his self-awareness and perceptivity and the issues with which he struggled. Two weeks after greeting Gerrit Smith's project with such excitement, he wrote again to convey greetings of the season and closed the letter with mixed emotions as he looked back over 1846:

> The veil of night is gradually closing over the old year, sad memories of crushed hope, of national shame, of ensanguined fields, will ever crowd around it, yet amid all, there are one or two generous Deeds about which it will be pleasant to linger, and they will be swept from the earth before the Colored People of this state and country will forget how you remembered them in their bonds.[9]

Gerrit Smith's generosity was one of the only encouraging memories in a year of setbacks.

The "national shame" and "ensanguined fields" were references to the onset that year of the Mexican–American War, which most abolitionists saw as a cynical land grab whose real purpose was the expansion of slave territory. When the Senate refused to pass the Wilmot Proviso, which prohibited slavery in any territory taken from Mexico and had been approved by the House of Representatives, the abolitionists felt that their suspicions had been confirmed. Clearly this was McCune Smith's view. And at least one of his "crushed hopes" would have been the complete failure of a referendum in New York State that fall to equalize the suffrage requirements for black and white males. Another may well have been the results of the diocesan convention, for which his congregation had had such optimism; but again, McCune Smith never mentioned this struggle explicitly in his correspondence with Gerrit Smith despite the importance of their shared Christian faith.

McCune Smith began his meditations on the year in response to a request from Gerrit Smith that he write something for "the colored men of the state." McCune Smith confessed, "I have not heart to write it. Each succeeding day, that terrible majority falls sadder, heavier, more crushingly on my soul. . . . There is in that majority a hate deeper than I had imagined." He could not believe that prejudice against African Americans was of greater import than the availability of their votes to any party, which was only further evidence that such prejudice outstripped all other considerations for so many white Americans. "Laboring under these views," he felt, "I cannot write a cheerful word and will not write a discouraging one."[10]

Though he refused Gerrit Smith's invitation to publish an address on the subject, he warmed to it on this personal level:

> The direction in which our people must labour is a point on which I am not certain. The heart of the whites must be changed, thoroughly, entirely, permanently changed . . . and men, colored men, must go to work to produce that conviction—of the eternal equality of the Human Race—which is the first principle of Good Government—of Bible Politics. This must be done, but how?

The concept of "Bible politics" was one McCune Smith shared with Gerrit Smith, and pointed to their efforts to understand the application of their faith to the workings of society. Thus his conclusion: "Of course it is mind-work. Physical force has no place in it."[11] Though he would later turn to supporting force as a justifiable means of ending slavery, here McCune Smith was concerned with the human heart, with inculcating a commitment to Christian faith and social good that would alter the very humanity of white America.

Yet such a broad picture inevitably stumbled upon his personal experience of prejudice. The law in New York State required black men to own $250 worth of taxable property and prove three years of residency in the state, while white men had no property requirement and had only to demonstrate one year's residency. For McCune Smith (who owned his own New York City home), this implied that land was of greater value than African American life:

> My personal influence, manhood, presence at the ballot box is utterly destroyed when the earth-owning oath is thrust at me. The negro Man is merged into the negro Landowner. The point of the moral is dipped into poison. It is established by the solemnity of an oath that the vile earth has rights superior to Manhood! That "the dust of the earth" is the greater, without "the breath of life." What horrible mockery! Is it right to be a party in such Blasphemy?[12]

The thought so enraged him that he had to break off the letter and continue it two days later.

In a calmer frame of mind, McCune Smith returned to what always was his highest hope for improving the lot of African Americans: educational opportunities. He bemoaned the absence of such facilities in so many of the state's rural areas, and asserted, "The mere possession of land by our people, even if cultivated by them, must be associated with equal educational privileges." Only in such a manner might black New Yorkers truly develop, and thus demonstrate their adequacy to enjoy social and political equality: "If five thousand souls advance from five to fifteen years old, without learning to read and write, they will indeed form a lower grade in the classes of mind which make up our state. Along with the effort to make voters, therefore, we must labour to spread intelligence in the state."[13] Thus McCune Smith concluded this rambling epistle by seeking Gerrit Smith's assistance in forcing the state legislature to open more schools for African Americans. The return to the pragmatic, to looking at concrete tasks and potential movements, brought McCune Smith back to a place of active engagement with his society.

It was precisely this engagement, however, that forced McCune Smith to continually interact as an oppressed man with his oppressors. Every possible movement, every idea for the improvement of conditions or the amelioration of prejudice, required negotiation with white men. When that white man was Gerrit Smith, such negotiation and interaction brought hope and pleasure; but too often it was with men whose hearts were unchanged and unchanging. The results then were limited voting rights, a dismal lack of educational facilities, expansion rather than contraction of slave power, prejudice on the basis of skin color, and a set of Christians that could not allow themselves to recognize their brethren in faith. It is a wonder, then, that James McCune Smith never succumbed completely to despair but instead remained thoughtful, articulate, and oddly hopeful throughout his lifelong struggle for justice and equality.

CHAPTER 18

~~~~~~~~~~

The Beauties of Freedom

On Saturday July 10, 1847, the Brazilian ship *Lembranca* docked at the Roosevelt Street pier in New York City. Word soon reached the offices of the American Anti-Slavery Society that three slaves, owned by the ship's captain, were on board. A crowd of African Americans and antislavery activists quickly gathered at the pier in protest. John Jay rushed to court for a writ of habeas corpus, and had the three slaves brought before a judge. Anticipating the argument of the Dred Scott case ten years later, Jay insisted that the slaves were free by virtue of having been brought by their owner into free territory. So, indeed, read the state law that had ended slavery twenty years earlier: "every person born within this state, whether white or colored, is FREE; every person who shall hereafter be born within this state, shall be FREE; and every person brought into this state as a slave, except as authorized by this Title, shall be FREE."[1]

The Brazilian captain argued that a treaty between his nation and the United States prevented anyone from tampering with his property, so the judge remanded the three slaves to the custody of the sheriff while he pondered his decision. According to the *New York Herald*, numerous African Americans gathered around the three as they were taken to jail and tried, "by all sorts of signs, as they could not speak each others' language, to impress them with the beauties of freedom."[2]

The slaves languished in jail for a month while their case was brought before three different judges. The first ruled in favor of the Brazilian captain on the strength of the treaty, the second declined to review that decision, and before the third could hear the case, the slaves mysteriously escaped from jail. There was no sign of violence or forced entry or exit. Jay could barely contain his glee over this result, as no actual crime could be said to have been committed in the escape, since the slaves were in jail only to keep them out of their owner's possession until the case was resolved.[3]

While this odd chain of events was running its course, Sydney Gay—the editor of the American Anti-Slavery Society's newspaper, the *National Anti-Slavery Standard*, and fundraiser for the society—appealed to the vestry of St. Philip's for a donation to defray legal expenses in the ongoing case. This would seem a reasonable appeal on Gay's part, given the parish's connection to Jay and the number of parishioners active in the Anti-Slavery Society. The vestry, however, dismissed it, recording their response in the minutes of their August 12 meeting:

> A letter was received from Sydney H. Gay requesting that this church do join other *colored* churches in this city in raising One Hundred Dollars for carrying on the suit in the case of the Brazilian slaves. *Moved*, that in the opinion of this vestry the question is one that concerns all men regardless of complexion, and that this vestry cannot by word or deed assent to the doctrine that it is a matter particularly pertaining to colored churches. *Agreed*.[4]

The language and sentiment here are once again those of the secretary of the vestry, James McCune Smith. Yet the sentiment is clearly shared, as the vestry minutes use the term "agreed" to indicate a unanimous vote, and there is no record of any discussion or disagreement. Most white Americans understood the issues of slavery, freedom, and prejudice to be problems for African Americans, not themselves. The vestry saw that attitude reflected in Gay's appeal to the "colored" churches, and repudiated it. This group of African Americans understood the Brazilian slaves to be human beings whose welfare should have been the concern of all humanity.

Did McCune Smith convince the rest of the vestry to take this position? Or were they all truly offended by the implication of Gay's appeal that the case of the Brazilian slaves was something only "colored" churches would want to support? The minutes do not record Gay's letter in full, only Smith's summary of it, but the vestry clearly understood him to be applying only to African American churches. Most of the Anti-Slavery Society's members were white church leaders; would not their churches have wanted to contribute to this case, or were they more interested in the principles of antislavery than in the reality of three Brazilians?

This intriguing incident is open to a variety of interpretations, none of them conclusive beyond the association with an attitude for which McCune Smith, at least, had become well known. At a minimum, however, it can be seen that once again those on the white side of the racial divide—even those working to end slavery—were constantly reinforcing that divide, even if unintentionally or unconsciously, while those on the other side were trying their best to blur it. Thus the approach to the question of the Brazilian slaves can be plausibly attributed to the people of the parish, not just their elected parish leaders.

In the circumstances of constant racial encounters and tension such as those of the people of St. Philip's, it is tempting to see the individuals involved only through the lens of race. Certainly Gay was guilty of that limited perspective, and the vestry rejected it. But the same myopia is possible when looking back historically on those circumstances. African Americans in New York City, as anywhere else in mid-nineteenth-century America, lived under conditions fraught with such circumstances. Yet it is easy to forget that their lives also had joy and accomplishment and entertainment and all the other pieces that make up life. They were individuals leading lives as best they could, under conditions that were certainly better than those of other African Americans still in slavery. The "beauties of freedom" that the crowd attempted to convey to the Brazilian slaves may have been defective, but they were appreciated nonetheless for the opportunities they created for individuals to carve out lives and identities defined by more than race.

Who, then, were these people? Picture a Sunday morning in 1847, or any year thereabouts; due to the vagaries of city directories and other forms of record keeping in the mid-nineteenth century, what follows will have to be a bit of a composite portrait. The Rev. Alexander Frazer, having finished the early service at the Sailors' Snug Harbor on Staten Island, the home for retired sailors where he was the chaplain, has hurriedly caught the ferry across the harbor to the city. Hailing a carriage at the ferry landing, he rides the twenty-some blocks north to 85 Centre Street, the site of St. Philip's Episcopal Church. Though white, he has been serving as officiating minister since February of 1842. Donning his cassock, surplice, preaching bands, and tippet, Frazer strides into the sanctuary to begin the service of morning prayer. As he surveys the congregation he has seen Sunday after Sunday (though seldom otherwise) for five years, how well does he know the individuals that make up this remarkable congregation?[5]

Maria Wright is the organist for St. Philip's; her husband died in 1843, the year she took on the position at the church. Her tenure is apparently not without some dissatisfaction: a few years hence, in 1852, she demands a raise, is rebuffed, resigns, and the vestry passes a resolution that "Miss Wright be not employed as organist under any circumstances." At the moment, however, she is at the keyboard of the instrument built by Henry Erben, who also built

Trinity Church's organ. Leading the choir is Robert Hamilton, who works as a porter and lives around the corner on Leonard Street. He too is not as popular with the vestry as he might wish, but then he succeeded one of the city's best-known black composers, William Brady, who then returned to the position briefly in 1848. Brady was described by one contemporary as "very much esteemed as a composer, being the author of many fine pieces of music, such as quadrilles, polkas, waltzes, marches, and songs. He also essayed more elevated work with fine success, having been the composer of a musical service for the Episcopal Church, and a beautiful Christmas anthem."[6] The negotiations over these personnel moves regarding worship music, as recorded in the vestry minutes, were quite complex, and indicate the importance of this aspect of the parish's life.

St. Philip's, in the standard practice of the time, charged its parishioners for the pews they occupied: this "pew rent" was the primary source of income for the parish. No records exist of who rented which pews, or for how much, but Philip Lacy is the parish sexton at this time, and thus in charge of collecting the rents. For motivation, he receives a commission of six percent in addition to his small yearly salary of $72.00.[7] Lacy lives on Orange Street, in the heart of the Five Points slum and hard by the African Society Hall, headquarters of the African Mutual Relief Society. As sexton, he is well positioned to know the economic circumstances of his fellow parishioners.

By the 1840s, some parishioners are quite successful. Thomas Downing, the wealthy restaurateur, is here this morning in his pew with his wife Rebecca. Their five children are all grown now, and while son Henry is working at the family restaurant (and living with his parents), George has moved on to open his own oyster supply business. Thomas and Rebecca at this time are living at 4 Temple Street, a quiet lane behind Trinity Church. Seated nearby is parish treasurer Henry Scott, whose pickling business supplies ships for their ocean voyages; he owns both his downtown business establishment on Water Street and his home uptown on West Fifteenth Street.[8] Peter Ray, the warden, lives on the premises of the tobacco factory he supervises on Wooster Street; within a few years, he and his wife Ann will move to Williamsburgh in Brooklyn. Their son, Peter Williams Ray, was tutored by James McCune Smith and then went to Bowdoin College; he is currently serving his internship at Massachusetts General Hospital, and will become a wealthy and famous doctor in Brooklyn. Albro Lyons, in another nearby pew, also studied with Smith (working as a "segarmaker" in the meantime) and was the first African American to graduate from the

New York College of Pharmacy in 1844; his drugstore on Frankfort St. has become a large retail and wholesale business (it is destroyed in the Draft Riots of 1863, but Lyons and family escape to Brooklyn). Lyons and his wife, Mary, were married by Peter Williams just before the rector's death, with Smith serving as best man.[9]

The rector's widow, Sarah Williams, owns a home around the corner from the church on Leonard Street, which home she shares with her late husband's adopted sister, Mary. The parish pays Sarah an annuity, but her financial circumstances are such that she often donates it to the Female Assistance Society (which then occasionally loans it back to the church). Sarah and Peter have one daughter, Amy Matilda, who will marry Charles Lenox Remond, the famous African American abolitionist speaker. They live in Salem, Massachusetts, and are perhaps contributing to Sarah's financial stability.[10]

Other parishioners are less fortunate and are therefore less regular in their pew rent payments, but are in attendance this morning nonetheless. Alexander Elston, who was the second warden with Ray for the past two years but lost the election this year, is currently living on Leonard Street next door to Sarah Williams and just a few doors down from Robert Hamilton, whom he will replace briefly as chorister in 1850. Elston and his wife, Mary, have moved nine times in the past twenty years, a sure sign of the financial instability of his bootmaking business. Indeed, Mary has been taking in washing, and sons Alexander and Barzillai are old enough now to be making their own ways in the world. Thomas Hoffman, another former vestryman, is working as a porter and living hard by the west side docks on Albany Street. Others working the same profession include Felix Guinan, John Berrian, Gabriel Bowyer, Isaac Matthews, and Henry Carter—all of whom must be struggling to make ends meet with this low-paying occupation. On the other hand, John Marander lists himself in the city directory as a porter, yet he seems to have put some money by: he was a trustee of the lease for the land on which St. Philip's sits, served on the first vestry, and at one point loaned the parish $460, on which he is still paid annual interest.[11] He and his wife Elizabeth are among the most respected elders of the church.

The range of lower-income occupations represented in this congregation is quite impressive: Francis Harley is a "clothes scourer," John Robertson is a whitewasher, Francis Bastien works as a bootblack, John Brown is a clerk, and Daniel Burry is a seaman. Some simply list their positions as "laborer": John Morgan, George Potts, and William Curtiss all fit this category. Isaac Gosiah is, like Elston, a bootmaker, and he too eventually serves as warden; he and his wife Hester move frequently as well. And then there are the barbers and hairdressers: William Poyer, George Chatters, Lorenzo Coggar, and William Innis. Charles Hamilton works as a waiter and lives in the same building as Elston, Robert Thomas is a coachman, and while Edward Cills leaves no record of his own employment, his wife Phebe runs a toy store. Nancy Van Dyke, whose son Peter works as a waiter and owns his house on York Street, takes in sewing at her home on Wooster Street, and Christina Nathan is a dressmaker living on Thomas Street.

As Frazer looks out at this congregation, he also sees those who have tried to make something different of themselves. John Peterson, who has taught for years at the African Free School, also serves as a layreader, warden, vestry member, and convention delegate at St. Philip's, and after the Civil War, he is ordained a perpetual deacon.[12] Ransom Wake is the other longtime teacher at the African Free School; he and his wife Mary live on Thompson Street just above Canal Street. Theodore Vidal has done sufficiently well as a hairdresser that he owns his house on Duane Street; Moses Burns has achieved the same goal as a waiter, owning his home on Leonard Street—though he is on the other side of Centre Street from the church (and Sarah Williams's home), which puts him in the Five Points district. Nonetheless, the building was recently assessed by the city at a valuation of $2,000.[13] Daniel Tilghman is a tailor, Thomas Zabriskie has developed his position at a livery stable into a thriving coach business, George Lawrence has parlayed his experience working for Henry Scott earlier in the decade into running his own dry goods shop, and Samuel Ennals has a grocery on Laurens Street and owns his house on Franklin Street, two blocks up from the church.

Thus on this typical Sunday morning, as he preaches and leads the prayers, Frazer looks out on a wide range of humanity. They come from all walks of life, are in all sorts of financial conditions, and a large proportion of them have served on the vestry or taken some other position of parish leadership. There are also some figures of more than passing historical interest, of whom Frazer is probably aware. James McCune Smith, of course, has made himself well known by this time; he and his wife Malvina are sitting with their three children this morning. Behind them is seated Philip Bell, cofounder of the *Weekly Advocate* and still proprietor of the Hutson and Bell Intelligence Agency (an employment service founded by one of the parish's first vestrymen, William Hutson) on Pearl Street. Bell has lived at 15 St. John's Place, behind the elegant St. John's Chapel, for the past fifteen years; in the late 1850s, however, he moves to San Francisco and founds two more newspapers, becoming an eloquent spokesman for black migrants to the West Coast. In New York, Bell was a founding member of the Philomathian Society, a director of the Phoenix Society, and an agent for Garrison's *Liberator*—and just this year has helped create the New York Society for the Promotion of Education Among Colored Children. The trustees of this organization are a veritable who's who of St. Philip's parishioners, including Smith, George Downing, Lyons, Ray, Scott, Philip White, and Patrick Reason.[14]

Another trustee is William Powell; he and his wife Mercy are seated amidst this array of friends. Powell is the founder and keeper of the Colored Seaman's Home, by the east side docks on Cherry Street; the home takes in both retired and active sailors, and has never turned anyone away because of an inability to pay. Powell created the institution because Frazer's other employer, the Sailors' Snug Harbor, will not admit African Americans. Powell is one of the more radical members of the congregation, involved in the fledgling black labor movement and a vocal opponent of slavery. When the Fugitive Slave Law is passed in 1850, Powell publicly advocates disobeying it. That law, however, finally does him in: later that year he gives up his brief tenure as warden at St. Philip's, turns the Colored Seaman's Home over to his friend Albro Lyons, and moves to England for ten years, stating that he has lost all hope that racial conditions in this country will ever improve.[15]

Boston and Charity Crummell, Alexander's parents, are present this morning; so are George and Maria DeGrasse. Both couples have been with the parish since its earliest years. Sitting with the DeGrasses are their daughter Theodocia and her husband Peter Vogelsang (their other daughter, Serena, is married to George Downing). Vogelsang has been working for the steamers on the Albany line, and he eventually creates his own highly successful shipping business. The "beauties of freedom" take on special significance for Vogelsang during the Civil War, when he enlists with the Fifty-fourth Massachusetts Regiment. He is the oldest member of what becomes the first African American regiment mustered for combat, and is wounded in its famous assault on Fort Wagner, South Carolina.[16]

Of the hundreds of individual parishioners of St. Philip's in its first decades of existence, these are among the few whose names—and a few other details—are known to the historical record. Most have passed into obscurity; many of them were undoubtedly important to the life of the congregation and the community despite the absence of enduring notice. To mark the names and lives of those that are known, however, is to be reminded of the individuality and humanity that composed this congregation—a perspective too often lost to the white population that surrounded them. Even the American Anti-Slavery Society too often forgot this simple truth, and assumed along with most other white Americans that the primary datum of identity about any African American was his or her race. Sidney Gay addressed the congregation of St. Philip's from such a perspective and was quickly rebuffed; it is worth noting that in no account of the Brazilian slaves, whether by Gay or in newspapers of the time, does anyone mention their names.

CHAPTER 19

Economic Opportunity and Religious Choice

Despite how little the historical record contains about most of the in-dividuals whose worship Alexander Frazer led that Sunday morning, some conclusions can be drawn about them and their circumstances. Though small, the list of names that can be definitively attached to St. Philip's and the addresses and occupations associated with those names in city directories over the years provide a means of exploring the economic conditions of the congregation relative to African Americans in other urban centers, to those in New York City itself, and even to one another. For in exploring the human-ity and individuality of this congregation, one lingering question is whether these Episcopalians were different from their fellow black New Yorkers only in their choice of religious affiliation, or whether they were (or believed themselves) distinct from that population in other ways as well.

A first look at this question is provided by examining where parishioners lived in relation to the rest of the city's black population. What various studies have made clear is that at no time prior to the Civil War did any particular African American ghetto exist in New York City, neither among the poor nor those better off. One ward-by-ward analysis of the city from 1790 to 1860 suggests that over the first half of the nineteenth century "the areas with the greatest concentration" of African Americans "shifted slowly westward and northward." Yet this movement of black New Yorkers was matched by a sim-ilar movement among white New Yorkers: as the city grew, downtown gave way to businesses, and residential areas spread ever further north. While preju-dice and discrimination did generally condemn African Americans to renting airless, overcrowded tenements in back alleys and unsavory neighborhoods, these neighborhoods were never predominantly black. Even the infamous Five Points slum district, located immediately adjacent to St. Philip's Church, was always racially and ethnically mixed. There were a couple of occasions in the late eighteenth and early nineteenth centuries when a three- or four-block area was known as "Little Africa," but such designations were short lived and narrow; these areas never contained more than a small percentage of the African American population of the city. The aforementioned study thus asserts that "Negroes and whites resided in the same houses even in the areas of the greatest concentration of the Negro population and often as boarders in the same apartment, if some of these hovels can be so described."[1]

The members of St. Philip's with known addresses fit these conclusions quite well. The majority did live on the west side of Broadway, Manhattan's north-south axis: three-fifths of the addresses were located in the Fifth and Eighth Wards, which had the highest numbers of African Americans from 1840 to 1850. Yet parishioners can be found to have been living in nearly every ward of the city. Henry Scott was a pioneer in moving well north to Fifteenth Street in the Sixteenth Ward in the 1830s, when the area was still largely a bucolic suburb, while three of the parish's porters—Thomas Hoffman, Henry Carter, and John Berrian—resided throughout the 1840s in the First Ward, at the city's southern tip. A dozen members lived on St. John's Place, which took its name from the imposing chapel on the west side; the street, however, actually abutted the rear of the church building, and thus had no connection to the stately homes and park in front of it. Several other parishioners lived on the opposite side of town, in the neighborhoods stretching to the east that now make up the Lower East Side.

While there were some congregants who lived near the church, including those who lived in the Five Points neighborhood, the wide scattering of the members across the city effectively thwarts the possibility that the church's location was central to its members. The church moved three times, leaving Centre Street in 1856 for Mulberry Street, then to West Twenty-fifth Street in 1886, and finally to 134th Street in Harlem in 1910.[2] It is certainly plausible that these moves followed the northward migration of the city's African American population, but not until the last move could one claim that the church occupied a primarily black neighborhood. During this early period, it is fairly clear that people did not choose St. Philip's by whether or not it was conveniently located in the part of town in which they lived: people came from all over the city to attend this parish. It is also important to note that there were other black churches located both near St. Philip's and sprinkled around the city's neighborhoods. Those who attended St. Philip's, then, did so because they chose to be Episcopalian, not because it was the nearest black church.

But did they choose to be Episcopalian because of its class associations in white America, and because they were, many of them, part of the first generation of middle-class African Americans? This is a valid question: certainly the

Episcopal Church, especially in the Northeast, was associated with middle- and upper-class identities or aspirations among European Americans. The rise of Victorianism occasioned an accompanying Anglophilia among those who aspired to status, culture, economic stability, and comfort, and the Episcopal Church was not one to hide its Anglican roots. Did St. Philip's attract, then, a particular group of black New Yorkers who aspired to the cultural and economic status of the bourgeoisie—and who saw this denomination as another means to that end? McCune Smith and Crummell both articulated such goals on many occasions; their admiration for Victorian ideals informed their faith in the divine progress of history and improvement of the race through education, and these were values they had learned at Peter Williams's knee. Was their attachment to the denomination—as well as that attachment of the congregation as a whole—determined by these values and hopes, rather than by any specifically religious perspective?

It is difficult to make sweeping generalizations about the economic status of the members of St. Philip's. As has been noted, those whose names and professions are known cover an enormous range. It is particularly important to remark, in addition, that these names of actual parishioners come primarily from two sources: the minutes of vestry meetings and an open letter written in support of John Jay's relationship with the parish. As will be seen, both of these sources should be understood to skew toward the leadership of the parish, rather than being seen as representative of the rank and file. Nonetheless, this is the data available, and it should be explored as fully as possible.

Any discussion of a rising black "middle class" must be understood only in relative terms: relative to other African Americans, not relative to any white middle class. The overall economic context for black Americans, as for black New Yorkers, was simply several steps below that of white Americans, and the majority lived in abject poverty. The delineation of that context has been aptly accomplished by Leonard Curry in a study of the economic and occupational status of African Americans in fifteen cities in the first half of the nineteenth century. Curry divides the occupations of urban free blacks into eight categories ranging from "unskilled" through "professional managerial, artistic, clerical, scientific, etc.," and then groups the categories "into three blocks of occupations roughly corresponding to low, medium, and high occupational achievement and economic opportunity."[3] He argues that "the greater the percentage of black males engaged in group A [low opportunity] occupations in a city . . . , the less likely it is that that particular population block will advance economically." Curry is less straightforward regarding the consequences of the high-opportunity block, arguing that the top two categories of "entrepreneurial/mercantile" and "professional managerial, artistic, . . . , etc." were impaired because racial conditions were such that the target market for those occupations was almost exclusively a poor black population, and thus not a strong indicator of economic opportunity. Instead, he relies on the sixth category of "artisan" as the indicator of a population's greater opportunities.

From these factors, then, Curry creates an "Index of Occupational Opportunity" and compiles statistics for fifteen cities from the 1850 census to establish a comparative range along a scale from 0.00 to 1.00, higher numbers indicating a population's greater opportunity.[4] The actual range he computes is from a high in New Orleans of .7316 to a low in Pittsburgh of .1366, and a pattern becomes evident: free African Americans in the mid-nineteenth century had greater economic opportunities in the cities of the South than in those of the North. In fact, the situation generally worsens the farther north the cities are found. New York City's index is calculated at .1584, ranking it higher than only Providence, Boston, and Pittsburgh. Curry argues that this pattern is no surprise, for while Southern cities legally restricted employment possibilities by directly prohibiting blacks from certain kinds of jobs, the social restrictions of Northern cities were actually more effective in limiting opportunities for African Americans. Thus more than two-thirds of the black males in nine Northern cities were employed in low-opportunity-block jobs, and Curry sees simple discrimination as the primary cause.

It is also true, however, that Curry's statistics for the South—as he himself notes—are significantly affected by the fact that slavery still existed there. The free black communities of Southern cities, then, were created by the emancipation of its members through purchasing their own freedom or being rewarded with freedom for their labor, loyalty, or familial relationships. Such individuals thus can be understood to be the most energetic and talented members of the slave population, with greater access to higher-opportunity occupations. Therefore, the figures for Southern cities reflect a set of conditions that created a group of greater achievement (the manumitted) that was more visible than the wider population of lesser achievement (those still slaves).[5] This is a situation that is analogous, to a degree, to that of the members of St. Philip's.

Applying Curry's methods and statistics to the men of St. Philip's is informative only if the issue of date is simply ignored: there are not sufficient data for any one year to be useful. Instead, the ninety-nine occupations that can be definitively linked to parishioners between the years of 1820 and 1856 must be elided together. Doing so yields an index of .3850, which is staggeringly higher than the .1584 that Curry found for New York City as a whole. Two factors account for this disparity, however, and the first is somewhat trivial: Curry's statistics were drawn from the 1850 census. When he compared information from the city directory for 1852, he found an index for the city of .2377 (indicating that the directory listings either included more artisans or fewer low-opportunity-block occupations). The parish's index, based on data from city directories, is still significantly higher than this number, but the difference is not as shocking.

The more important factor has to do with the issue of class distinctions within the congregation. The data for the parish, again, reflects the congregation's leadership group rather than its population as a whole, and it is not surprising that this group would be perceptibly higher on the economic and opportunity scale. Thus the analogy to the situation in Southern cities: the group of greater achievement here, the leaders, have been made more histori-cally visible than the wider population of lesser achievement—simply because historical data tend to lean in that direction.

The disparity between the congregational leadership and the congrega-tion as a whole is made even clearer by breaking the available data into two groups: those who actually served on the vestry, and those who did not. The former group comprises forty-four known individuals between 1820 and 1859, and their index is .4100. This is slightly higher than the parish as a whole, and almost impressive compared to Curry's figures for New York City. The index for those on the list who did not serve on the vestry, on the other hand, is .3000, which, though lower than that of the vestry members, is still slightly higher than that for the city. Due to a variety of historical gaps, however, it is highly possible that some of the people included on this list served on the vestry at some point. An even clearer distinction, then, is found by restricting this group to those who ran for the vestry but were not elected: though a small group, it yields an index of .2775, much closer to Curry's fig-ure for the city and vastly lower than that of those who served on the vestry. Those who ran for the vestry but failed to be elected, then, would seem representative of the wider population of the city, while those who did get elected were of a significantly higher economic or social level. This is largely due to the fact that the vestry members were proportionally far less employed in occupations in the low-opportunity block than either the city's population as a whole or the group that never served on the vestry.

Altering Curry's approach somewhat can also emphasize this disparity. Curry felt that the top two categories, the entrepreneurs and the profes-sionals, had their opportunities severely limited by racial prejudice. It is hard to imagine, for example, that James McCune Smith had any white patients among his medical practice. Yet it has been noted that many of the members of St. Philip's were self-made men who worked their ways up from lower-category jobs to higher ones or who turned entrepreneurial opportunities into thriving businesses. In this situation may be found the businessmen Thomas Downing, Henry Scott, and Peter Vogelsang, and Moses Burns and Thomas Zabriskie serve as examples of those who created something stable and relatively remunerative out of lower-category occupations (Burns started as a waiter and eventually ran his own restaurant, and Zabriskie began as a carter and ended up with a livery stable of his own). In addition, these top two categories of occupations include those that had a great deal of social respect whether they were economically profitable or not, such as teacher, musician, and clergyman. It would be useful, therefore, to recalculate the opportunity index by including all of the high-opportunity-block occupations, rather than just those in the category of artisan.

To alter the index in this fashion—by including in the positive calculations all of the high-opportunity-block occupations—points to the educational and creative achievements of the African American population, as well as its relative economic levels. Reworking Curry's numbers for New York City results in an index of .1830, which is not a significant improvement. But the figure for the parish is astonishing: .5450, a positive ratio of high-opportunity occupations that displays the congregation's commitment to education, artistic talent, and economic drive. Comparing the indexes for vestry and nonvestry members points to the class disparity within the congregation: for the vestry, the index is .6250, while that for nonvestry members is .4250—and the index for those who ran for the vestry but were never elected is .3600. Fully twice as many members who ran for the vestry and lost were in low-opportunity occupations as compared to those who served on the vestry, and twice as many vestry members were in high-opportunity occupations as compared to those who were not elected. This gap clearly indicates that those chosen for the vestry—for the designated leadership of the parish—were generally members of educational or economic achievement, while those who are not chosen were those without such accomplishments.

This analysis points to the qualities of the people who made up the leadership of St. Philip's. They were men of the economic and cultural elite of New York City's black population. The disparity between them and the rest of the city's population, however, seems to be replicated by the disparity between them and the rest of the congregation. Thus the people of St. Philip's, as a whole, cannot be seen as significantly different in economic status from their fellow black New Yorkers, and their choice to be Episcopalian cannot be asserted to have been made on that basis.

It can also be seen here that achievement, whether economic or cultural, led to a kind of power within the community, and appears also to assume a greater level of interaction with the surrounding white community. McCune Smith may or may not have had any white patients,[6] but his intellectual and cultural status was such that he was expected to be both an example for white New Yorkers of what African Americans could achieve and also a spokesperson to that white population on behalf of the black community. His role on the St. Philip's vestry manifested these expectations as well, as he often served as the contact person for dealings with the diocese. Yet higher achievement did not always lead to any greater power in relation to the oppressing culture: Downing, for example, was a powerful figure in the black community precisely because of his successful interaction with the white world, yet his power to run his own establishment was constrained by the white prejudice that prevented him from serving his fellow African Americans in the restaurant. And although achievement often led to degrees of power within the black New York City population, it did not necessarily follow that an individual would choose to exercise such power. While Downing was involved in the leadership of several political and cultural organizations, Henry Scott, whose pickling business was also successful and well known, seems to have had no involvement with such organizations. Scott is visible only in his leadership at St. Philip's, not in the surrounding community, pointing again not only to how racial conditions affected the lives of African Americans, but also to the wide range of individual choices that were being made within those conditions. Once again it is clear that the people of St. Philip's cannot be easily categorized or explained, particularly when it comes to their choice of religious expression.

CHAPTER 20

Attentive to Their Devotions

A s Alexander Frazer began the service on that imaginary but typical Sunday morning in 1847 (or thereabouts), he looked out on a congregation that was just as religiously odd as the rest of his denomination. The Episcopal Church, even in its most evangelical parishes and dioceses, stood largely apart from the revivalist, democratizing fervor that American Protestantism was bringing to the still-new nation in the middle of the nineteenth century. The denomination had grown significantly over the first half of the century, but it had not seen anything like the growth of the evangelical denominations—the Baptists, the Methodists, and even the Presbyterians and Congregationalists. The Episcopal Church was bucking a powerful trend, and yet this black congregation and all the other white congregations had chosen to make the formal liturgies of Anglicanism their own. In this context particularly, the people of St. Philip's were defined less by their race than by how they expressed their Christian faith.

Frazer instructed his congregation to turn to the first page of their prayer books for the opening of the service of morning prayer.[1] This form of worship was the standard for Sunday mornings; even if Holy Eucharist was being celebrated (as it was once a month), it would be attached seamlessly to the conclusion of morning prayer. Frazer began by reciting one of the Biblical verses assigned as a call to worship; perhaps today it would be: "From the rising of the sun even unto the going down of the same, my Name shall be great among the Gentiles; and in every place incense shall be offered unto my Name, and a pure offering: for my Name shall be great among the heathen, saith the Lord of hosts" (Malachi 1:11). He then introduced the general confession with a prescribed formula of penitence, and the congregation responded by kneeling and reciting the confession together: "Almighty and most merciful Father: We have erred and strayed from thy ways like lost sheep. We have followed too much the devices and desires of our own hearts. We

have offended against thy holy laws ... And there is no health in us. . . ."
This opening certainly was as penitential as any evangelical could wish, but
its general and formulaic nature permitted no room for the actual confession
of individual and specific sins, nor did it lead to a personal conviction of sin;
rather, it led directly to a statement of God's absolution from the minister.

Remaining on their knees, the congregation next recited the Lord's
Prayer. Then all stood, and Frazer led them into a series of exchanges between minister and congregation to begin the part of the service that focused
on Bible readings (beginning with, "O Lord, open our lips. *Answer:* And our
mouth shall show forth thy praise."). The congregation said together Psalm
95, known as "the *Venite*" from the Latin for its opening word ("O come, let
us sing unto the Lord ... "), and then the three psalms assigned for the day;
one or more of these might be sung this morning. Each psalm was concluded
with a recitation of the Gloria Patri, the ancient Trinitarian statement: "Glory
be to the Father, and to the Son, and to the Holy Ghost. . . . " Two passages
from the Bible—one from the Old Testament, and one from the New—were
read with the congregation seated; each alternated with a canticle, a short
song either from the Bible or from an ancient liturgy. The Apostles' Creed,
a confession of faith developed in the first or second century, was then recited while standing (unless Frazer had chosen this morning to substitute
the Nicene Creed). As the people again knelt, Frazer offered several prayers
known as "collects"—accent on the first syllable—which served to sum up
the prayers of the individuals gathered for worship: one collect was specifically assigned for the day in the church year being marked, and then there
were collects for peace, grace, and the President of the United States and all
in authority.

The congregation next turned to page 24 for the Litany, assigned by the
prayer book for use on Sundays.[2] This was a long series of responsive prayers
for the church, the world, and particularly for deliverance from the human
condition of sinfulness; the congregation's first four responses ended with
the phrase "have mercy upon us miserable sinners." The service concluded
with the congregation saying "A General Thanksgiving," a prayer of praise
and gratitude for the assurance of God's forgiveness and sustaining love, and
Frazer's pronouncement of Paul's benediction from First Corinthians: "The
grace of our Lord Jesus Christ, and the love of God, and the fellowship of the
Holy Ghost, be with us all evermore. Amen." Frazer then left the sanctuary,
exchanged his cassock and surplice for a black preaching gown, and offered
a sermon based on the Biblical passages previously read.

If it was the second Sunday of the month, Frazer would delay his sermon a bit longer and instead proceed to the opening of the service of Holy Communion.[3] This consisted of a collect for the inspiration of the Holy Spirit, originally composed by the architect of the English Reformation, Thomas Cranmer, archbishop of Canterbury, and the recitation by Frazer of the Ten Commandments, with each followed by a congregational response of "Lord have mercy upon us, and incline our hearts to keep this law." Then came the reading of a nongospel passage from the New Testament (generally from one of Paul's letters, though sometimes from other epistles or Revelation); and then a passage from one of the gospels (again, assigned according to that Sunday's place in the liturgical year). Then Frazer would preach his sermon.

Following the preaching, bread and wine were brought to the altar, and Frazer consecrated them with a long prayer that included the "institution narrative," the story of the Last Supper and Christ's actions in instituting the practice of communion—taken both from the gospel versions and from Paul's narrative in First Corinthians. The people knelt to receive the bread and wine, joined Frazer afterward in saying again the Lord's Prayer, then a prayer of thanks, and finally were blessed by the priest and sent on their way.

Nearly every step of this order of worship was, in its own way, anathema to evangelical Protestantism. The printed prayers for the minister that left no room for spontaneity, the ancient sources for so much of the liturgy, the use of Latin names, the calendar of readings assigned for each Sunday of the church year, and the monthly rather than quarterly celebration of the eucharist—not only were these elements contrary to the trend against formal liturgies found in evangelical Calvinism, they also were shockingly Roman in appearance and history. Yet it was precisely because the congregation of St. Philip's followed so carefully this structured worship, based on the Book of Common Prayer, that they were so frequently praised by both Hobart and Onderdonk on their visits. And lest it be thought that they cleaned up their liturgy when they knew the bishop was to be in attendance, two white observers whose attendance was not expected in advance offered a parallel assessment: "I was with an English friend, and we both remarked that all who were present were particularly attentive to their devotions and respectable in appearance. I can truly say that I never saw the church service better performed, more devotion and regularity in the responses, or a purer spirit of Christian charity and concord."[4] While the racist implications behind the sense of surprise here echo those noted earlier in the observations of the visiting bishops, so also do these visitors comment on the strict observance of the formal liturgy. The people of St. Philip's prized their Episcopal worship, and show no evidence of tinkering with it to add evangelical elements or impulses.

The loyalty of the congregation to the prayer book is underscored by two occasions when they made donations to the New-York Bible and Common Prayer Book Society, a pet project of Hobart's that was continued by Onderdonk. While most evangelical denominations were blurring their sectarian lines by joining forces in such organizations as the American Bible Society, Hobart had founded his own specifically Episcopal society to emphasize denominational distinctiveness. While many Low Church leaders and congregations joined the ecumenical group despite Hobart's urgings, St. Philip's and others in the High Church wing supported his organization instead. In 1827, the black newspaper *Freedom's Journal* reported on the collection made by the congregation for Hobart's society, noting that "the amount collected was $35.54. As the Sunday schools, and indigent members of this Church, had been gratuitously supplied by this society, with Bibles and Common Prayer Books, for a number of years, the congregation felt it their duty to offer a collection in aid of its funds." From this notice it can be gleaned that, whether they purchased the books themselves or had them donated by the society, members of St. Philip's had their own prayer books for regular use. Nearly twenty years later, the vestry minutes recorded another such donation; it can be assumed that the same conditions applied. The practice of owning a prayer book—as opposed to today's normal practice, in which Episcopal parishes simply fill their pews with books for anyone's use—reinforces the sense that the formal and ordered nature of their liturgy was a significant part of its appeal to this congregation.[5]

Another significant difference from evangelical worship, and therefore perhaps another aspect of its appeal to this congregation, was the degree of participation in Episcopal services by the people. In most Protestant liturgies, the people were largely spectators; efforts to reform evangelical worship practices in the 1850s moved to include at least a congregational "Amen" at the end of prayers, as not even that degree of participation was the norm.[6] The Book of Common Prayer, on the other hand, included numerous opportunities for vocal participation by the congregation: the prayers said in unison with the priest, the recited psalms, and the mandated responses to prayers such as in the Litany. While evangelical Protestants emphasized the "new measures" of Charles Finney as the means by which the minister acted nearly alone to bring about the proper spiritual state (which then should lead to spontaneous individual responses), the Episcopal liturgies assumed that worship comprised constant interaction between the priest and the people who had gathered. From a Hobartian perspective, this meant that the emphasis was on the church as a body of people (the Body of Christ) and its common actions as the locus of God's grace. From the congregation's perspective, so much participation may well have hastened the desire to own a prayer book, so as to make oneself as familiar with the services as possible.

Another significant aspect of Sunday mornings was the education of the parish's children. This too can be seen to reinforce the orderly practice of worship, the right understanding of theological and denominational issues, and the identity of the children as Episcopalians. These values received their culmination in the rite of confirmation, which was generally undertaken at the age of fourteen.

Confirmation, in Hobart's words, was "a rite . . . in which baptized persons take upon themselves their baptismal engagements; and . . . are certified of God's favor and goodness; of the grace of his Holy Spirit; and of all the other privileges of their baptism." In general, then, confirmation was used in the Episcopal Church to have individuals "confirm" that the baptismal vows made for them when they were infants or young children by their parents were now understood and assented to by them. This then "confirmed" that the new state of being, engendered by baptism (controversially termed "regeneration," at Hobart's insistence), had been brought to pass and was recognized as such by the church hierarchy.[7] The essential action of the rite of confirmation is that the bishop lays his hands upon the heads of the confirmands, which meant, in the most literal sense, that the bishop would come to the parish of St. Philip's and recognize the baptized, Christian, and Episcopal identity of each of the children and adults whose heads he touched. This must have been a most gratifying annual ritual for the parish, and the congregation prepared its confirmands most assiduously.

At the very beginning of its existence, St. Philip's created a Sunday school for this purpose. Peter Williams described it in the first parochial report he submitted to the diocese: "there are about eighty scholars, with a sufficient number of teachers, selected from among the most capable of our young people." The curriculum of the school is not known, but it is likely to have had as much to do with reading and writing as with religious or ecclesiastical issues: Williams asserted that the school was "of great utility . . . to the cause of literature, morality, and religion." In 1843, the vestry reported that the secretary of the Sunday school, John J. Brown, had requested funds for books for the students. Certainly Bible stories and the prayers and psalms found in the Prayer Book would all have been included in their studies. The most direct teaching tool, however, was the catechism in the prayer book, and Williams described the process of testing the scholars in that area himself every Sunday, following the afternoon service.[8]

Alexander Frazer celebrated the thriving Sunday school in his reports to the diocese as well—there were 150 students in 1843 and 140 in 1844, the last year before midcentury for which there are statistics—and he too maintained the practice of catechizing the children "publicly in the church, by the minister." He was assisted in the preparation of the students by "24 catechists, who are teachers in the Sunday School," which suggests that they were responsible for teaching the catechism, while he was in charge of testing their learning in front of the congregation and clarifying any particular issues or confusions. The results of this process were apparently quite gratifying, for Frazer that same year reported forty-five confirmations, "the greater part of them the most intelligent of the youth of the congregation."[9] Those not part of the "youth" were most likely adults who had never had the opportunity to be confirmed or who had joined the church recently but had been baptized in another denomination.

The educational scheme, then, as was most likely the case at Episcopal parishes in general, was designed to move linearly toward confirmation: the children began in Sunday school, and as they became old enough to understand the theological and ecclesiastical issues raised, they took on the catechism class as well. Those who could demonstrate their understanding of the creed, the Lord's Prayer, the Ten Commandments, and the sacraments—not just know what they were, but be able to explain them as the catechism did, and know what the explanations meant—were then brought before the bishop for confirmation. The parish as a whole was involved in every step: the older and brighter students served as Sunday school teachers, an administration of adults oversaw their efforts (the school had a superintendent and a secretary), the vestry kept track of the progress being made through reports from the administrators and occasional visits, and the congregation heard the youth tested in the catechism each Sunday.

But while the immediate aim of the educational process was the rite of confirmation and the marking thereby of their youth as full Episcopalians, it also served to reinforce everyone's denominational identity. A congregation that expected its young scholars to demonstrate their proficiency before them would have needed also to see itself as examples of what those youth were learning to become. Proper conduct of worship would have been essential to such a vision, as well as clarity and pride in one's denominational identity.

Equally important to the shape of worship on this and every Sunday morning was the strength of the congregation's marking and use of the sacred space of the building itself. When consecrated by Bishop Hobart in 1819 according to the rite prescribed in the prayer book,[10] the building had been expressly set apart from all worldly uses: it was dedicated to the service of God for services of worship. The one surviving engraving of the church shows a large brick edifice of roughly Federal style, with a window over the central door and another tall window on either side. As was typical of the time, there were no overt signs that this was a church: no steeple, no visible cross. The interior contained wooden pews, a raised chancel with a pulpit and reading desk, and a communion table that in 1849 received a new marble slab for the top. The pulpit and desk had decorative "drapery," and the walls were painted "in imitation of Portland Stone and blacked off"—a rather mysterious description! The damage caused by the 1834 riots attests to the presence of stained-glass windows, brass candelabra, altar candlesticks, altar hangings, and vestments.[11] Though most Episcopal churches were quite plain both inside and out in the early nineteenth century, these details indicate that St. Philip's marked its sacred space in a number of visual manners.

This marking and setting apart of the church, however, caused for the congregation some conflicts, which illuminate other dimensions of the question of religious identity. The building contained, in addition to the sanctuary, a basement room used for Sunday school and other meetings, and a vestry room for the deliberations of that body. Were these sacred spaces as well? And what constituted "worldly" uses? After the riots of 1834, Bishop Onderdonk had been quite explicit about keeping divisive social issues out of Episcopal churches, yet from 1843 through the middle of the next decade, the vestry rented out space for an annual "Tappan Society meeting," which, with that name, can only have been antislavery related.[12] Given the centrality of that struggle to the people of this parish, was this not a proper use of the space? Yet conflicts arose: in 1850, in the aftermath of the Fugitive Slave Law and parishioner William Powell's advocacy of disobedience to the same, he and George Downing, along with nonparishioner Lewis Putnam, requested "use of the church for a public meeting." It is hard to imagine that anyone involved thought this would not be of some political bent, and the vestry denied the request—but did so with a split vote, indicating their disagreement about proper use of the space under their charge.[13]

Perhaps not surprisingly, several of the conflicts over sacred space that were recorded in the minutes of vestry meetings had to do with music. It is difficult to say how much of a role music played in the regular worship services: there was a hymnbook available to Episcopal parishes, though it stipulated that the singing of hymns was to be added to the singing of psalms, not replace it. Peter Williams was remarked to have "lined-out" hymns for his congregation: he sang a line or two, which the congregation then repeated. This practice was quite common for establishing the proper melody, and, more importantly, for teaching the hymns to those who could not read or did not have hymnals, both of which were frequent problems in black churches.[14] And the congregation had an organ, which was a source of some pride in the parish, and was also a means of enforcing proper singing—again, supporting the orderly nature of worship at St. Philip's. However, the presence of an organ and the importance of music to the religious and social lives of the parishioners occasioned some difficulties when it came to determining what was the proper sort of music for this sacred space.

In 1827, the parish held a "Concert of Sacred Music," with vestry members William Hutson and John Marander selling the tickets. Such concerts were important to African American communities in the first half of the nineteenth century, as they offered opportunities for black musicians to present themselves in a serious context. By the 1830s, they were often sponsored by black literary and cultural societies, but churches continued to be regular venues. The question was whether there was a clear line between a "sacred" concert and a "serious" one. The 1827 concert at St. Philip's followed a typical pattern for the former sort: first the congregation sang a classic hymn, "Old Hundred," then an orchestra played an overture, a chorus sang a piece entitled "Lord of all power and might," and a duet and solo followed; the first part then closed with a choral anthem, "Christ Our Passover"—the words coming from a portion of the service of Holy Communion. The second half of the concert opened with an organ voluntary, and then three choral anthems alternated with two solos and a duet. All of these had Biblical or liturgical themes: "Praise Ye the Lord," "O had I Jubal's lyre," and "Prayer for the Commonwealth" are among those listed. It is hard to imagine that anyone would have considered such a concert inappropriate for a church.[15]

Yet other instances proved to be quite controversial. In 1846, the vestry minutes record a rancorous dispute over the hiring of Robert Hamilton to serve as choir leader; one stipulation was that he was to have "the use of the church, for a concert, once a year." The motion carried, which indicates that the vote was split, and McCune Smith was clearly upset. As secretary, he recorded in the minutes that he and Thomas Downing were those who objected—this was a rare departure, as individual votes were almost never listed. More revealing is the way he wrote down the motion: he first wrote "basement" instead of "church." Though the former term is neatly crossed out, it is still easily legible. Clearly McCune Smith objected to this use of sacred space—though it is hard to say whether it was because he was concerned about the content of the planned concerts or about having them in the church at all.[16]

The same issue divided the vestry much more openly in 1855, when Peter Stevens, in his seventh year on the vestry, requested permission to put together a music concert "in the church." The motion in favor of this once again "carried," indicating a split vote. At the next month's meeting, Stevens read a letter from the wardens, Peter Ray and John Peterson, in which they refused to let him proceed with the concert. Peterson then presented a formal resolution arguing that "occupying the Church Edifice for concerts according to the present mode of conducting them is a use not contemplated in the consecration service ... and a desecration of the Sacred Edifice," and therefore moving that the permission given at the previous meeting be rescinded. This motion lost, and vestryman Philip White moved that the letter from the wardens be designated "uncalled for and impertinent," as the wardens had "transcended their authority." Ray, as warden and therefore chair of the meeting, refused to put the motion, so it was ignored (though dutifully recorded in the minutes!), and Stevens resigned the vestry immediately.[17] This is an unusually full and open account of a vestry dispute that demonstrates the degree of conflict over the use of sacred space. Peterson, one of the original members of the parish and soon to be ordained a deacon, held to a narrow definition of what was appropriate in the church, and appealed to the prayer book as his authority. Though the minutes imply that this was not to be a concert of sacred music, the majority of the vestry disagreed with Peterson and adhered to their original decision. Clearly some members of the parish were more comfortable with the intertwining of religious and cultural strands in the life of their community than others.

When Alexander Frazer led the congregation of St. Philip's in worship on that relatively typical Sunday morning, then, he did so with a people for whom some ways of expressing the sacred were quite straightforward, while for others the issue was complicated and in need of negotiation. The prayers and the order of worship were supplied by the denomination, and there is every evidence that they were attended to with devotion and a solid grasp of their importance to the parish's religious identity. This identity was reinforced through the education of children and new members, culminating in confirmation. But the roles of music and sacred space in the expression of faith and maintenance of religious identity were less obvious and less easily resolved. The mere fact of conflict, however, manifests the importance these goals of identity and expression had for this congregation. Such conflict also reinforces the perception of this group of people as one composed of myriad individuals struggling to make sense of various economic, social, political, and cultural elements in their lives—and of how those elements impinged upon or were influenced by their understanding of their faith and religious identity.

CHAPTER 21

The Express Wishes of Nearly All

The desire to see the people of St. Philip's as a monolithic body working steadily by predetermined methods toward a clearly defined goal is a seductive one, as it would provide a simple and clearly cut historical narrative. But the foregoing picture of a diverse body with differing interests amid varying life circumstances does not support such a heroic perspective any more than the actual history of the parish during the time of Peter Williams. It should not be surprising to realize that the battle to be fully accepted into the Diocese of New York and to be permitted to attend the diocesan convention like every other parish proceeded by fits and starts in the latter years of the 1840s, and was marked more by conflict and upheaval in the parish than by progress in the convention.

In preparation for the convention in the fall of 1847, the vestry of St. Philip's appointed McCune Smith and Peter Ray to serve as delegates. And despite the previous fall's refusal to acknowledge the majority report on their admission, Smith was now directed "to call the attention of the 63rd Convention of this Diocese to the misstatements contained in the report of the Majority" on this topic. What was not specified was whether this was meant to be a memorial to the convention presented by Frazer or something else entirely.[1]

The issue of the admission of St. Philip's was not brought to a vote at that convention, however, as the parish had hoped. Nor is there any immediate sign of what Smith might have produced. John King, the layman from Grace Church in Jamaica, Queens, and the other signer of the minority report, began this convention by moving that the two reports from the committee on St. Philip's be brought up. They were then read "in part" by the convention secretary. King and Johnson then discovered that the committee's majority had printed up copies of its report for distribution to the delegates, while they themselves had not realized that this was an option. William Jay, serving as a delegate from St. Matthew's, Bedford, recognized the strength of putting a written argument for admission into the hands of the convention members, and moved that the entire subject be tabled so that this might occur. The convention no doubt breathed a sigh of relief that they could avoid the topic altogether, and do so at the instigation of a Jay.[2]

Back at the parish, no mention was made of the convention during the ensuing vestry meeting. Instead, they became embroiled in their own conflict: this was the fall in which the controversy over whether or not to hire Alexander Crummell as an assistant broke out. Feelings ran high over this issue, with disagreements between vestry members and between the vestry and the officiating minister, Alexander Frazer. Whether because of lingering effects from this controversy (and Crummell's sudden departure in its midst for England), wider disagreements over the vestry's course of action regarding admission to convention, or something completely unrelated it is difficult to say, but the next year saw the vestry go through a radical upheaval.

On the Monday after Easter, as was their custom, the people of St. Philip's held their annual vestry election. The vestry minutes reveal somewhat obliquely what must have been quite a row: a written election result, signed by two parishioners designated "election inspectors" and by the assistant minister, Thomas Clark, was delivered by hand to Smith, who was still serving as secretary. This result was tabled at the vestry meeting two weeks later over two technicalities: the letter was not addressed to the vestry or any specific member, and it did not name the church—it only listed those who had been elected. These seem like trivial concerns, which suggest that the election itself had been a subject of dispute. Things grew rapidly worse: there was a call for a new election to be held two weeks later, which motion carried in a split vote, and the minutes then note, "At this stage of the meeting, several Vestrymen left the Vestry room, and the Meeting was left without a quorum for the transaction of any further business." The minutes then append a memorandum certifying that the election results were valid; presumably those elected felt that an outside judgment was needed. Ironically, the certification was signed by William Harison, comptroller of Trinity Church and one of the authors of the majority report, and David Ogden, another Trinity vestryman and convention delegate opposed to the admission of St. Philip's. The transcription of this memo in the vestry minutes is followed by a note to the effect that the new election was cancelled and the foregoing results stood. Both of these items are clearly later additions to the minutes, as they certainly do not reflect any action actually taken at the meeting itself. This last note concluded rather ominously by stating that "these minutes, the Draft Book, the Pew Book, and other papers belonging to the Corporation of St. Philip's Church are delivered to John Berrian and George D. Jamieson vestrymen elect, by the Secretary of the late vestry of said Corporation: New York City, May 21st, 1848." Since the minutes to which this note was appended were dated May 9, it is obvious that someone has attempted to clarify the record after the fact.[3]

And thus was marked a major transition of power. The change in personnel is quite astonishing: Warden Thomas Zabriskie, who had served on the vestry for twenty-five of the twenty-eight years the church had been incorporated, including the very first vestry, was voted out, returning only once three years later and then dying the following year. The fifty-three voting members could cast ballots for two wardens and eight vestry members, meaning that each person elected had the possibility of receiving up to fifty-three votes. Zabriskie received one vote. George Lawrence, a member of the last three vestries, was voted out, though he was reelected two years later. Ransom Wake, on three of the previous five vestries, received only four votes and never served again. Most striking, however, was the rejection of James McCune Smith, who received only twelve votes, and had to record into the minutes not only the dispute over the election, but the requirement that he himself turn over the parish books to his successor. Due to years of lost minutes, it is impossible to tell when Smith's tenure on the vestry had begun, but he had been secretary for the five consecutive years for which minutes exist. He continued to be appointed delegate to the convention almost every year until 1862, but he did not serve on the vestry again until 1855—after the battle for admission to the convention had been won.

With the death of John Robertson the previous July (he had served for four years), fully half of the previous year's vestry was gone. On the other hand, Peter Ray and Henry Scott continued their seemingly interminable regimes as warden and treasurer, respectively, and they were joined in returning by George Jamieson and Thomas Downing, both now in their fourth years of service, and Samuel Rankin, who had been newly elected in 1847. The newcomers were John Berrian, who became secretary for the next four years; Dunbar Brown, elected warden for two consecutive terms and then never heard from again; George Chatters, who was elected for three of the next four years; John Freeland, who also served for just two years; and Peter Stevens, who spent the next seven years on the vestry until he resigned during the 1855 disagreement about a musical concert.

This degree of turnover was truly remarkable. Though there are records for only the previous five years, those show a generally consistent vestry, with only minor changes from year to year. The minutes say nothing about why this shakeup occurred or what parish expectations might have led to it, but they do reveal some smoldering resentment: Berrian, the new secretary, noted in the minutes of the new vestry's first meeting (held two days after the mutinous meeting that attempted to overturn the election) that a committee had been formed to go see Smith and retrieve the parish's books and any "other property in his possession belonging to this Parish"—and the above-mentioned note indicates that it was another ten days before the transfer actually occurred. The next month's meeting recopied the election certification, claiming "an omission in the transcript entered by James McCune Smith, Sec'y to the late vestry," yet no actual change in wording can be found.[4] Either Smith had alienated a large number of parishioners or he was alienated by them: it is impossible to say which or why, but it is remarkable that a man who was so prominent in the community and had been so prominent in the parish was now being forcibly turned out to pasture.

Another tremor hit the parish later in May, and the new vestry immediately proved to be no more united than the old. Alexander Frazer, after seven years of service to St. Philip's, died on May 26. A special vestry meeting was held two days later, at which resolutions were passed expressing the parish's sympathy to Frazer's family and designating that the church be dressed in mourning, and assistant minister Clark read a last letter from Frazer requesting that the vestry attend his funeral service in St. John's Chapel. At the June meeting, Berrian moved that a committee be appointed "to make inquiries relative to the engagement of a clergyman." Incomprehensibly, the motion—just to start looking for a new priest—lost by a vote of five to four! The motion was brought up again at the next meeting, and this time passed unanimously.[5] Perhaps some of the veteran vestrymen had thought that June was too soon to begin trying to replace a still-mourned pastor, or perhaps the resolution passed this second time because it followed a resolution in which the vestry gave Clark notice of his dismissal effective at the end of the summer. Whatever the reason, this shaky start augured further conflict: as noted earlier, this vestry spent a year wrangling over the ministries of Clark and Samuel Berry until finally hiring William Morris in August of 1849.

In the meantime, the vestry got together in the fall to appoint convention delegates: Peter Ray, Henry Scott, and—out of favor in other areas but apparently not here—James McCune Smith. Smith actually sent a formal letter of acceptance of the post to the vestry, something never noted as having occurred on anyone's behalf before. The delegates, should they be admitted to the convention, were directed by the vestry to vote against any resolution calling for the resignation of Bishop Onderdonk, which decision occasioned no disagreement this time. The vestry met again two weeks later, in a special session, to adopt a statement in response to the majority report of 1846, and then moved to print five hundred copies of the statement for distribution to the delegates, along with copies of the church's consecration certificate and Williams's ordination certificate.[6]

No specific authorship of this statement is mentioned in the minutes, but it seems likely that it was the document Smith had been directed to draw up the previous year—perhaps newly edited by this group. The statement is recorded in full in the minutes, which is fortunate, since no mention is made of it in the convention journal. It is unclear how the statement might have been distributed, as Frazer was dead and a vestry motion requesting Clark (or anyone else) to present the materials of the parish to the convention is conspicuous by its absence.

The heart of the parish's statement was to refute the claim that either Williams or anyone in the parish had ever agreed not to attend diocesan conventions as a condition of his ordination, as the report had claimed. The vestry instead asserted that they were indeed acting on behalf of the parish in making their application for admission, and that they were not guilty of "violating good faith," as the majority report had charged: "This we solemnly deny. First because there was no law nor usage in the church by which a candidate for orders could by any act of his bind to perpetual disfranchisement a congregation to which he held only a probable relation as a minister." In other words, Williams would not have had the authority to make such an agreement on behalf of the parish at that time, as he held no official position in the parish. "Secondly because it is not true that the candidate for orders in question, nor that the Vestry of St. Philip's, nor the congregation of the same ever did become parties to such distinct understanding of their exclusion from the convention." Thus they assert that Williams made no such agreement regarding his ordination, nor did anyone make such an agreement on behalf of the parish. This is then reiterated as forcefully as possible:

> The Rev. Peter Williams within one year of his death denied all participation or knowledge of any such agreement to a credible witness now living. There are at least twenty respectable members of St. Philip's Church who were such in 1819 and are so still, who deny that any such understanding existed at the former date nor can any others be found who were aware of its existence, and at least one member of the vestry

from its early organization in 1817 until 1847—during the whole time an active participant in all the proceedings—denies that any such arrangement or understanding ever was named to the Vestry until the printing of the majority report.

It is ironic that the figure of Zabriskie, who had served for such a long time and had just been voted off the vestry, is invoked to offer as broad a denial as the vestry could muster. The vestry then took on the Standing Committee's records in support of their claim: "The distinct understanding therefore must have been confined to the minutes of the Standing Committee as a proposition never acted on for it is not therein reported as having been assented to by the parties most deeply interested." They conclude this section by maintaining that Hobart never enacted the agreement, but instead declared the parish to be in communion with the diocese at the consecration of the building.[7]

There is an unassailable logic to this argument, despite the fact that Williams certainly behaved during his tenure as rector as someone who had no intention of attending convention. It is true that no written record exists (or seems to have existed then) of the arrangement ever being agreed to by Hobart and Williams, let alone conveyed in any official fashion to the parish. Nonetheless, no effort was ever made by priest or vestry to be admitted into convention during Williams's lifetime, and thus it does seem highly likely that the arrangement had been made and agreed to, at least by him and at least verbally. It is also highly possible that Hobart conveyed the arrangement to Williams as a temporary accommodation, and that Williams did actually plan to seek admission to convention in his later years but died before he could do so. Whatever the story, however deliberately naive Smith and the vestry may have been trying to be, there was certainly cause for them to assert that they should not have been held any longer to an arrangement whose existence could not be documented and whose central parties were both long dead.

The vestry tried to present as united a front as they could, stating that their application to the convention for admission was "in conformity with the express wishes of nearly all the members and seat holders of said Church." This, of course, begs the questions of which members were not in support of this action—is it possible that some members of the previous vestry were voted off because they did not support this issue, or was there a faction in the congregation that just wanted to leave well enough alone?—and to whom that lack of support might have been communicated, given that the vestry felt compelled to own up to it. Then, having dispensed with the accusation of "violating good faith," the statement concluded by returning to the present:

"By these plain statements we trust that we have reduced the matter of this application to its own merits." This would ultimately prove to be an essential strategy: to get the convention simply to consider the case of St. Philip's without freighting in all the broader issues that caused such anxiety and irritation. The vestry hoped that the members of the convention would do so with a view to living up to their professed beliefs: "Whatever be your decision we humbly trust that it will be made in fear of him who is no respecter of persons and in the prayer that His Kingdom may come and his will be done on earth as it is in heaven." This finish wonderfully echoed the theological grounding that Evan Johnson had provided in the minority report.[8]

The vestry also had a new cause for hope that year—and included the fact in their statement—in that there now existed two precedents for their admission to convention. In 1843, the Diocese of Rhode Island had admitted the parish Crummell founded into its convention, and just this year, the Diocese of New Jersey had followed suit. The parish of St. Philip's in Newark was admitted to its convention that fall, to the great approval of its bishop, the Rt. Rev. George Washington Doane: "A sure token from God for good," he applauded the approving gathering.[9]

Despite these precedents and the vestry's cogent arguments, the matter went untouched at that year's convention. There is no mention of any motion, discussion, or any other progress at all. The vestry minutes are silent on the topic as well, so it is not even certain that the five hundred copies were ever distributed, nor what happened with the printing of the minority report. And the year ended on a sour note, as the vestry acknowledged that its finances were in an "embarrassed state" and that they could not afford to hire a new minister—thus forcing them to keep Clark on in his part-time status long after they had hoped to send him packing.[10]

The same inertia held the following year, when once again the issue seems to have never come up at the convention, and no mention was made of any plans, responses, or hopes in the vestry minutes. Adding to the parish's discouragement must have been the news out of Philadelphia, where the bid by St. Thomas's Church—the first black Episcopal church in the country—for admission to their convention had failed as well. William Jay reported on the impassioned plea on that church's behalf made by the bishop of Pennsylvania, Alonzo Potter, who argued that rejecting their application was:

A step that no one of us but would wish to recall when we came to stand in the presence of Him who sitteth upon the throne, at the last great day. We shall then feel that we should have had more faith in our religion, more trust as Americans in our institutions, than to fear the admission of a few poor negroes would be sufficient to shake these institutions to the centre.

The clergy responded strongly to this plea, voting in favor of St. Thomas's, but the laity voted it down despite them.[11]

The vestry ended the decade on a stronger note, though, as it settled its clergy quandary. Not finding a suitable African American to serve as rector, they hired William Morris to fill Frazer's post of "officiating minister." Morris was the rector (headmaster) of Trinity School in Manhattan from 1838 through 1857, but notwithstanding this position, felt he had the time to take on St. Philip's as well. Trinity Church had founded the school in 1709 as a free school for the poor of the city; it had gone through a few changes since then, however, and was by this time an elementary school with fee-paying students. One happy result for the parish was that Morris's position at the school afforded him with a wonderful network of church connections: trustees during that era included Bishop Onderdonk, the Rev. Benjamin Haight of Trinity Church, the Rev. John McVickar of Columbia College, the Rev. Samuel Seabury (editor and publisher of the *Churchman*, the High Church journal), and the Honorable Samuel Jones, who headed up the Committee on the Incorporation of Parishes year after year. This was a powerful collection of Episcopalians, and they clearly thought highly of Morris, as they retained him as headmaster for nearly twenty years.[12] Perhaps with his leadership, the parish's fortunes would change.

CHAPTER 22

Injurious to the Cause of Religion

The people of St. Philip's came to midcentury with a new and well-connected minister, a significantly changed vestry, and mixed signals from the wider church about the full inclusion of African Americans in denominational gatherings. They had also seen two years of inactivity by the diocesan convention regarding their situation, so they must have been discouraged about how best to proceed. The new decade would ultimately prove fruitful in this regard, but these years would also make it ever clearer that the vestry and John Jay were not really working in concert on the admission of the parish to the convention.

The vestry election of 1850 manifested continued uncertainty in the parish about who would provide the best leadership. Warden Dunbar Brown and vestrymen George Chatters and John Freeland, elected in the upheaval of 1848, were all voted out, with the latter two disappearing from the historical record. George Lawrence was returned to the vestry after a two-year hiatus; Philip White, who had studied with Smith and then opened his own pharmacy, joined the vestry for the first time; Smith himself received only three votes. As usual, Peter Ray was elected warden (along with George Jamieson), but he then resigned the post a week later with no explanation offered in the minutes. William Powell was elected to replace him—the only time he served on the vestry—but the election was not held until two months after Ray left. Adding to the sense of upheaval is the fact that on several occasions after this election there were too few vestry members present at the meeting to constitute a quorum. One such occurrence was in September, which would account for the fact that the vestry failed to appoint convention delegates for the first time since they began pressing the diocese for admission.[1]

On the other hand, John Jay, who had been noticeably silent in convention the previous two years, briefly returned to the attack that fall. According to the *Morning Courier and New-York Enquirer,* Jay "called up the former report of the Committee on the Incorporation of Churches [it was actually the special Committee on St. Philip's Church], in which the Alumni of the colored churches of St. Philip's and Messiah was disapproved. Mr. Jay read a long and elaborate speech in confutation of the majority report." Did Jay's speech perhaps incorporate some of the arguments the vestry had made in their statement the previous year? There is no way of knowing. But Harison, Spencer, and Livingston, the writers of the majority report, were joined by two others in putting a quick end to Jay's effort: they argued that the issue was out of order, "not having been continued in the regular way as unfinished business from 1847 to 1850." The chair upheld their view, and Jay responded that he would return to the question in some different form. Nothing further, however, was heard from him, and the convention successfully dodged the issue once again on a procedural technicality.[2]

William Jay attributed the convention's approach to its domination by "politicians" who did not want to take a public stand that might hurt them elsewhere:

> A gentleman . . . remarked that he did not mean to be a delegate to the next Convention. On being asked why? He replied that the question of the colored churches would come up; that he could not in conscience vote against them, and that by voting for them, he would prejudice an application he had then pending in Washington.

The elder Jay went on to argue that the problem was that of "conscience vs. cotton," and suggested that it was Southern connections that militated against the admission of African Americans to the New York and Pennsylvania conventions.[3] This is a striking echo of Isaiah DeGrasse's conviction that it was Northerners' concerns about Southern sensibilities that had removed him from the General Seminary nearly twenty-five years earlier.

That October, the General Convention passed a canon permitting the election of a provisional bishop in the case of an indefinite suspension of a sitting bishop. Finally the pleas of the Diocese of New York had been heard: they could stop stewing about Onderdonk's status and get a bishop in place to lead the diocese. A second diocesan convention was immediately called for the end of November, for the election of said bishop.

The vestry at St. Philip's were not going to be caught napping again, especially since—as a result of Jay's initiative in September—they now knew what problem to address. They promptly elected Scott and Smith to be delegates. Smith then drafted a letter to the convention replying to the assertion that the parish's desire for admission had not been continually pursued. The communication began by rehearsing the history of their application since 1846, noted that they had elected delegates to the convention each year since in anticipation of their application's approval (glossing over September's misstep), and insisted that their interest had never waned:

> If their [the parish's] claims have not been urged upon the attention of said Convention, it has been their hope that a sense of justice would, before now, have brought the matter up, and would have led to the only decision at which a due regard to the right could possibly arrive. But the recent announcement, that the matter is not before the Convention, shows that the silence of St. Philip's Church has been misinterpreted; and that her delegates have not only been deprived of admission during these years, but the very existence of the Church attempted to be ignored in Convention, in consequence of this non-obtrusion.

The letter concluded with reference to the immediate convention's business: "they would more earnestly press this claim upon your attention at this time, when a Diocesan [bishop] is about to be elected, under whose charge said congregation must come, and in the choice of whom they are therefore specially interested in having a voice."[4]

The letter was signed by Smith and Scott. Oddly, it was not entered into the vestry minutes as the previous letter to the convention had been, nor was there any resolution on their part calling for its composition. Is it possible that Smith composed the letter (rather than Berrian, the current secretary) without the vestry's knowledge? Or did the vestry turn the job over to Smith and Scott as the delegates, and not bother to enter either the task or the result into the minutes? Whatever circumstances surrounded this communication, it was clearly the boldest challenge the parish had yet made to the convention regarding their status, or lack thereof.

It is significant that this letter was printed in full in the convention journal, unlike the previous missive. It is possible that Morris, present at the convention, was able to see that their communication was not ignored. In any case, the letter was read to the convention, but then the order of the day was called for—to wit, the election of a bishop. Jay attempted to intercede, however, moving that the order of the day be suspended so that a response could be made to the parish's letter. Livingston, the parish's nemesis, had this motion tabled. A "Rev. Hill, from Zion Church in Morris, New York," moved again to suspend the order of the day so that the 1846 reports could be considered;

Livingston again had the motion tabled. The convention then cast its first ballots for provisional bishop. While they were being counted, the Committee on the Incorporation of Churches made its report, admitting three new parishes. Jay then moved the admission of St. Philip's, but this time Livingston's rector, the Rev. A. J. Bleecker, had the motion tabled. The convention met the next day as well, but failed to achieve an election, and the issue of St. Philip's Church did not come up.[5]

This latest effort on Jay's part cannot have pleased the convention delegates at all. The sole purpose of the special convention was to elect a bishop; no other business was to be brought before it, as that year's regular convention had already been held. Jay's tactic seems obvious: to try to get the convention to approve the motion in their haste to move on to the larger question before them. Instead, he appears only to have annoyed people by bringing the matter up. Evidence that some were getting sick of his advocacy of St. Philip's and his antislavery activities in general can be seen in the correspondence between Jay and one James Monroe in January of 1851. Narrating the latter's effort to sponsor Jay for membership in New York City's venerable Union Club, the correspondence was published by Monroe for the information of his fellow club members. Jay wrote to inform Monroe that he had heard "that an election had occurred at the Union Club, at which I was blackballed by five votes out of fifteen." Jay reminded Monroe that he had not wanted to join the club in the first place, but had applied only at Monroe's urging, and that Monroe himself had warned him of possible difficulties: "you sent for me to say, that to your surprise, you had received intimations of an intention to blackball me, on the ground of my advocacy in the Episcopal Convention, of the admission of St. Philip's Church, and of my anti-slavery views generally." Monroe replied that he was appalled that "on mere political grounds a gentleman is to be chosen or otherwise," arguing that he himself disagreed completely with Jay on the issue of slavery, but that he considered the Union Club to be a social gathering and wished his friend to be a member.[6] Some nineteenth-century Americans apparently found it easier to separate their political opinions from their social connections than others.

Jay nevertheless pressed on. At the 1851 convention, however, he pursued the admission of the Church of the Messiah without mentioning St. Philip's at all. Alexander Crummell was in England, trying to raise money for this parish and pursuing a degree from Queen's College, Cambridge, while subsisting largely on financial grants from Jay; perhaps the latter felt he needed to shepherd the troubled flock in its rector's absence—though he was actually serving as a delegate from his own parish, the Church of the Intercession in Manhattan. Whatever the cause, Jay adapted the argument from St. Philip's of the previous year, that they wanted to participate in the election of the bishop who would preside over them, but applied it to Messiah instead. He got no further this time than last: the Rev. Hill once again moved the admission of the parish, but the Rev. Alexander Leonard, of Emmanuel Church, New York City, moved that the subject be tabled "to avoid an exciting debate at this stage of the proceedings." Jay attempted to force a vote by protesting that Hill's motion should come first, but was overruled by the chair. A large majority tabled the motion.[7] Since the convention had failed to elect a bishop the previous year, that was first and foremost on everyone's minds once again—and Jay's efforts were shown little patience as a result.

The vestry at St. Philip's, meanwhile, had again appointed Scott and Smith as delegates to this convention. They had also formally requested that Morris, their officiating minister, "urge the admission of St. Philip's into the Diocesan Convention by bringing the matter before said Convention and pressing the same to a favorable issue"—but there is no sign of Morris's participation in the discussion at the convention, and no report back to the vestry on the topic.[8]

By now one begins to ask just what Jay and St. Philip's were each up to. Jay had pursued the fight once again, but this time on behalf of another parish; why did he not mention St. Philip's at all? On the other side, why did the vestry never pass a resolution thanking Jay for his efforts, as they did for Johnson and King when they argued for the parish's admission in 1846? Why did they regularly request their minister to either "present their materials" or "urge their admission," yet the minutes indicate no formal communication with or even mention of Jay regarding this campaign? These oddities suggest that the parish leadership and Jay, while moving in the same direction, were operating on separate tracks.

Those historians who have written about this struggle of St. Philip's with the diocese (largely in passing) have uniformly credited Jay with bringing about the parish's success.[9] While it is certainly true that he brought up the issue regularly, developments in the 1850s make it clear that his strategy and that of the parish had indeed diverged—and that Jay was actually becoming more of a hindrance to the congregation's goal than a help. The first hint is a rather cryptic statement in the minutes of the April vestry meeting of 1852, when a motion was passed stating that "the course pursued by the Rev. William Morris since his connection with St. Philip's Church as Pastor thereof meets with the entire and full approbation of this vestry."[10] There is no indication of what prompted this vote of confidence, nor to what in particular it might refer, but what becomes clear in the minutes that autumn is that Morris was working in his own way toward the admission of the parish. It is therefore highly likely that this statement was meant to encourage those efforts. It is intriguing that the motion did not pass unanimously, which suggests that there was still disagreement among the vestry about the best course of action to pursue. Perhaps there was even conflict over whether to support Jay's approach or Morris's.

The vestry itself went through another turnover that year; again there is the sense that the parish was uncertain about its leadership. Peter Ray, who had resigned as warden two years earlier (and had not been appointed a convention delegate since then), had apparently resurfaced and was returned to his usual post. John Peterson, who had not served on the vestry since 1844, was also elected warden, signaling his return from the Church of the Messiah, where he had served as warden during some of the intervening years. These two would serve as wardens together for the next seven years. John Berrian, who had been secretary since the upheaval of 1848, was voted off the vestry this year and replaced in that office by Philip White, who had been a vestryman for the two previous years. Dunbar Brown was returned to the vestry, though only for this year; he and Berrian then both vanish from the parish record. Smith narrowly missed returning to office, losing a special runoff election to Peter Stevens held in May. Thomas Hoffman, elected for the first time, died in June and was replaced in July by George Jamieson—who had fared poorly in the April election despite serving five of the previous seven years. And in a further sign of leadership instability, Ray and White were named as the delegates to the convention that fall—the first time that Smith was passed over for this position.[11]

The vestry once again requested that the Rev. Morris "urge the admission" of the parish to convention, and this time Morris made his first public attempt. The delegates came to the 1852 convention eager to try again to elect a provisional bishop; having twice failed, this time they succeeded, electing Jonathan Wainwright, assistant rector of Trinity, Wall Street, to serve in this new office.[12] With this issue pending, Morris moved "to receive the Church of St. Philip's (colored) into union with the convention." Jay leapt to second the motion, adding that "he considered the example hitherto set by this Convention, with regard to the colored Churches, to be highly injurious to the cause of religion."[13] This description comes from the day's report in the *New-York Daily Times*, and apparently it was rather understated. Jay himself, in a draft of an article on the St. Philip's story that does not appear to have been published, characterized his statement rather more forcefully:

The motion was seconded by Mr. John Jay, who remarked that the example set by the convention on this subject was not only at variance with the clear intention of the Constitution and Canons [the foundational documents of the denomination], and derogatory to their own character, but widely injurious to the cause of Religion, and most oppressive in its influence upon the Colored people.[14]

Here the diverging strategies begin to become visible. While Morris carefully moved the admission of the parish with no further comment, thus keeping the issue neatly circumscribed, Jay used the motion as an opportunity to issue a diatribe about race and religion, chastising the very delegates whose support he sought.

The Hon. Thomas J. Oakley, delegate from Manhattan's Calvary Church, protested that this resolution was out of order. Jay disagreed, but William Creighton, still chairing the convention as the diocese's senior clergyperson, ruled that the motion was out of order now but could be brought up the next day. Jay then took over from Morris completely, returning the next day to make an even more bombastic resolution:

Resolved, that this Convention think it proper to declare . . . in reference to all Parishes at present legally existing, or which may be hereafter duly organized in this Diocese, composed wholly or in part of colored persons, that this Convention, here assembled in God's name and presence, recognise among parishes applying for admission no distinction or caste based upon natural complexion or social position; but utterly reject and repudiate such tests, as unknown to the Articles, the Constitution, the Canons, and the Liturgy of our Church; as contrary to her primitive and apostolic usage; as absolutely violative of her Catholic unity; and in defiance of the precepts, the spirit, and the example of Christ her head.[15]

It is hard to imagine that Jay thought such an approach would win him friends and supporters: he is asking the convention, in essence, to apologize for its past behavior.

Not surprisingly, Spencer—whom Jay described as having "distinguished himself by his bitter opposition to the Coloured Churches"—objected to the convention even receiving Jay's resolution, and added that "he wished to keep this subject entirely out of the Convention, and especially to keep it out of their minutes." Oakley and others supported this desire, and when Jay attempted to object, he was interrupted by numerous calls for the question (of whether to receive his resolution), and Creighton obliged. Jay narrated himself what followed:

> Mr. Jay immediately called for the vote by orders and was seconded by the requisite number. . . . The [chair] now changed his mind, and refused to put the question, and ruled that the original resolution was out of order. Dr. Tyng, in order to have the house sustain the decision of the Chair, appealed from the decision. The question on the appeal was taken and the Chairman was sustained by a large majority.

Jay's every effort was to force delegates to take a public stand, and the repudiation of that effort here required rather contorted invocations of the rules of order. A motion was made to table the admission of St. Philip's, but Morris withdrew his motion "for the present" and the convention proceeded to elect Wainwright provisional bishop.[16]

Just prior to adjournment, Jay tried one last time: he gave notice of proposing an amendment to Canon IV, "Of the Admission of a Church into Union with the Church in this Diocese," which he planned to offer at the next convention. By the rules, such notice needed to be placed on the record the year before it would be brought to a vote; this move of Jay's would at least get the issue entered into the convention journal. But he was stymied once again, for "in accordance with [Spencer's] suggestion the Record was mutilated the next morning." Thus while three newspapers and the *Churchman* reported on these maneuvers and debates in full, the convention journal makes no mention of Morris's motion, Jay's resolution, or the proposed amendment.[17]

Morris reported back to the vestry with a letter read into the October minutes. It is explicit about the distinctions he saw between his approach and Jay's:

> Rev. Mr. Morris begs leave to say to the Vestry . . . that he presented to the convention their application for admission into the diocese. He endeavored to bring the matter plainly before the Convention on its proper merits and to have a hearing. He . . . asked the convention if there was a single member who felt that there was any objection on the ground of irregularity in the organization of St. Philip's and was not answered. He then sought a vote from this Convention of the Diocese but finding that a member wished to assume to be the defender of St. Phil-

ip's Church and under this name to introduce another subject foreign to the application of St. Philip's Church . . . and seeing that numbers of friends of St. Philip's who would vote for it on its own claims would not vote for it connected with a creed written out by that member, Dr. Morris withdrew the resolution he proposed amidst the kindest remarks of his brethren of the clergy in reference to St. Philip's Church and the assurances of their support when coming to claim its rights.[18]

Morris is here asserting that he actually had the votes lined up to admit the parish, but that Jay's support twisted the issue into something much broader and killed the chance of success.

Morris, then, was pursuing a course of quiet networking, building support for the parish if it could be considered "on its proper merits"—that is, devoid of any explicit association with the broader issues of race and slavery, "subject[s] foreign to the application" and posed by Jay as a "creed." Was this the plan Morris had outlined to the vestry earlier in the year and to which they had given a vote of confidence in April? If so, that would add to the implication that a significant portion of the parish now saw Jay's efforts as hindrances. It is hard from a twenty-first-century perspective to disagree with Jay's opinions and goals in this matter, but it is also easy to see how his manner and approach—that of turning the parish's status into a soapbox for the condemnation of the church's and society's racism and prejudice—had actually become detrimental to the interests of the parish. The people of St. Philip's, it would seem, were less interested in apologies for past behavior or grand statements about their racial oppression than in achieving a present acknowledgment of their Episcopal identity.

CHAPTER 23

A Fulness of Assent

The people of St. Philip's had built a church and had it consecrated by an Episcopal bishop to be an Episcopal house of worship. They had worshiped with order and devotion according to the rites of the Book of Common Prayer. They had been led for many years by a minister of their own color who had been ordained as an Episcopal priest, and they continued to seek another such person. They had been confirmed, many of them, by a bishop who came to their parish, laid his hands upon them, and thereby acknowledged their essential Christian nature as attached to the Episcopal Church. They had defined themselves and carried themselves as Episcopalians for many years. Why, then, given the response they received year after year, did they so wish to attend diocesan convention? This annual meeting was a contentious wrangle of men who, in the heat of the High Church–Low Church battles, could barely be civil to one another. Why did this one remaining criterion for becoming fully Episcopalian loom so large that this parish would repeatedly endure the demeaning racial insults put so openly and so frankly?

This question makes manifest the paradoxes at the heart of the history of the relationship between the parish and the diocese. On the parish's side, the paradox lay between their struggle to develop an independent and self-sufficient African American congregation and their commitment to do so within the confines of an overwhelmingly white, hierarchical denomination. On the part of the denominational leaders, the paradox resided in their Christian desire to have an Episcopal presence among the city's "Africans and their descendants," combined with an even stronger social desire to keep that presence separated from themselves—while the denomination's self-conception made such a separation ultimately sinful and horrifying. The resolution to these paradoxes, however, was precisely in the recognition, by both sides, of the importance of unity to Episcopal denominational identity.

These annual diocesan conventions and the triennial General Conventions were not simply bureaucratic gatherings to handle budgets and administrative matters. They were demonstrations of the Episcopal Church's unity, and therefore of its identity. To be denied admission to convention was to be held as separate from the diocese, and therefore, in a very powerful sense, from the denomination. Convention journals for several of these years listed St. Philip's as "not in union with the convention." This singled out the parish as occupying a different status from any other Episcopal church in the diocese except the Church of the Messiah, the other black congregation.[1] Thus an equation was made and published, year after year: black parishes were not truly Episcopal parishes. After spending thirty years building what they believed to be an Episcopal congregation and an Episcopal parish life, the people of St. Philip's remained highly motivated to remove the stigma of enforced separation from their diocese and from their denominational identity. This year, 1853, they would see that finally come to pass.

At their May meeting in 1853, the vestry of St. Philip's recorded their pleasure with the work in all capacities of their officiating minister, William Morris, by rescinding the previous month's offer of a three-year contract and replacing it with one for an indefinite period. In his letter of acceptance recorded in July, Morris assured the vestry that "My earnest desire is to see St. Philip's Church arrived at that prosperity which ought to belong to it. And I will be glad to aid in bringing it about."[2] There were no doubt literal components to this wish, as the parish continued to have financial difficulties and desired to grow and prosper in every way, but surely Morris's intent was more largely metaphorical, referring to the relationship of the parish to its diocese. There is a lovely sense of a unity of purpose here between vestry and priest, even more than was the case under the stewardship of Alexander Frazer.

In September, the vestry launched its campaign for admission to convention once again, appointing Ray, Scott, and White to be its delegates. They again formally requested that Morris "urge the admission" of the parish; they also again did not mention John Jay and his efforts toward the same.[3]

The diocesan convention, held September 29 and 30, attracted the attention of four local newspapers—the *New-York Daily Times*, the *Morning Courier and New-York Enquirer*, the *New-York Commercial Advertiser*, and the *Evening Post*—and both the High and Low Church denominational journals, the *Churchman* and the *Protestant Churchman*, respectively. Their reports of the convention all outline the same basic order of events, but the *Evening Post*, William Cullen Bryant's paper, established a rather lighter tone regarding the proceedings than the rest. Describing the opening of the convention, their reporter noted that "the lower floor of the chapel was filled with the delegates and members of theological schools, and the galleries made a fair display of ladies." He then opined:

> From what we saw of the bishops and the other members, we should judge that clerical life has a beneficial effect on the health, inasmuch as the elders presented as rosy, rotund, and comfortable appearance as could be desired, while the young candidates just starting on the profession showed every symptom of decline.[4]

It would seem that some took the august Episcopal gathering rather less seriously than it took itself.

Late on the first afternoon, Jay took the floor to give notice that the next day he would move a new version of the amendment that he had attempted to enter into the previous year's record:

> No Church applying for admission, which shall have been fully incorporated as above provided [in the Canon as it existed], shall be refused admission into union with the Convention of this Diocese, on account of the race, lineage, color, or complexion of the congregation so applying, or any part thereof, or of the minister presiding over the same—nor on account of any social or political qualifications of any kind whatsoever, that may attach, or may be supposed to attach to them without the Church—and all churches admitted into union with said convention, shall be admitted—without any condition or qualification establishing or recognizing caste in the Church—upon a footing of catholic equality and Christian brotherhood.[5]

In his lawyerly verbosity, Jay was hoping to build a nondiscrimination clause into the laws of the diocese itself. He once again demonstrated that his priority was less the admission to the convention of a specific parish than the alteration of the attitudes and practices of his denomination. The principle mattered more to Jay than what any actual people might have wanted. This was hardly a bad choice, but it was not the one most helpful to the congregation of St. Philip's.

The *Times* confirmed that Jay had offered this amendment at the end of the last convention, but that "by some mischance [it] had slipped out of the minutes." The *Commercial Advertiser* was less circumspect, reporting, "Mr. Jay said that the same amendment was offered at the last convention, but by some

mischance it had slipped out of the minutes. (Laughter.)"[6] There had been
no "mischance," of course; John Spencer had made sure that nothing on the
topic would appear in the convention journal. Yet it is reassuring that both Jay
and the delegates at large had found some sense of humor about his continual
efforts to force this issue upon the convention.

The same "mischance" was to occur this year as well: the Rev. Alex Leonard the next morning proposed to amend the previous day's minutes to elimi-
nate the text of Jay's amendment, claiming that the notice of the proposal of
an amendment was a sufficient record, and the actual text of the amendment
was unnecessary. Impressively, Henry Anthon, the Low Church leader, objected to this "mutilation of the minutes." The Rev. William Richmond thought
that all references to Jay's amendment, even including his notice of offering
it, should be struck from the record—or none of it should be. Evan Johnson,
from whom nothing had been heard on the subject since the writing of
the minority report in 1846, rose to speak in favor of altering the minutes,
but from a rather different perspective: he "did not wish anything to appear
on the minutes which was not strictly· true. He knew of no canon which
excluded any Church." Thus he argued that there was no need to amend
a canon that already provided for the admission of churches; the problem
was for the convention to live up to that canon. It would appear that he too
wished to distance himself from Jay's strategies, despite his agreement with
the principles involved. After further discussion, a close vote by the delegates
resulted in the minutes being wiped clean of the entire issue, and Jay's amendment once again lacked any official written record.[7]

The Committee on the Incorporation of Churches reported next, and
included St. Philip's among those it had approved for union. Morris clearly
was at work here, for he must have presented the parish's documents to that
committee once again, as if the question had never come up before—thereby
preventing anyone from complaining that the question was not in the "unfinished business" category. The *Evening Post* reporter announced breathlessly
that "the question on the admission of colored church members to the convention's deliberations will probably come up this afternoon, and an exciting debate may be expected."[8] Apparently his deadline prevented him from
remaining to see how it turned out.

The reporter would have been disappointed. With Jay's amendment in
limbo, the question of the admission of St. Philip's was finally separated from
all statements of broader principle. Upon the report of the committee, eighteen parishes were joined to the convention. Regarding the nineteenth, St.
Philip's, no record was made of who put the motion for admission—most

likely it was Morris—but Henry Anthon immediately "called for the ayes and nays," demanding thereby a vote by orders. Five delegates seconded his call; tellingly, Jay was not among them. Instead, he rose to announce that he would make his amendment the next day "specially applicable to that Church." Anthon responded that if there was to be any discussion, he would move to table the question until later. Here again, Jay was actually proving to be an obstacle to the parish's desires! According to the *Morning Courier*, "several members rose to speak, but cries of 'question, question' arising from all parts of the Convention, it was clear that the members were generally ready and anxious to vote at once, without debate." It was bad enough that they would have to vote by orders and thus have individual votes recorded in the minutes; the delegates therefore shied from any further forms of public record about where they stood or how intensely they felt about the issue.[9]

The vote was called, and St. Philip's Church was admitted to the diocesan convention by an impressive margin. The laity voted by parish delegation, and passed the motion by more than two to one, 75 to 33; the clergy were overwhelmingly in favor, with a vote of 140 to 13. Significantly, thirty-seven clergy refused to vote at all—oddly, these included Ralph Hoyt, who had once served as Frazer's assistant minister at St. Philip's. There was a final intriguing footnote: one of Jay's fellow delegates from the Church of the Incarnation, Murray Hoffman, insisted that the minutes record his dissent from his parish's affirmative vote. On an issue Jay had pursued for years, his own parish delegation could not unite behind him. The issue was brought to a close when Jay withdrew his amendment from consideration.[10]

Thus three black men—Peter Ray, Henry Scott, and Philip White— walked into St. John's Chapel on that September afternoon and took their seats among the five hundred white clergy and lay delegates who had finally recognized the right of their parish to attend their diocesan convention.

The Rev. Samuel Seabury, grandson of the denomination's first American bishop and editor of the *Churchman*, commented in his report: "We hardly know whether our colored brethren or the Diocese is more to be congratulated on this result. If the triumph of genuine Christian principle have been long delayed, it has at length come with such a fulness of assent as more than pays for the waiting." It seems doubtful that the people of St. Philip's would agree with this dismissal of their long wait, but it is certain that they felt the triumph of "Christian principle." The vestry of St. Thomas's Church in Philadelphia sent a message of congratulations to their counterparts at St. Philip's, which was most gratefully received. Others were not so pleased: sometime (but not this year) delegate George Templeton Strong, no friend of Jay's, remarked in his diary, "Another Revolution. John Jay's annual motion carried at last, and the nigger delegation admitted into the Diocesan Convention. John Jay must be an unhappy, aching void, as when one's stomach, liver, and other innards have been dexterously taken out." Though Strong was antislavery by this time, he was no happier than most of the other white delegates to be actually associating with African Americans.[11]

Strong, like many others since, attributed the victory to Jay and assumed it was his motion that had carried the day. The vestry of St. Philip's, however, tendered its deepest thanks to William Morris, "for his services in securing the admission of this Church in the late convention."[12] They knew that what had finally worked was not the attempt to force a diocese (and by implication a denomination) to face its racism and address the issue of slavery, but rather the call of Morris—and Evan Johnson seven years earlier—for the delegates to decide quite simply whether St. Philip's was an Episcopal church or not. This may seem to minimize their triumph to a rather selfish one, but the actual presence of individual African Americans in a diocesan convention would have its own far-reaching implications.

In 1854, Bishop Jonathan Wainwright died, and the vestry of St. Philip's posted notices of condolence in both the *Churchman* and the *Protestant Churchman*. James McCune Smith, who had not been present to enjoy the triumph the year before, was this time returned to his post as convention delegate, and was joined by warden John Peterson. They reported back to the vestry that, in the balloting for a new provisional bishop, they had voted for Benjamin Haight on the first three ballots, and Alexander Vinton on the next six, but that Horatio Potter of Albany had finally been elected. More importantly, they informed the vestry that "their credentials were received and they were entered on the roll. They were well received and fraternised with both by clergy and laity."[13] That simple statement must have meant the world to the parish. They were finally in union with their diocese, and their identity as Christians practicing their faith as Episcopalians was fully recognized.

CHAPTER 24

But One Fold and One Chief Shepherd

In 1883, the Rt. Rev. William M. Green, bishop of Mississippi, invited the Episcopal bishops of the former slave states to a gathering at the University of the South in Sewanee, Tennessee. The purpose was to address "the relations of our Church to the late slave population of our States, and the best means that can be adopted for their religious benefit." He encouraged them to bring along any of their clergy or lay leaders "who, either from much experience in instructing the negro, or from a becoming interest in his behalf, may be qualified to aid us by his counsel."[1] That July, what became known as the Sewanee Conference heard a variety of propositions from those gathered, and then delegated a committee to consider the propositions and issue a plan of action. As the committee's report made clear, the agenda of the conference was less a "becoming interest" in the religious life of African Americans than a desire to legislate on a national level the same state of separation that St. Philip's had endured.

The report began, however, by denying that any such separation or schism based upon race was envisioned:

> Your Committee believes that because of the Apostolic character of the Episcopal office, which has been received "always and everywhere and by all men"; because of the Ecclesiastical unity thereby maintained and exhibited, which may not be broken; and because of the truest welfare of all mankind,—there can be but one fold and one Chief Shepherd for all the people in any field of Ecclesiastical designation.... Therefore your Committee would report, that in its judgment it is entirely inexpedient, both on grounds of Ecclesiastical polity, and also of a due consideration of the interests of all concerned, to establish any separate, independent Ecclesiastical organization for the colored people dwelling within the territory of our constituted Jurisdictions.[2]

The understanding of the importance of unity as central to denominational identity has here made strange bedfellows of the language of theology and the language of social expediency, forestalling a simple racial division—it would seem. The Civil War, after all, had been fought and lost, and the realities of the culture's social distinctions were no longer sufficient grounds for this committee to simply suggest casting out their black congregants.

But these Southern gentlemen, while still professing their "real belief in the brotherhood of all men in Christ," were not going to acquiesce so easily to the new order. They again brought together theological belief and what they hoped was mere social realism, stating:

> Your Committee is of the opinion that because of the peculiarity of the relations of the two races, one to the other, in our country, because of their history in the past and hopes of the future, there is needed special legislation, appointing special agency and method for the ingathering of these wandering sheep into the fold of Christ.

This "special agency" was a proposal to keep African Americans in the Episcopal Church, but only by creating a church within a church, a denomination within a denomination: "In any Diocese containing a large number of persons of colour, it shall be lawful for the Bishop and Convention of the same to constitute such population into a special Missionary Organization under the charge of the Bishop." This missionary organization was to be overseen by a committee appointed by the bishop. The clergy and laity so "missionized" would meet in a convocation convened by the bishop, and they could be "received into union with the Convention of the Diocese on such terms and by such process as are provided by the said Diocesan Convention."[3] In other words, the black population of any diocese could be disenfranchised and segregated at the will of their bishop and with the support of his convention.

The proposed separation may have differed from schism only semantically—certainly the spirit was the same—but the care lavished on those semantics and on the logic behind them was a product of the recognition of denominational realities by these Southerners. Black congregations had been slowly admitted to conventions, yet racial divisions were still openly acknowledged; the Sewanee Conference's argument was couched carefully to take both factors into account. The conference was not to succeed on such an official level, however, for the post–Civil War triumph in the denomination of the Broad Church movement over the divisiveness of both Low and High Churchmen meant that a theology of inclusiveness had taken the day.

The Committee on Canons of the General Convention that year rejected the conference's proposed canon in part because of a wish to eschew making such divisions explicit in church structure: "In the judgment of the Committee, the Church cannot too carefully avoid the appearance of drawing lines of classification and distinction between the followers of our common Lord; and they fear that the proposed Canon, if adopted would tend to such a result." The theology of catholicity was here joined to the fear of legislating a bifurcation, for the High Church horror of sundering the apostolic church was still of equal importance to any Biblical injunctions about being one in Christ. The Committee on Canons felt compelled to respond by submitting its own resolution to the General Convention, moving that "the work of the Church among the colored people ought to be regarded as a common work of our whole body, and, as such, ought to receive a large share of the cares and benefactions of our Board of Missions, and the sympathy and assistance of all Churchmen."[4] Racism and paternalism can still be seen as predominant elements in the dealings of white Episcopalians with their black brethren, but there were also beliefs about the nature of Christianity and of the Episcopal Church itself that played significant roles in this debate.

The genesis, presentation, and rejection of the Sewanee Conference proposal parallel rather neatly the struggle that St. Philip's Church had won thirty years earlier. The effort to create an ecclesiastical structure that would encode pragmatic social realities and the intersection between social expediency and religious belief are apparent in both stories. There is even a striking echo by the Committee on Canons of the language of James McCune Smith in his response to the case of the Brazilian slaves: both professed the importance of racial issues to all Americans, regardless of color. The most significant parallel, however, is the foundering of racism in the face of Episcopal polity. Once again, the centrality of unity to the Episcopal identity militated against desires to codify a social separation. Once again, the structures of a hierarchical denomination forced those white Americans who wished to distance themselves from black Americans into constant interaction instead.

The elements of the case of the Sewanee Conference are rendered more visible through the lens of the history of St. Philip's. The local circumstances of the latter point to the individual lives and congregations behind the conference's attempt to treat African Americans as a population to be managed, and reveal larger movements and motives common to the history of the denomination and of African American religion in the nineteenth century. The combination of self-reliance and interaction with the existing social and denominational powers, the paradox of establishing "a distinct congregation" while nonetheless demanding inclusion in the wider church, and the response by the white hierarchy of attempted separation defeated by the actualities of their professed faith—these elements so carefully and contradictorily illustrated by the parish's history are also important to understanding broader movements such as the Sewanee Conference.

But seeing these similarities crop up in later and larger movements also highlights the remarkable nature of the St. Philip's story. Theirs was not a unique struggle and their oppression was not peculiar in any way, but such a realization renders the congregation's ability to use the polity of a conservative denomination for their own empowerment all the more impressive. Compromises were made in the pursuit of their goal, most visibly in acquiescing to the separation of the issue of their admission to convention from broader principles about race and slavery, but such compromises are no more than expected in the negotiations between an oppressed group and their oppressors. In fact, they serve to reinforce the sense of surprise that an oppressed group could achieve anything under such conditions.

There are no simple heroes or villains in the tale of St. Philip's and the diocese. A careful examination of this history instead reveals the players to have been conflicted, contradictory, ambiguous, and altogether human. John Jay was adamant and obnoxious, principled and humorless, enormously helpful to the parish but in the end often an obstacle; James McCune Smith was articulate, powerfully faithful, supremely concerned about the advancement of his people, but not always the leader his parish wanted him to be; Peter Williams was devout and dutiful, an inspiration to an entire generation, but castigated for his reticence and misunderstood for his loyalty to parish and priesthood. Such figures and so many more showed themselves over the course of this story to be deeply and irretrievably individual. Yet despite and amidst these quirks of personalities, everyone involved managed to set aside— even if only briefly and partially—the basic division of race for the unity of the "one fold and one chief shepherd." Religious faith did not resolve the social reality of nineteenth-century racism, but the structure that faith found in the Episcopal Church did at least prevent its institutional legitimization. For these antebellum New Yorkers, both black and white, a creative tension between race and religion produced results that may have been limited but were certainly profound.

The desire of the members of St. Philip's to claim an Episcopal identity for their faith was certainly entwined with a variety of other motives and agendas, such as the improvement of the lives of African Americans through education, seen powerfully in the life and work of Peter Williams; the striving for economic wealth and status, exemplified by Thomas Downing; and the aspirations for Victorian ideals so clearly articulated by James McCune Smith and Alexander Crummell. But if their religious desires cannot be disentangled from such other motives, neither can they be subsumed by them. The choice to be Episcopalian was made by too many different individuals in this congregation, living in too many different ways, having differing approaches to how to improve not only their own lives but also those of their congregation and their people, to be neatly relegated to the service of another somehow larger agenda.

In the end, the triumph of St. Philip's Church not only affirmed its members' desire to be Episcopalians who happened to be African American, it also pointed out the ways in which they were African Americans who happened to be Episcopalian. Du Bois's "double consciousness" is exposed in all of its complexity in this history, for the efforts of the people of this parish to assert a religious identity were ultimately entwined most firmly with their efforts to establish their identities as Americans and as African Americans. No such difficulties existed for white Episcopalians of the period: for them, the choosing of their faith and its expression was simply another aspect of their American identity. For the people of St. Philip's, making such a choice was just as fraught with oppression, negotiation, compromise, and self-pride as was asserting their rights and abilities to be Americans. In this instance, they succeeded in forcing at least a portion of the surrounding culture to acknowledge that they belonged.

Parishioners of St. Philip's Church

This table lists all those whose names can be connected to St. Philip's Church from 1818 to 1860, to the extent that such information is available. The "Relation to Church" category designates what could be learned about each person's connection to the parish, either by what the vestry minutes said about him or her or by the fact that he signed the open letter to John Jay (some of these signatories are also mentioned in the vestry minutes, and some are not). The occupations are those listed in the city directories for the indicated years; there will be more than one listing for those individuals whose occupations change significantly.

NAME	OCCUPATION	YEARS	RELATION TO CHURCH
Annin, John	sexton	54–56	pew rent collector/sexton
Anthony, Joseph	shoemaker	43–44, 48–49	pew rent collector
Bastian, Francis	bootblack	44	Jay letter
Bastian, Francis	barber	57	Jay letter
Bees, John	fruiter	18	Lorillard trustee
Bell, Philip	intelligence/ newspaper	37–54	runs for vestry
Berrian, John	porter	43–54	secretary of vestry
Bowers, Jeremiah	barber/ hairdresser	43–54	runs for vestry
Bowyer, Gabriel	porter	44	runs for vestry
Brady, William	musician	48–54	chorister
Brown, Dunbar	bootblack	48–54	warden, vestry
Brown, John J.	clerk	50–54	vestry, chorister
Burgalew, Richard	eating house	43–45	vestry
Burns, Moses	waiter	30–36	warden, vestry
Burns, Moses	caterer	43–56	warden, vestry
Burry, Daniel	seaman	43–44	pew owner
Burry, Daniel	steward	48–54	pew owner

Name	Occupation	Years	Relation to Church
Carter, Henry	whitewasher	43–44	runs for vestry/pew rent collector
Carter, Henry	porter	53–54	runs for vestry/pew rent collector
Chatters, George	barber	38–49	vestry
Coggar, Lorenzo	barber	39–57	runs for vestry
Conner, John D.	musician/ teacher	42–53	chorister
Cowes, James C.	barber/ hairdresser	42–44	Jay letter
Crosby, Edward	hotelkeeper	55	Jay letter
Crummell, Boston	oysters	42	Jay letter
Curtiss, William	laborer	51–52	vestry
Curtiss, William	jeweler/plater	52–64	vestry
Downing, George	oysters/caterer	43–57	Jay letter
Downing, Henry	coachman	43–44	member
Downing, Henry	refectory	48–49	member
Downing, Thomas	oysterer	21–35	vestry
Downing, Thomas	oyster house	35–60	vestry
Elston, Alexander	shoemaker	25–60	warden, vestry
Elston, Daniel	sugar refiner	44–46	Jay letter
Elston, Daniel	porter	50–51	Jay letter
Ennals, Samuel	grocer	43–44	warden
Gosiah, Isaac	shoemaker	43–54	warden, vestry
Green, George	teacher	43–44, 52–54	Jay letter
Guinan, Felix	porter	43–54	runs for vestry
Hamilton, Charles	waiter	48–49	runs for vestry
Hamilton, Charles	laborer	53–54	runs for vestry
Hamilton, Robert	porter	43–49	chorister
Harley, Francis	clothes cleaner	44–51	runs for vestry, Jay letter
Hoffman, Thomas	porter	43–49	vestry
Hoffman, Thomas	barber	53–54	vestry
Hutson, William	intelligence	18–30s	vestry
Innis, William	barber	44–55	Jay letter
Jackson, William	musician	43–44	organist
Jackson, John H.	liquors	53–54	runs for vestry
Jennings, Thomas Jr.	artisan	42–44	Jay letter
Lacy, Philip	sexton	42–51, 56	sexton, pew rent collector
Lawrence, George	steward, pickler (for Scott)	35–36, 43–49	vestry

NAME	OCCUPATION	YEARS	RELATION TO CHURCH
Lawrence, George	grocer, threads, drygoods	38–39, 49–59	vestry
Lawrence, George Jr.	editor	61	vestry
Lyons, Albro	segarmaker	43–44	vestry
Lyons, Albro	porter	48–49	vestry
Lyons, Albro	sailor's home	53–54	vestry
Marander, John	porter	10–14, 20–37	vestry
Marander, John	mariner/ laborer	17–18, 44–52	vestry
Matthews, Isaac	porter	48–49	election inspector
McDougall, Robert	carman	43–44	vestry
Morgan, John	laborer	43–44	pew owner
Myers, Francis	barber	48–54	runs for vestry
Peterson, John	teacher	25–54	warden, vestry
Peterson, John V.	sexton	53–54	sexton
Potter, Ellis	coachman	48–49	runs for vestry
Potts, George	laborer	48–49	election inspector
Powell, William	boarding house	43–49	warden, election inspector
Poyer, Aaron	hairdresser	43–49	runs for vestry
Poyer, William	barber	21	runs for vestry
Poyer, William	musician	43–44	runs for vestry
Poyer, William	carpenter	48–49	runs for vestry
Rankin, Andrew	waiter	18	vestry
Ray, Peter	factory supervisor	43–62	warden
Ray, Peter Williams	doctor	50–60	vestry
Reason, Charles	teacher	43–44	lay reader
Reason, Patrick	artist/engraver	43–44	member
Robertson, John	whitewasher	43–44	vestry
Scott, Henry	mariner	23–26	treasurer of vestry
Scott, Henry	grocer, pickling business	30–54	treasurer of vestry
Seaman, Timothy	clerk	44	election inspector
Smith, James McCune	printer	25–26	secretary of vestry
Smith, James McCune	doctor/ newspaper editor	32–54	secretary of vestry
Stevens, Peter	musician	43–54	vestry
Thomas, Robert	coachman	43–44	vestry
Thomas, Robert	mariner	53–54	vestry
Tilghman, Daniel	tailor	36–49	Jay letter

NAME	OCCUPATION	YEARS	RELATION TO CHURCH
Van Dyke, Peter	waiter	48–49	vestry
Van Dyke, Peter	cook	53–54	vestry
Vidal, Theodore	hairdresser	43–54	Jay letter
Vogelsang, Peter	porter	53–54	runs for vestry
Wake, Ransom	teacher	43–54	warden, vestry
Waldron, Samuel	musician	52–56	organist
White, Philip	druggist	48–54	secretary, vestry
Willets, Charles	sexton	52–54	sexton
Williams, Henry	porter	44	Jay letter
Zabriskie, Thomas	livery stable	22–42	warden, vestry
Zabriskie, Thomas	coachman/ carman	42–53	warden, vestry
Zuille, John	printer/teacher	42–55	Jay letter

NOTES

1. Improper Associates

1. Accounts of conditions between the races in early nineteenth-century New York City are numerous. Those used most particularly in researching this book include Rhoda Golden Freeman, *The Free Negro in New York City in the Era Before the Civil War* (Ph.D. diss., Columbia University, 1966); George E. Walker, *The Afro-American in New York City, 1827–1860* (New York: Garland, 1993); and Tyler Anbinder, *Five Points: The Nineteenth-Century New York City Neighborhood That Invented Tap Dancing, Stole Elections, and Became the World's Most Notorious Slum* (New York: Free Press, 2001). A broader perspective is found in Donald R. Wright, *African Americans in the Early Republic, 1789–1831* (Arlington Heights, Ill.: Harlan Davidson, 1993).

2. This account will make use of traditional masculine nouns ("churchmen," "laymen," etc.) and masculine pronouns in order to call attention to the exclusively male leadership in the denomination—and generally in the wider culture—that was the case in this period. Women could neither hold official leadership positions nor be ordained in the Episcopal Church in the nineteenth century. Any discussion of a gathering of Episcopal leaders, then, will be about a male group. One particularly unfortunate result of this exclusivity is the absence of historical records describing the enormous contributions women made to the life of the individual churches and even the denomination as a whole in the early nineteenth century.

3. A "diocese," in the Episcopal Church, comprises the churches within a specific geographical area overseen by a bishop. The Diocese of New York originally covered the entire state, but it was split in half in 1838, so after that date the name refers to the denominational entity in the eastern half of the state.

4. The primary source for the names of members of St. Philip's Church is the collection of minutes of the vestry's meetings, which lists vestry members and those who ran for election to the vestry; various other names are also referred to in the minutes when the individuals were involved in the business of the parish: *Vestry Minutes of St. Philip's Episcopal Church*, St. Philip's Episcopal Church Records, Manuscripts, Archives,

and Rare Books Division, Schomburg Center for Research in Black Culture, the New York Public Library, Astor, Lenox, and Tilden Foundations, box 74. All information regarding addresses and employment in the following pages, unless otherwise noted, is from the New York City directories. These are as follows (the directories were published annually): for 1800–1811 and for 1813–1841, *Longworth's New-York Register, and City Directory* (New York: Thomas Longworth); for 1812, *Elliot's Improved New-York Double Directory* (New York: William Elliot); for 1842–1844, *The New-York City and Co-Partnership Directory* (New York: Doggett); for 1845–1851, *Doggett's New York City Directory* (New York: John Doggett Jr.); for 1852, *New York City Directory* (New York: Doggett and Rode); and for 1853–1859, *Trow's New-York City Directory* (New York: John F. Trow).

5. *Journal of the Proceedings of the 62nd Convention of the Protestant Episcopal Church in the State of New York, 1846* (New York: Henry M. Onderdonk, 1846), 73. After 1819, these journals were all published for the diocese in New York City by various printers in the year of the convention, and will hereinafter be referred to as *Journal of the Nth Convention.*

6. There have been four efforts to write overall histories of the parish, all of which suffer from both brevity and inaccuracy regarding the antebellum period: Benjamin F. DeCosta, *Three Score and Ten: The Story of St. Philip's Church, New York City* (New York: Printed for the Parish, 1889); Shelton H. Bishop, "A History of St. Philip's Church, New York City," *Historical Magazine of the Protestant Episcopal Church* 15 (December 1946): 298–317; *Reaching Out: An Epic of the People of St. Philip's Church* (Tappan, N.Y.: Custombook, for St. Philip's Church, 1986); and John H. Hewitt, *Protest and Progress: New York's First Black Episcopal Church Fights Racism* (New York: Garland, 2000). Hewitt, a former clerk of the vestry at St. Philip's, was the unacknowledged author of much of *Reaching Out*, and his own work is actually composed of a series of previously published articles. All of these accounts were produced by people connected to the parish. For example, DeCosta's piece was actually a lengthy talk given at the opening of the parish's new building on West Twenty-fifth Street in 1868, and Bishop was the rector of the parish at the time he wrote his article.

7. Population statistics are taken from Leonard P. Curry, *The Free Black in Urban America, 1800–1850* (Chicago: University of Chicago Press, 1981), 245–261. Additional data for New York City is from Freeman, *Free Negro*, 439–447.

8. Curry, *Free Black*, 217–219.

9. Curry, *Free Black*, 18.

10. Curry, *Free Black*, passim.

11. Curry, *Free Black*, 120–121.

12. Curry, *Free Black*, 121. Another perspective on this point is offered in Nathan I. Huggins, *Protestants Against Poverty: Boston's Charities, 1870–1900* (Westport, Conn.: Greenwood, 1971).

13. Freeman, *Free Negro*, 375–423.

2. Freedom's Defects

1. Peter Williams, "Slavery and Colonization," in Carter G. Woodson, *Negro Orators and Their Orations* (Washington, D.C.: Associated Publishers, 1925), 78.

2. The best source of biographical information on Peter Williams Sr. is J. B. Wakeley, *Lost Chapters Recovered from the Early History of American Methodism* (New York: Printed for the Author, 1858), 438–473. Wakeley, a white Methodist minister, clearly knew Williams personally, for his account is quite anecdotal and inflected with effusive appraisals of Williams's character. This is the primary source for the information provided in John H. Hewitt, *Protest and Progress: New York's First Black Episcopal Church Fights Racism* (New York: Garland, 2000), 13–16. See also the unsigned article "Peter Williams," in Kenneth T. Jackson, ed., *The Encyclopedia of New York City* (New Haven, Conn.: Yale University Press, 1995), 1263.

3. Hewitt, *Protest and Progress*, 13, says that Williams Jr. was born "probably in 1780." Wakeley, *Lost Chapters*, 446, does not give a year for his birth but states that "he was born in New Brunswick during the war of the Revolution," but both appear to be wrong. A date of 1786 is more firmly attested: first, Williams's passport, dated 1836, gives his age as fifty. See George E. Carter and Peter C. Ripley, eds., *Black Abolitionist Papers, 1830–1865* (Sanford, N.C.: Microfilming Corp., microform, reel 1, #2123). Second, a death notice in 1840 gives his age as 54. See *Colored American* (October 24, 1840): 3. Third, a nineteenth-century biographical sketch confirms the date of the passport and states that Williams was born in December of 1786, though it still claims that he was born in New Jersey, while the family is clearly living in Manhattan by that time. See William C. Nell, *The Colored Patriots of the American Revolution, with Sketches of Several Distinguished Colored Persons* (Boston: Robert F. Wallcut, 1855), 320, indexed and microfilmed in Randall K. Burkett, Nancy Hall Burkett, and Henry Louis Gates Jr., eds., *Black Biography 1790–1950: A Cumulative Index* (Alexandria, Va.: Chadwyck-Healey, 1991).

4. Wakeley, *Lost Chapters*, 469.

5. Wakeley, *Lost Chapters*, 449, 446.

6. The following account of the creation of the new church is based on that given in William J. Walls, *The African Methodist Episcopal Zion Church: Reality of the Black Church* (Charlotte, N.C.: A.M.E. Zion Publishing House, 1974), 43–75.

7. On this latter point, see Harry V. Richardson, *Dark Salvation: The Story of Methodism As It Developed Among Blacks in America* (Garden City, N.Y.: Anchor, 1976), 148–150.

8. Wakeley, *Lost Chapters*, 453–454.

9. Wakeley, *Lost Chapters*, 446; Benjamin F. DeCosta, *Three Score and Ten: The Story of St. Philip's Church, New York City* (New York: Printed for the Parish, 1889), 31–33.

10. The work of Elias Neau is covered in John H. Hewitt, "New York's Black Episcopalians: In the Beginning, 1704–1722," *Afro-Americans in New York Life and His-*

tory (January 1979): 9–22. This is based in large part on Sheldon S. Cohen, "Elias Neau, Instructor to New York's Slaves," *New York Historical Quarterly* 50 (January 1971): 12–16. See also James Elliott Lindsley, *This Planted Vine: A Narrative History of the Episcopal Diocese of New York* (New York: Harper and Row, 1984), 31–33.

11. Edmund Gibson, quoted in Hewitt, "New York's Black Episcopalians," 14; originally quoted in Winthrop D. Jordan, *White Over Black* (Chapel Hill: University of North Carolina Press, 1968), 191.

3. Hobart and the High Church

1. Accounts of the role of Anglicans in the American Revolution and of the formation of the Episcopal Church in the Revolution's aftermath can be found in a number of histories. The best treatments are in Robert Prichard, *A History of the Episcopal Church* (Harrisburg, Penn.: Morehouse, 1991), 73–104; and David L. Holmes, "The Episcopal Church and the American Revolution," *Historical Magazine of the Protestant Episcopal Church* 47 (Summer 1978): 261–291.

2. Explanations of the doctrine of apostolic succession are numerous in the literature of church history, especially in the Anglican and Episcopal traditions. One of the more amusing versions is found in George Parkin Atwater, *The Episcopal Church: Its Message for Men of Today* (Milwaukee: Morehouse, 1917), 101–104.

3. This is neither the time nor place for a detailed explanation of the circumstances and arguments that led to the existence of what were known as "non-juring bishops," a group comprising all of the Scottish bishops and several English bishops who refused to swear allegiance to William III and Mary II, joint British monarchs, when they ascended the throne in 1688. See, for example, Prichard, *History*, 21–25. Suffice to say here that this controversy provided a "dissenting church" that suited the new American needs rather neatly.

4. A useful discussion of how Hooker elucidated this point in his *Of the Laws of Ecclesiastical Polity* (1593–1597) is offered in John E. Booty, *The Church in History* (New York: Seabury, 1979), 60–61.

5. See Charles Finney, *Lectures on Revivalism* (1835), cited in Sydney E. Ahlstrom, *A Religious History of the American People* (New Haven, Conn.: Yale University Press, 1972), 460.

6. For my discussion of the "new measures" and the ways in which they shaped regular worship services, I am indebted to Ralph Gerald Gay, *A Study of the American Liturgical Revival, 1825–1860* (Ph.D. diss., Emory University, 1977).

7. A nuanced portrait of the issues summarized here is provided in Diana Hochstedt Butler, *Standing Against the Whirlwind: Evangelical Episcopalians in Nineteenth-Century America* (New York: Oxford University Press, 1995).

8. This discussion of Hobart's "High Church theology" and its implications is dependent upon Robert Bruce Mullin, *Episcopal Vision/American Reality: High Church*

Theology and Social Thought in Evangelical America (New Haven, Conn.:Yale University Press, 1986). Also quite helpful is E. Clowes Chorley, "Outline of Two Hundred and Fifty Years of Trinity Parish in the City of New York," *Historical Magazine of the Protestant Episcopal Church* 16 (March 1947): 39–42.

9. John H. Hobart, *The Candidate for Confirmation Instructed* (New York: T. and J. Swords, 1816), 23.

10. John H. Hobart, *The Churchman: The Principles of the Churchman Stated and Explained, in Distinction from the Corruptions of the Church of Rome, and from the Errors of Certain Protestant Sects* (1819), quoted in Chorley, "Outline," 40.

4. One of Their Own Colour

1. There are three significant efforts exploring the history of this remarkable parish: William Berrian, *An Historical Sketch of Trinity Church, New York* (New York: Stanford and Sons, 1847); Morgan Dix, ed., *A History of the Parish of Trinity Church in the City of New York*, 5 vols. (New York: G. Putnam's Sons, 1898–1906); and E. Clowes Chorley, *A Quarter of a Millennium: Trinity Church in the City of New York, 1697–1947* (Philadelphia: Church Historical Society, 1947). Also very useful is James Elliott Lindsley, *This Planted Vine: A Narrative History of the Episcopal Diocese of New York* (New York: Harper and Row, 1984). I have drawn on these works throughout.

2. This is stated in Benjamin F. DeCosta, *Three Score and Ten: The Story of St. Philip's Church, New York City* (New York: Printed for the Parish, 1889), 13–14; and Berrian, *Historical Sketch*, 367, says in an appendix listing grants, gifts, and loans made by the parish that "at one time [the vestry] appropriated £200 towards furnishing land for a Negro Burial-ground." This latter statement is undated, but comes between entries for 1805 and 1807. A search of Trinity's vestry minutes, however, does not turn up any entry on the topic.

3. In 1807, Trinity made the first grant to the African Episcopal Catechetical Institution, for $25, for an instructor. There is no evidence of any such organization prior to this date, and it is the name by which the grantee was known to Trinity—at least in its fiduciary records—until 1826, when it was changed to "St. Philip's Church." See *Gifts to Churches, Organizations and Persons Outside the Parish of Trinity Church, 1697–1965* (Archives of Trinity Parish, New York City, printed 1965), unpaginated.

4. DeCosta, *Three Score and Ten*, 14, says that the congregation met at Trinity "prior to 1810," suggesting that the separation occurred that year; Shelton H. Bishop, "A History of St. Philip's Church, New York City," *Historical Magazine of the Protestant Episcopal Church* 15 (December 1946): 302, agrees. John H. Hewitt, in "Unresting the Waters: The Fight Against Racism in New York's Episcopal Establishment, 1845–1853," *Afro-Americans in New York Life and History* 18, no. 1 (January 1994): 7, states that the congregation began meeting separately in 1809; and Jonathan Greenleaf, *A History of the Churches of All Denominations, in the City of New York, From the First Settlement to the*

Year 1846 (New York: E. French, 1846), 79, concurs with the earlier date. The communication with the diocesan convention, cited below, was made in 1809, which affirms the earlier date definitively. It should be noted here that DeCosta, in a preface dated 1868, laments that the early records of St. Philip's Church had disappeared (DeCosta, *Three Score and Ten*, 4). As a result, all assertions regarding the parish's first years are deductions from what sources do exist.

5. DeCosta, *Three Score and Ten*, 14; an entry in Trinity's vestry minutes in 1807 refers to paying "James McCoon" as the instructor of the African Episcopal Catechetical Institution: *Minutes of the Vestry, the Corporation of Trinity Church*, vol. 2, December 19, 1807 (Archives of Trinity Parish, New York City). Greenleaf, *History of the Churches*, 79, refers to him as "Mr. McCoombs."

6. *Journals of the Conventions of the Diocese of New York: 1800–1819* (New York: E. French, 1846), 191.

7. *Journals of the Conventions*, 191.

8. *Journals of the Conventions*, 205.

9. DeCosta, *Three Score and Ten*, 15; Greenleaf, *History of the Churches*, 79. Both imply that Williams's tenure began around 1812, with the death of McCombs. As there is no diocesan record of his licensing, it could have been anywhere between the convention of 1810 (which was in the fall) and 1812.

10. James McCune Smith, quoted in William C. Nell, *The Colored Patriots of the American Revolution, with Sketches of Several Distinguished Colored Persons* (Boston: Robert F. Wallcut, 1855), 321, indexed and microfilmed in Randall K. Burkett, Nancy Hall Burkett, Henry Louis Gates Jr., eds., *Black Biography 1790–1950: A Cumulative Index* (Alexandria, Va.: Chadwyck-Healey, 1991).

11. Peter Williams Jr., "An Oration on the Abolition of the Slave Trade, delivered in the African Church in the City of New York, January 1, 1808," in Carter G. Woodson, *Negro Orators and Their Orations* (Washington, D.C.: Associated Publishers, 1925), 32–41. It is also anthologized in Philip S. Foner and Robert James Branham, eds., *Lift Every Voice: African American Oratory, 1787–1900* (Tuscaloosa: University of Alabama Press, 1998), 66–79. Parishioner Smith, quoted in Nell, *Colored Patriots*, 321, asserts that the speech "was discredited as having emanated from his pen—and it was deemed necessary that his certificate to that effect should be published, confirmed by Rt. Rev. Benjamin Moore, Bishop of the Protestant Episcopal Church, and others." See also John H. Hewitt, *Protest and Progress: New York's First Black Episcopal Church Fights Racism* (New York: Garland, 2000), 18.

12. Peter Williams to the Citizens of New York (open letter), July 14, 1834, in Carter G. Woodson, ed., *The Mind of the Negro As Reflected in Letters Written During the Crisis, 1800–1860* (1926; repr., New York: Russell and Russell, 1969), 632.

13. DeCosta, *Three Score and Ten*, 15.

14. *Journals of the Conventions*, 265.

15. *Journals of the Conventions*, 265.

16. *Minutes of the Proceedings of the Standing Committee of the Protestant Episcopal Church in the State of New York* (Archives of the Diocese of New York: Standing Committee, Minutes #1), November 3, 1813.

17. *Minutes of the Proceedings of the Standing Committee*, December 1, 1813.

18. Harold T. Lewis, *Yet With a Steady Beat: The African American Struggle for Recognition in the Episcopal Church* (Valley Forge, Penn.: Trinity Press International, 1996), 29–30. See also George F. Bragg, *History of the Afro-American Group of the Episcopal Church* (1922; repr., Baltimore: Church Advocate Press, 1968), 59–80.

19. *Minutes of the Proceedings of the Standing Committee*, December 1, 1813.

5. An Orderly and Devout Congregation

1. Benjamin F. DeCosta, *Three Score and Ten: The Story of St. Philip's Church, New York City* (New York: Printed for the Parish, 1889), 15; he cites parishioner John Peterson as his source.

2. *Gifts to Churches, Organizations and Persons Outside the Parish of Trinity Church, 1697–1965* (Archives of Trinity Parish, New York City, printed 1965), listing for the year 1814.

3. William S. Pelletreau, *New York Houses, with Historical and Genealogical Notes* (New York: Francis P. Harper, 1900), 1; DeCosta, *Three Score and Ten*, 18–19; and *Reaching Out: An Epic of the People of St. Philip's Church* (Tappan, N.Y.: Custombook, for St. Philip's Church, 1986), 18. Pelletreau gives the date and lot numbers, but lists Lewis Francis as "Linn Frances." DeCosta and Hewitt (the unacknowledged author of most of *Reaching Out*) both give these same names, but add that of George Lawrence, and list William Hutson as "William Whitson." As most of the same names are listed on the document of incorporation (cited below), this is certainly the most accurate list.

4. *Christian Journal* 3, no. 8 (August 1818): 256, cited in DeCosta, *Three Score and Ten*, 20; see also *Gifts to Churches, Organizations and Persons*, listing for the year 1818. As to Sherred's involvement, see William Berrian, *An Historical Sketch of Trinity Church, New York* (New York: Stanford and Sons, 1847), 363, which lists Sherred as a vestryman from 1812 to 1821. DeCosta, *Three Score and Ten*, 20; *Reaching Out*, 18; and Shelton H. Bishop, "A History of St. Philip's Church, New York City," *Historical Magazine of the Protestant Episcopal Church* 15 (December 1946): 300 all state that Sherred left the donation in his will. However, since he was a vestryman until 1821 and is listed as a painter and glazer living at 31 Broad Street in the city directories for the years 1819 through 1821, he was still alive in 1819, when it appears the donation was made. The directory has the following listing at the same address in 1822: "Sherred, widow of Jacob." Both Berrian, *Historical Sketch*, 372 (an undated listing stating "additional sum guaranteed to [the congregation] of $2500") and *Gifts to Churches, Organizations and Persons*, listing for the year 1819 ("$2,500") would seem to be listing Sherred's donation under the aegis of the parish on whose vestry he served. Both list Trinity's grant

for that year toward ground rent separately from this figure, which accords with what DeCosta says Sherred gave.

5. *Gifts to Churches, Organizations and Persons*, listing for the year 1819; *Minutes of the Vestry, the Corporation of Trinity Church*, vol. 2, December 19, 1807 (Archives of Trinity Parish, New York City): "Upon the application and petition of Peter Williams Jun... . Resolved, that this Vestry will assume the payment of the rent of the ground on which their new church is erected for the term of seven years unless the Vestry shall see proper sooner to discontinue such payment."

6. *Certificates of Consecration and Incorporation of St. Philip's Church, dated respectively 1819 & 1820 (copy)*, Archives of the Diocese of New York, box 69: Manhattan, St. Philip's, 1. This is a typed copy, but there is no reason to doubt its accuracy, particularly as its version of the certificate of incorporation matches perfectly with a copy made by hand, dated September 26, 1853, and certified for authenticity by Bishop Jonathan Wainwright, found in the same location.

7. *Christian Journal* 3, no. 8 (August 1818): 256.

8. *Certificates of Consecration*, 1.

9. *Commercial Advertiser* (New York), July 6, 1819, cited in DeCosta, *Three Score and Ten*, 22.

10. *Christian Journal* 3, no. 8 (August 1818): 256.

11. *Journals of the Conventions of the Diocese of New York: 1800–1819* (New York: E. French, 1846), 451–452.

12. Gary Nash, *Forging Freedom: The Formation of Philadelphia's Black Community, 1720–1840* (Cambridge, Mass.: Harvard University Press, 1988), 213.

13. Robert E. Hood, "From a Headstart to a Deadstart: The Historical Basis for Black Indifference Toward the Episcopal Church, 1800–1860," *Historical Magazine of the Protestant Episcopal Church* 51 (September 1982): 269. The quote attributed to Washington is cited in Harold T. Lewis, *Yet With a Steady Beat: The African American Struggle for Recognition in the Episcopal Church* (Valley Forge, Penn.: Trinity Press International, 1996), 1.

14. *Minutes of the Proceedings of the Standing Committee of the Protestant Episcopal Church in the State of New York* (Archives of the Diocese of New York: Standing Committee, Minutes #1), March 6, 1819.

15. *Minutes of the Proceedings of the Standing Committee*, April 7, 1819.

16. *Journals of the Conventions*, 451.

17. DeCosta, *Three Score and Ten*, 23–24. *Reaching Out*, 18, claims that Williams applied to the General Theological Seminary for his studies, but this institution—which claims its beginnings in 1817—was in such flux (particularly regarding location) prior to the 1820s as to have been impractical for most candidates.

18. *Journals of the Conventions*, 451–452.

19. *Journals of the Conventions*, 452.

20. See, for example, *Journals of the Conventions*, 458, 480. The latter instance, under

the "List of Clergy in the Diocese of New York" heading, reads: "Peter Williams, jun., a coloured man, a candidate for Orders, is licensed by the Bishop as a Lay Reader and Catechist, to officiate when no clergyman is present, in St. Philip's Church, New York, the congregation of which is composed of coloured members of the Protestant Episcopal Church."

21. *Journals of the Conventions*, 468.

22. *Commercial Advertiser*, October 21, 1820, cited in DeCosta, *Three Score and Ten*, 23–24; *Christian Journal* 4, no. 11 (November 1820): 351–352.

23. *Journals of the Conventions*, 474–476, contains instructions for the incorporation of churches, as detailed by act of state legislature and the canons of the Episcopal Church. Wardens are the officers of the vestry; two are elected, and one usually serves as chair of the meetings in the absence of a rector.

24. *Certificates of Consecration*, 3–4. The Biblical reference is Acts 8:26–40.

25. *Journal of the 35th Convention* (1821), 13. See note 5, chapter 1 for additional bibliographic information.

26. *Journal of the 37th Convention* (1822), 14; *Journal of the 38th Convention* (1823), 14; and *Christian Journal* 7, no. 1 (January 1823): 30–31, cited in DeCosta, *Three Score and Ten*, 29.

27. *Gifts to Churches, Organizations and Persons*, listings for the years 1819–1826.

28. William Jay to Anna Jay Balch, November 4, 1840, The Papers of John Jay, Rare Book and Manuscripts Library, Columbia University (italics are in the original).

29. *Minutes of the Proceedings of the Standing Committee*, July 1, 1826.

30. *Christian Journal* 10, no. 8 (August 1826): 253–254, cited in DeCosta, *Three Score and Ten*, 30.

31. Peter Williams Jr. to John Henry Hobart, August 14, 1826, The Archives of the Episcopal Church: The Francis L. Hawks Collection, box 49, folder 49.

32. *Journal of the 41st Convention* (1826), 17, 26, 54.

6. A Bitter Thralldom

1. Accounts of the antislavery and abolitionist movements are numerous. The most important for this account is John R. McKivigan, *The War Against Proslavery Religion: Abolitionism and the Northern Churches, 1830–1865* (Ithaca, N.Y.: Cornell University Press, 1984). It should be noted that "abolitionism" is used here to denote those who called for an immediate end to slavery, while "antislavery" refers to a much wider array of positions on how to bring slavery to an end. On the signatories of the Constitution of the American Anti-Slavery Society, see George E. Carter and Peter C. Ripley, eds., *Black Abolitionist Papers, 1830–1865* (Sanford, N.C.: Microfilming Corp., microform, reel 1), December 4, 1833.

2. Accounts of the antiabolitionist riots in New York City, July 4–14, 1834, can be found in a number of sources, including Tyler Anbinder, *Five Points: The Nine-*

teenth-Century New York City Neighborhood That Invented Tap Dancing, Stole Elections, and Became the World's Most Notorious Slum (New York: Free Press, 2001), 7–13; Leonard L. Richards, *"Gentlemen of Property and Standing": Anti-Abolitionist Mobs in Jacksonian America* (New York: Oxford University Press, 1970); and Luc Sante, *Low Life: Lures and Snares of Old New York* (New York: Farrar, Straus, Giroux, 1991), 342–344.

3. In addition to the accounts noted above, details regarding the attack on the church can be found in John Hewitt, "The Sacking of St. Philip's Church, New York," *Historical Magazine of the Protestant Episcopal Church* 49 (March 1980): 7–20, where Hewitt (as does Anbinder) summarizes reports from several newspapers.

4. Anbinder, *Five Points*, 12.

5. William Hamilton, *An Oration Delivered in the African Zion Church, on the fourth of July, 1827, in commemoration of the abolition of domestic slavery in the State* (New York, 1827), quoted in Rhoda Golden Freeman, *The Free Negro in New York City in the Era Before the Civil War* (Ph.D. diss., Columbia University, 1966), 1.

6. Peter Williams Jr., "An Oration on the Abolition of the Slave Trade, delivered in the African Church in the City of New York, January 1, 1808," in Carter G. Woodson, *Negro Orators and Their Orations* (Washington, D.C.: Associated Publishers, 1925), 36–38, 41. It is also anthologized in Philip S. Foner and Robert James Branham, eds., *Lift Every Voice: African American Oratory, 1787–1900* (Tuscaloosa: University of Alabama Press, 1998), 66–79.

7. Foner, *Lift Every Voice*, 80.

8. James Weldon Johnson, *Black Manhattan* (1930, repr. New York: Da Capo Press, 1991), 38.

9. Peter Williams, *A Discourse Delivered on the Death of Captain Paul Cuffe, Before the New York African Institution, in the African Methodist Episcopal Zion Church, October 21, 1817* (New York, 1817). See also *Black Abolitionist Papers*, reel 1, for a letter of Williams to Cuffe dated March 22, 1817, in which the friendship between the two men is made quite clear.

10. Freeman, *Free Negro*, 28–29.

11. Harry A. Reed, *Platform for Change: The Foundations of the Northern Free Black Community, 1775–1865* (East Lansing: Michigan State University Press, 1994), 196.

12. Johnson, *Black Manhattan*, 40–41.

13. The origins of the American Colonization Society have been documented (and rather oversimplified) in a number of places; one of the earliest works to capture the complex array of movements that resulted in this organization is Henry Noble Sherwood, "The Formation of the American Colonization Society," *The Journal of Negro History* 2, no. 3 (July 1917): 209–228. (This article is available electronically, courtesy of the University of North Carolina, at http://docsouth.unc.edu/church/sherwood/sherwood.html.) The galvanizing effect this organization had on New York City's African American community is discussed in Johnson, *Black Manhattan*, 39–46;

Freeman, *Free Negro*, 24–63; and George E. Walker, *The Afro-American in New York City, 1827–1860* (New York: Garland, 1993), 149–161.

14. The implications of the colonization and emigration movements for African American thought are discussed most thoroughly in Patrick Rael, *Black Identity and Black Protest in the Antebellum North* (Chapel Hill, N.C.: University of North Carolina Press, 2002). The transition from "African" to "colored" in self-references among African Americans in this period is discussed particularly in pages 83–115.

15. Peter Williams, "Slavery and Colonization: A Discourse delivered at St. Philip's Church, July 4, 1830," in Woodson, *Negro Orators*, 80.

16. This is a major thrust of Richards, *Gentlemen of Property*.

7. A Godly Admonition

1. See Robert Bruce Mullin, *Episcopal Vision/American Reality: High Church Theology and Social Thought in Evangelical America* (New Haven, Conn.: Yale University Press, 1986); and James Elliott Lindsley, *This Planted Vine: A Narrative History of the Episcopal Diocese of New York* (New York: Harper and Row, 1984), 102–123.

2. Lindsley, *This Planted Vine*, 124–150.

3. Onderdonk's letter and Williams's reply were both printed in several newspapers, including the *New York Spectator*, the *Morning Courier and New York Enquirer*, and the *African Repository*. They are reprinted in Carter G. Woodson, ed., *The Mind of the Negro As Reflected in Letters Written During the Crisis, 1800–1860* (1926; repr., New York: Russell and Russell, 1969), 629–634.

4. Woodson, *The Mind of the Negro*, 630.

5. Alexander Crummell, "Reply to Bishop Onderdonk," The Papers of John Jay, Rare Book and Manuscripts Library, Columbia University, cited in Wilson J. Moses, *Alexander Crummell: A Study of Civilization and Discontent* (New York: Oxford University Press, 1989), 24; *Liberator*, July 19, 1834, quoted in Rhoda G. Freeman Manuscript and Research Collection, 1956–1985, Manuscripts, Archives, and Rare Books Division, Schomburg Center for Research in Black Culture, The New York Public Library, Astor, Lenox, and Tilden Foundations, box 7; Carter G. Woodson, *The History of the Negro Church*, 3rd ed. (1945; repr., Washington, D.C.: Associated Publishers, 1992), 83.

6. *The Book of Common Prayer, and Administration of the Sacraments; and Other Rites and Ceremonies of the Church, According to the Use of the Protestant Episcopal Church in the United States of America* (New York,: E. & J. B. Young, 1881). This version of the prayer book was approved for use in the Episcopal Church in 1789 and was not altered until the revision of 1892, so all editions between those years are precisely the same. This title will not be italicized in the text, but will be referred to variously as "the prayer book," "the common prayer book," or " the Book of Common Prayer."

7. All quotations in this paragraph and the next three are from Williams's letter in Woodson, *The Mind of the Negro*, 630–634.

8. Peter Williams to Gerrit Smith, July 26, 1834 and September 4, 1834, Gerrit Smith Papers, Bird Library, Syracuse University, microform: reel 19.

9. Lewis Tappan, *Life of Arthur Tappan* (1871), note in Freeman Collection.

10.. *Churchman* 4 (July 19, 1834): 695. I am indebted to Mullin, *Episcopal Vision*, 128, for this citation.

11. *Journal of the 52nd Convention* (1837), 27n–28n, italics in the original. See note 5, chapter 1 for additional bibliographic information.

12. Woodson, *The Mind of the Negro*, 629–630.

13. W. E. B. Du Bois, *The Souls of Black Folk* (1903; repr., New York: Bantam Books, 1989), 3.

14. Robert Trendel, "John Jay II: Antislavery Conscience of the Episcopal Church," *Historical Magazine of the Protestant Episcopal Church* 45 (September 1976): 237–252.

15. William Allen Butler, Charles A. Peabody, Thomas C. Acton, "Union League Club: Memorial to the Hon. John Jay, June 1894" (printed by the Club, 1894), 2, in The Papers of John Jay.

16. Moses, *Alexander Crummell*, 28.

8. Peculiar Circumstances

1. The most reliable sources of information on Thomas Downing have been summarized in John H. Hewitt, "Mr. Downing and his Oyster House: The Life and Good Works of an African-American Entrepreneur," *New York History* (July 1993): 229–252. The reliability of these sources, however, is not impeccable, and at least one, S. A. M. Washington, *George Thomas Downing: Sketch of His Life and Times* (Newport, R.I.: The Milne Printery, 1910), is riddled with errors. Nonetheless, the sources do all agree about the factors that led to Downing's fame and the various manifestations of his reknown.

2. Quoted in Hewitt, "Mr. Downing," 229.

3. Hewitt makes this assertion ("Mr. Downing," 240) based on the conditions that prevailed in New York City during this period, which is quite reasonable. Contemporary references to Downing's restaurant establish its popularity with white patrons and never remark on any racial mixing, which would have been sufficiently unusual to have caused comment. Washington implies (*George Thomas Downing*, 11) that Downing's son George worked under similar conditions, and by his tone suggests that the reader will have already assumed this to be true.

4. Washington, *George Thomas Downing*, 7. Again, because this source has so many factual errors, it is hard to fully credit its accuracy, but there is certainly no reason for the author to knowingly dissemble about the DeGrasse family heritage.

5. See, for example, 'A Churchman' [John Jay], *Caste and Slavery in the American Church* (New York: Wiley and Putnam, 1843); and William Jay to Anna Jay Balch, November 4, 1840, The Papers of John Jay, Rare Book and Manuscripts Library,

Columbia University: "Verily the spirit of caste in the Church has not been rebuked in vain."

6. Peter Williams to Gerrit Smith, September 4, 1834, Gerrit Smith Papers, Bird Library, Syracuse University, microform: reel 19; *Emancipator*, September 7, 1837, quoting "an article that appeared in the Boston *Liberator* in the year 1831," Rhoda G. Freeman Manuscript and Research Collection, 1956–1985, Manuscripts, Archives, and Rare Books Division, Schomburg Center for Research in Black Culture, The New York Public Library, Astor, Lenox, and Tilden Foundations, box 7.

7. Peter Williams to Gerrit Smith, September 4, 1834, Gerrit Smith Papers.

8. The principal source for the history of DeGrasse and his conflict with the diocese is Jay, *Caste and Slavery*. This work is primarily focused on the subsequent conflict between Alexander Crummell and his bishop, but it cites portions of a lost diary of DeGrasse's regarding his difficulties. It is upon this account that all later efforts have depended, including those found in Wilson J. Moses, *Alexander Crummell: A Study of Civilization and Discontent* (New York: Oxford University Press, 1989), 27–30; George E. Walker, *The Afro-American in New York City, 1827–1860* (New York: Garland, 1993), 106; Robert Trendel, "John Jay II: Antislavery Conscience of the Episcopal Church," *Historical Magazine of the Protestant Episcopal Church* 45 (September 1976): 237–241; and Leon Litwack, *North of Slavery: The Negro in the Free States, 1790–1860* (Chicago: University of Chicago Press, 1961), 201–203. This summary is also dependent upon Jay's version of the story (unless otherwise noted), but it must be said that this pamphlet was produced with a polemical intent and is therefore to be treated with some suspicion.

9. Washington, *George Thomas Downing*, 8, does not consider DeGrasse to have any African heritage and affirms that he attended Geneva College and then asserts that "Bishop Onderdonk offered him the Rectorship of [Trinity Church, Wall Street], if he would renounce the colored Americans." This is highly implausible, given DeGrasse's youthful demise and his conflict with Onderdonk over admission to seminary. Moses, *Alexander Crummell*, 27, 309n, cites Crummell's comment on DeGrasse's complexion.

10. Cited in Moses, *Alexander Crummell*, 27.

11. Jay, *Caste and Slavery*, 14–17.

12. *Journal of the 54th Convention* (1838), 32. See note 5, chapter 1 for additional bibliographic information.

13. Jay, *Caste and Slavery*, 16.

14. *Journal of the 54th Convention* (1838), 32.

15. *Journal of the 57th Convention* (1841), 76. The convention journals for the years between ordination and death list DeGrasse's church connections.

16. Crummell, Alexander, *Jubilate: 1844–1894, The Shades and Lights of a Fifty Years' Ministry* (Washington, D.C.: St. Luke's Church, 1894), 6, in Moses, *Alexander Crummell*, 25. Moses has gone over Crummell's life quite carefully, and I am dependent on his account for most of these details.

17. Alexander Crummell, "Reply to Bishop Onderdonk," Jay Family Papers, in Moses, *Alexander Crummell*, 25.

18. Moses, *Alexander Crummell*, 12.

19. Crummell, *Shades and Lights*, 7–8, in Moses, *Alexander Crummell*, 27–28.

20. Alexander Crummell to John Jay, October 29, 1834, The Papers of John Jay, in Moses, *Alexander Crummell*, 29.

21. John Jay, "Mem. Of Geo. DeGrasse," August 16, 1846, The Papers of John Jay. This notice discusses the several-year history of a legal dispute of DeGrasse's and suggests therefore that the two had been connected for some years.

22. Trendel, "John Jay II," 244.

23. Moses, *Alexander Crummell*, 38–39.

9. The Chains That Bind

1. "John Bolding," *The National Anti-Slavery Standard*, September 4, 1851, 58.

2. "John Bolding," 58.

3. Mss. Census, New York County, 1855. Note in Rhoda G. Freeman Manuscript and Research Collection, 1956–1985, Manuscripts, Archives, and Rare Books Division, Schomburg Center for Research in Black Culture, The New York Public Library, Astor, Lenox, and Tilden Foundations, box 7.

4. Charles C. Andrews, *The History of the New-York African Free Schools* (New York: Mahlon Day, 1830), 58. There has been very scattered and scanty notice of Smith in the past century until the recent work of John Stauffer, *The Black Hearts of Men: Radical Abolitionists and the Transformation of Race* (Cambridge, Mass.: Harvard University Press, 2002). This work neatly summarizes the available biographical information, working with many of the same sources I had uncovered and directing me to some others. Stauffer's work places Smith in a powerful intellectual and activist context. Surprisingly, though, he is unaware of Smith's affiliation with St. Philip's, and thus misses that aspect of his faith. The only prior work focused on Smith is David W. Blight, "In Search of Learning, Liberty, and Self Definition: James McCune Smith and the Ordeal of the Antebellum Black Intellectual," *Afro-Americans in New York Life and History* 9, no. 2 (July 1985): 7–25, which also summarizes these early years. Smith is an important figure as well in Patrick Rael, *Black Identity and Black Protest in the Antebellum North* (Chapel Hill: University of North Carolina Press, 2002). Biographical sketches of Smith were abundant in the nineteenth and early twentieth centuries, however, including Benjamin Brawley, *The Negro Genius: A New Appraisal of the Achievement of the American Negro in Literature and the Fine Arts* (New York: Dodd, Mead, & Co., 1937), 44–46; William Wells Brown, *The Rising Son; or, the Antecedents and Advancement of the Colored Race* (Boston: A. G. Brown & Co., 1876), 453–454; Martin Robison Delany, *The Condition, Elevation, Emigration, and Destiny of the Colored People of the United States, Politically Considered* (Philadelphia:

printed for the author, 1852), 110–112; John A. Kenney, *The Negro in Medicine* (n.p., 1912), 6; William C. Nell, *The Colored Patriots of the American Revolution, with Sketches of Several Distinguished Colored Persons* (Boston: Robert F. Wallcut, 1855), 352–355. These sources are all indexed and microfilmed in Randall K. Burkett, Nancy Hall Burkett, Henry Louis Gates Jr., eds., *Black Biography 1790–1950: A Cumulative Index* (Alexandria, Va.: Chadwyck-Healey, 1991).

5. *Colored American,* April 15, 1837, cited in George E. Walker, *The Afro-American in New York City, 1827–1860* (New York: Garland, 1993), 77; and Rhoda Golden Freeman, *The Free Negro in New York City in the Era Before the Civil War* (Ph.D. diss., Columbia University, 1966), 430; *Medical Register for 1866,* 202, and *Emancipator,* September 7, 1837, 73, in Freeman Collection; Peter Williams to Gerrit Smith, September 4, 1834, Gerrit Smith Papers, Bird Library, Syracuse University, microform: reel 19; Blight, "In Search of Learning," 21n.

6. George W. Forbes, *Biographical Sketch of James McCune Smith* (typescript, Boston Public Library: Rare Books and Manuscripts, n.d.) in Blight, "In Search of Learning," 8–9, who finds this source "somewhat mysterious"; Stauffer, *Black Hearts,* 88, 124.

7. Smith, letter to the editor, *Colored American,* September 23, 1837, 3; Blight, "In Search of Learning," 9.

8. For the newspaper advertisement, see, for example, *The Colored American,* March 11, 1840, 3; Stauffer, *Black Hearts,* 125; James McCune Smith to Gerrit Smith, May 12, 1848, Gerrit Smith Papers.

9. James McCune Smith, "The Abolition of Slavery and the Slave Trade in the French and British Colonies," in Carter G. Woodson, *Negro Orators and Their Orations* (Washington, D.C.: Associated Publishers, 1925), 123. The *Liberator* (June 1, 1838) lists the program for the day, with this speech given in the afternoon and Gerrit Smith speaking in the morning.

10. Blight, "In Search of Learning," 9; Stauffer, *Black Hearts,* 127.

11. James McCune Smith to Gerrit Smith, July 31, 1839, Gerrit Smith Papers.

12. James McCune Smith to Gerrit Smith, July 31, 1839, Gerrit Smith Papers.

13. Stauffer, *Black Hearts,* 125–127; James McCune Smith to Gerrit Smith, July 31, 1839, Gerrit Smith Papers.

14. *Colored American,* August 15, 1840.

15. Freeman, *Free Negro,* 136.

16. James McCune Smith to Gerrit Smith, May 12, 1848, Gerrit Smith Papers.

17. Nell, *Colored Patriots,* 354–355; Walker, *Afro-American,* 56; Freeman, *Free Negro,* 247.

18. James McCune Smith to Gerrit Smith, May 12, 1848, Gerrit Smith Papers.

19. Stauffer, *Black Hearts,* 8–10.

20. James McCune Smith, *Frederick Douglass' Paper* (May 12, 1854), in Rael, *Black Identity,* 12–13. Rael does a marvelous job of outlining Smith's contributions to African American intellectual thought in this period.

21. The vestry minutes show that Smith served in this capacity from at least 1843 (the year the extant minutes begin) through 1846, and then was a vestryman from 1855 until 1858.

22. James McCune Smith, *A Lecture on the Haytien Revolutions; with a Sketch of the Character of Toussaint L'Ouverture; Delivered at the Stuyvesant Institute (for the benefit of the Colored Orphan Asylum), February 26, 1841* (New York: printed for the Colored Orphan Asylum, 1841), 28; Woodson, *Negro Orators,* 124.

23. Stauffer, *Black Hearts,* 125; Mss. Census, 1855, New York County, note in Freeman Collection; Forbes, *Biographical Sketch,* in Blight, "In Search of Learning," 21n.

24. James McCune Smith to Gerrit Smith, May 12, 1848, and February 6, 1850, Gerrit Smith Papers.

25. The reconstruction of the births and deaths of Smith's children is based on snippets of information in the letters cited and those of March 1 and October 6, 1855, and April 9, 1858; in notices in *National Anti-Slavery Standard* (August 13, 27 and September 19, 1854); and Mss. Census, 1855, note in Freeman Collection.

26. James McCune Smith to Gerrit Smith, March 1, 1855, Gerrit Smith Papers.

27. James McCune Smith to Gerrit Smith, December 28, 1846, Gerrit Smith Papers.

10. *Promoting Improvement*

1. Roi Ottley and William J. Weatherby, eds., *The Negro in New York: An Informal Social History* (New York: New York Public Library, 1967), 60–61; Rhoda Golden Freeman, *The Free Negro in New York City in the Era Before the Civil War* (Ph.D. diss., Columbia University, 1966), 236–239.

2. Freeman, *Free Negro;* George E. Walker, *The Afro-American in New York City, 1827–1860* (New York: Garland, 1993); James Weldon Johnson, *Black Manhattan* (1930, repr. New York: Da Capo Press, 1991); and Ottley and Westherby, *Negro in New York,* all document these organizations quite well. They also all display a tendency to see the "black community" in the city as monolithic.

3. James Abajian, *Blacks in Selected Newspapers, Censuses, and Other Sources: An Index to Names and Subjects,* 3 vols. (Boston: G. K. Hall, 1977), 3:568.

4. All assignments of occupations are based on the listings in the city directories discussed in note 4 of chapter 1, unless otherwise noted.

5. The statistics for St. Philip's are based on reports included in the diocesan convention journals for the relevant years. The statistics for other churches are from Freeman, *Free Negro,* 385, 386, 405, 401, respectively.

6. *The Anniversary Book of St. Philip's Church, New York, 1943* (no publisher, 1943), 40; *Vestry Minutes of St. Philip's Episcopal Church,* St. Philip's Episcopal Church Records, Manuscripts, Archives, and Rare Books Division, Schomburg Center for Research in

Black Culture, The New York Public Library, Astor, Lenox, and Tilden Foundations, box 74, January 11 and February 9, 1848.

7. *Journals of the Conventions of the Diocese of New York: 1800–1819* (New York: E. French, 1846), 468–469; *Journal of the 54th Convention* (1838), 77. See note 5, chapter 1 for additional bibliographic information.

8. Freeman, *Free Negro*, 319–335; Carleton Mabee, *Black Education in New York State: From Colonial to Modern Times* (Syracuse, N.Y.: Syracuse University Press, 1979), 21–28.

9. Walker, *Afro-American*, 53, 59; Wilson J. Moses, *Alexander Crummell: A Study of Civilization and Discontent* (New York: Oxford University Press, 1989), 16; Freeman, *Free Negro*, 369–372. See also "An Appeal, from the Rector, Churchwardens, and Vestrymen of St. Philip's Church in the city of New-York, for the means of establishing a school for colored children," unsourced clipping in Archives of the Diocese of New York: box 69: Manhattan, St. Philip's.

10. Harry A. Reed, *Platform for Change: The Foundations of the Northern Free Black Community, 1775–1865* (East Lansing: Michigan State University Press, 1994), 144–46; Eric Foner, *History of Black Americans*, 3 vols. (Westport, Conn.: Greenwood Press, 1975, 1983), 2:312.

11. This movement is amply covered in numerous works, including Freeman, *Free Negro*, 126ff; Foner, *Black Americans*, 2:300ff; Reed, *Platform for Change*, 144–146; Walker, *Afro-American*, 111ff.

12. Freeman, *Free Negro*, 430–431; *Colored American*, April 15, 1837; Abajian, *Blacks in Selected Newspapers*, 1:501.

13. Freeman, *Free Negro*, 431–434.

14. Freeman, *Free Negro*, 171–190.

15. Freeman, *Free Negro*, 328–329; see also 315–318.

11. *Partaking of the Heavenly Gift*

1. William Jay to Anna Jay Balch, November 4, 1840; John Jay, "Funeral of Rev. Peter Williams, New York," 1840 ms., The Papers of John Jay, Rare Book and Manuscripts Library, Columbia University.

2. J. B. Wakeley, *Lost Chapters Recovered from the Early History of American Methodism* (New York: Printed for the Author, 1858), 447–448; *National Anti-Slavery Standard*, August 30, 1856, 3, in Rhoda G. Freeman Manuscript and Research Collection, 1956–1985, Manuscripts, Archives, and Rare Books Division, Schomburg Center for Research in Black Culture, The New York Public Library, Astor, Lenox, and Tilden Foundations, box 7.

3. *Colored American*, October 24, 1840, 3.

4. *Colored American*, November 7, 1840, 1.

5. William Jay to Anna Jay Balch, November 4, 1840.

6. William Jay to Anna Jay Balch, November 4, 1840.

7. Jay, "Funeral of Peter Williams," The Papers of John Jay.

8. *Colored American*, November 7, 1840, 1.

9. *Colored American*, November 7, 1840, 1.

10. *Journal of the 57th Convention* (1841), 77–78. See note 5, chapter 1 for additional bibliographic information.

11. *Colored American*, October 24, 1840, 3.

12. To Employ a Colored Clergyman

1. *Colored American*, October 24, 1840, 3.

2. *Journal of the 57th Convention* (1841), 78. See note 5, chapter 1 for additional bibliographic information.

3. James Elliott Lindsley, *This Planted Vine: A Narrative History of the Episcopal Diocese of New York* (New York: Harper and Row, 1984), 137–138.

4. Frazer's early career is reconstructed from the clergy lists in the diocesan journals for the years 1837–1848.

5. This sequence is reconstructed from the vestry minutes and diocesan journals for the relevant years. Benjamin F. DeCosta, *Three Score and Ten: The Story of St. Philip's Church, New York City* (New York: Printed for the Parish, 1889), 34–36; and Jonathan Greenleaf, *A History of the Churches of All Denominations, in the City of New York, From the First Settlement to the Year 1846* (New York: E. French, 1846), 81, both support this sequence without having it complete. The end of Morris's tenure is attested in *Weekly Anglo-African*, February 4, 1860, 3, in Rhoda G. Freeman Manuscript and Research Collection, 1956–1985, Manuscripts, Archives, and Rare Books Division, Schomburg Center for Research in Black Culture, The New York Public Library, Astor, Lenox, and Tilden Foundations, box 8.

6. From Alexander Frazer's parish report in *Journal of the 58th Convention* (1842), 89.

7. *Vestry Minutes of St. Philip's Episcopal Church*, St. Philip's Episcopal Church Records, Manuscripts, Archives, and Rare Books Division, Schomburg Center for Research in Black Culture, The New York Public Library, Astor, Lenox, and Tilden Foundations, box 74, September 12, 1843; November 14, 1843.

8. *Vestry Minutes*, September 14, 1843; October 10, 1843.

9. *Vestry Minutes*, October 10, 1843; October 13, 1843.

10. *Vestry Minutes*, November 14, 1843.

11. "St. Matthew's Free Church [Protestant Episcopal]," *Colored American*, June 27, 1840. The vestry announcement is signed by Samuel S. Rankin, "secretary to the vestry of St. Matthew's."

12. Wilson J. Moses, *Alexander Crummell: A Study of Civilization and Discontent* (New York: Oxford University Press, 1989), 34–43.

13. *Vestry Minutes*, December 9, 1945; January 13, 1846; February 10, 1846; March 10, 1846.

14. *Vestry Minutes*, January 13, 1846; August 11, 1846; October 10, 1846; December 8, 1946.

15. *Vestry Minutes*, March 9, 1847.

16. *Vestry Minutes*, April 13, 1847.

17. *Vestry Minutes*, November 9, 1847.

18. *Vestry Minutes*, November 12, 1847.

19. *Vestry Minutes*, November 12, 1847.

20. *Vestry Minutes*, November 16, 1847.

21. *Vestry Minutes*, November 26, 1847.

22. *Vestry Minutes*, November 26, 1847; December 14, 1847.

23. *Journal of the 64th Convention* (1848), 32. Both *Reaching Out: An Epic of the People of St. Philip's Church* (Tappan, N.Y.: Custombook, for St. Philip's Church, 1986), 25; and George F. Bragg, *History of the Afro-American Group of the Episcopal Church* (1922; repr., Baltimore: Church Advocate Press, 1968), 191, state that Berry was ordained in 1846, but the minutes of the Standing Committee show him being approved for ordination in November of 1847 (*Minutes of the Proceedings of the Standing Committee of the Protestant Episcopal Church in the State of New York* [Archives of the Diocese of New York: Standing Committee, Minutes #1], November 4, 1847), and the convention journal cited then supplies the date of the ordination itself.

24. *Vestry Minutes*, January 11, 1848; May 11, 1848; August 8, 1848; December 12, 1848; May 8, 1849; June 12, 1849; August 14, 1849; Bragg, *Afro-American Group*, 191.

25. This intellectual perspective is visible throughout Moses, *Alexander Crummell*.

13. *A State of Schism*

1. *Journal of the 60th Convention* (1844), 47–48. See note 5, chapter 1 for additional bibliographic information.

2. Once the vestry is involved in the campaign for admission, it is mentioned regularly in the minutes, as noted below; thus the absence of any mention of Jay's motion, either beforehand or afterward, is notable.

3. Jennifer P. McLean, *The Jays of Bedford* (Katonah, N.Y.: Friends of John Jay Homestead, Inc., 1984), 3, 24.

4. McLean, *The Jays*, 1–24.

5. *Caste and Slavery* was published anonymously, credited only to "A Churchman," and when some intimated that they thought Crummell was the author, Jay publicly claimed authorship. See Robert Trendel, "John Jay II: Antislavery Conscience of the Episcopal Church," *Historical Magazine of the Protestant Episcopal Church* 45 (September 1976): 241–242.

6. McLean, *The Jays*, 23.

7. Allan Nevins and Milton Thomas, eds., *The Diary of George Templeton Strong*, 4 vols. (New York: Macmillan, 1952), 1:35, 1:12, 1:200.

8. Evan M. Johnson to John Jay, May 29, 1843, The Papers of John Jay, Rare Book and Manuscripts Library, Columbia University.

9. Wilson J. Moses, *Alexander Crummell: A Study of Civilization and Discontent* (New York: Oxford University Press, 1989), 44, 87.

10. Again, see John R. McKivigan, *The War Against Proslavery Religion: Abolitionism and the Northern Churches, 1830–1865* (Ithaca, N.Y.: Cornell University Press, 1984), on these issues.

11. Robert Bruce Mullin, *Episcopal Vision/American Reality: High Church Theology and Social Thought in Evangelical America* (New Haven, Conn.: Yale University Press, 1986), 161. I am indebted to Mullin for the foregoing, which is handled in his work with enormous depth and subtlety.

12. *Journal of the 60th Convention* (1844), 47–48.

13. *Journal of the 60th Convention* (1844), 64.

14. Moses, *Alexander Crummell*, 38; George F. Bragg, *History of the Afro-American Group of the Episcopal Church* (1922; repr., Baltimore: Church Advocate Press, 1968), 102–103.

14. A Bishop's Trials

1. James Elliott Lindsley, *This Planted Vine: A Narrative History of the Episcopal Diocese of New York* (New York: Harper and Row, 1984), 124–150, covers Onderdonk's rise and fall as bishop quite sympathetically, but with a balanced perspective. He points to many of the ways the bishop riled his colleagues (129–134, especially). I am indebted to both his overall account of Onderdonk's downfall for much of what follows, except where I have added contemporary perspectives, as well as to the account provided in Robert Bruce Mullin, *Episcopal Vision/American Reality: High Church Theology and Social Thought in Evangelical America* (New Haven, Conn.: Yale University Press, 1986), 161–166.

2. Lindsley, *This Planted Vine*, 134.

3. *The Book of Common Prayer*, 525. See note 6, chapter 7 for additional bibliographic information.

4. Lindsley, *This Planted Vine*, 146–48.

5. Lindsley, *This Planted Vine*, 149.

6. Allan Nevins and Milton Thomas, eds., *The Diary of George Templeton Strong*, 4 vols. (New York: Macmillan, 1952), 1:255, 1:249 (exclamation marks in the original).

7. *Vestry Minutes of St. Philip's Episcopal Church*, St. Philip's Episcopal Church Records, Manuscripts, Archives, and Rare Books Division, Schomburg Center for Research in Black Culture, The New York Public Library, Astor, Lenox, and Tilden Foundations, box 74, January 14, 1845.

8. *Vestry Minutes*, January 14, 1845.

9. *Vestry Minutes*, February 11, 1845.

10. *Vestry Minutes*, May 13, 1845.

11. *Vestry Minutes*, June 10, 1845; Lindsley, *This Planted Vine*, 153.

12. *Vestry Minutes*, September 9, October 10, 1845.

13. *Vestry Minutes*, September 22, 1845. Since Smith's vote is known, and the delegation was composed only of Smith and Ray prior to the meeting, it can be assumed that Ray did not agree with Smith, or there would have been no need for this meeting.

14. Undated newspaper clipping, John Jay II Scrapbook, John Jay Homestead, Katonah, N.Y.; copy in Freeman Collection: box 8, marked *National Anti-Slavery Standard*, May 29, 1845, 205.

15. Undated newspaper clipping, John Jay II Scrapbook, John Jay Homestead.

16. Undated newspaper clipping, John Jay II Scrapbook, John Jay Homestead.

17. Undated newspaper clipping, John Jay II Scrapbook, John Jay Homestead.

18. Lindsley, *This Planted Vine*, 153.

19. *Vestry Minutes*, October 14, 1845. The Jays, father and son, are listed as delegates in the *Journal of the 61st Convention* (1845), 10, 13. See note 5, chapter 1 for additional bibliographic information.

15. *Exciting the Deepest Feelings*

1. *Vestry Minutes of St. Philip's Episcopal Church*, St. Philip's Episcopal Church Records, Manuscripts, Archives, and Rare Books Division, Schomburg Center for Research in Black Culture, The New York Public Library, Astor, Lenox, and Tilden Foundations, box 74, September 15, 1846.

2. *Journal of the 62nd Convention* (1846), 1–18; *Morning Courier*, October 2, 1846, 2. See note 5, chapter 1 for additional bibliographic information regarding the convention journals.

3. *Journal of the 62nd Convention* (1846), 24–25.

4. *Journal of the 62nd Convention* (1846), 25; *Morning Courier*, October 2, 1846, 2.

5. Henry Stiles, quoted without citation in Paul Bosten, "The History of St. John's Church at Brooklyn," unpublished ms., Archives of St. John's Church, Brooklyn, N.Y., 2; Clifford A. Buck, *St. John's Church, Episcopal-Anglican, 1976: 150th Anniversary Year* (no publisher), 5–8; Records of St. John's Church, "Various Records, 1826–1863," Archives of St. John's Church, Brooklyn, N.Y.

6. *Morning Courier*, October 2, 1846, 2.

7. *Morning Courier*, October 3, 1846, 2.

8. *Morning Courier*, October 2, 1846, 2; *Journal of the 62nd Convention* (1846), 26.

9. *Morning Courier*, October 2, 1846, 2.

10. *Journal of the 62nd Convention* (1846), 26–30.

11. *Morning Courier*, October 2, 1846, 2.

12. *Journal of the 62nd Convention* (1846), 30, 47–49.

13. *Journal of the 62nd Convention* (1846), 60.

14. "Report: Committee on St. Philip's Church," *Journal of the 62nd Convention* (1846), 72–76. All subsequent quotations in this chapter, unless otherwise noted, are from this report.

15. Galatians 3:28.

16. *Journal of the 62nd Convention* (1846), 76–77.

16. Vouchsafed to All Men

1. "Minority Report," *Journal of the 62nd Convention* (1846), 77–79. All subsequent quotations, unless otherwise noted, are from this report, and all italics are in the original. See note 5, chapter 1 for additional bibliographic information.

2. *Morning Courier*, October 2, 1846, 2.

3. *Journal of the 62nd Convention* (1846), 79.

4. *Vestry Minutes of St. Philip's Episcopal Church*, St. Philip's Episcopal Church Records, Manuscripts, Archives, and Rare Books Division, Schomburg Center for Research in Black Culture, The New York Public Library, Astor, Lenox, and Tilden Foundations, box 74, October 20, 1846.

17. The Heart Must Be Changed

1. For example, see James McCune Smith to Gerrit Smith, December 28, 1846 and May 12, 1848, Gerrit Smith Papers, Bird Library, Syracuse University, microform: reel 19.

2. James McCune Smith to Gerrit Smith, December 17, 1846, Gerrit Smith Papers.

3. James McCune Smith to Gerrit Smith, January 25, 1847, Gerrit Smith Papers.

4. James McCune Smith to Gerrit Smith, December 17, 1846, Gerrit Smith Papers.

5. This extraordinary plan of Gerrit Smith's is outlined in John Stauffer, *The Black Hearts of Men: Radical Abolitionists and the Transformation of Race* (Cambridge, Mass.: Harvard University Press, 2002), 134–144.

6. James McCune Smith to Gerrit Smith, December 17, 1846, Gerrit Smith Papers.

7. James McCune Smith to Gerrit Smith, December 17, 1846, Gerrit Smith Papers.

8. James McCune Smith to Gerrit Smith, February 6, 1850, Gerrit Smith Papers.

9. James McCune Smith to Gerrit Smith, December 28, 1846, Gerrit Smith Papers.

10. James McCune Smith to Gerrit Smith, December 28, 1846, Gerrit Smith Papers.

11. James McCune Smith to Gerrit Smith, December 28, 1846, Gerrit Smith Papers. For a discussion of the "Bible politics" these men shared, see Stauffer, *Black Hearts*, 134ff.

12. James McCune Smith to Gerrit Smith, December 28, 1846, Gerrit Smith Papers.

13. James McCune Smith to Gerrit Smith, December 28, 1846, Gerrit Smith Papers.

18. *The Beauties of Freedom*

1. "A Novel Slave Case," *National Anti-Slavery Standard* 8, no. 7 (July 15, 1847): 27; *Revised Statutes of the State of New York*, Part I, Title VII, Chap. XX, Sect. 16 (December 3, 1827), cited in Rhoda Golden Freeman, *The Free Negro in New York City in the Era Before the Civil War* (Ph.D. diss., Columbia University, 1966), 5.

2. *New York Herald*, quoted in *National Anti-Slavery Standard* 8, no. 8 (July 22, 1847): 29.

3. "Brazilian Slaves," *National Anti-Slavery Standard* 8, no. 11 (August 12, 1847): 42.

4. *Vestry Minutes of St. Philip's Episcopal Church*, St. Philip's Episcopal Church Records, Manuscripts, Archives, and Rare Books Division, Schomburg Center for Research in Black Culture, The New York Public Library, Astor, Lenox, and Tilden Foundations, box 74, August 12, 1847 (italics in the original).

5. All information about the addresses and/or occupations of individuals is taken from the city directories (see note 4, chapter 1) from the relevant years, unless otherwise noted. In addition to the *Vestry Minutes* (as noted earlier), the other source for names of individuals who considered themselves members of St. Philip's is the open letter written to John Jay in 1845, as the letter states that all the signatories are parishioners: undated newspaper clipping, John Jay II Scrapbook, John Jay Homestead, Katonah, N.Y..

6. Regarding Ms. Wright's tenure as organist, see *Vestry Minutes*, October 12, 1852. On the purchase of an organ, see Benjamin F. DeCosta, *Three Score and Ten: The Story of St. Philip's Church, New York City* (New York: Printed for the Parish, 1889), 29; and *Reaching Out: An Epic of the People of St. Philip's Church* (Tappan, N.Y.: Custombook, for St. Philip's Church, 1986), 20. Both claim that an organ was purchased at some point between 1821 and 1826, and the latter source asserts it cost $1,000. No references are given for this information, but *Freedom's Journal* 1, no. 29 (September 28, 1827): 115 lists a concert in the church that features pieces played on the organ, so it must have been purchased before then. The vestry's financial reports from 1843 to 1854 list an annual payment to Henry Erben, in addition to the minutes indicating bills paid to him for tuning; this suggests that Erben was the builder. For Hamilton, see *Vestry Minutes*, January 11, 1848; for Brady, see James M. Trotter, *Music and Some Highly Musical People* (Boston: Lee and Shepard, 1885), 302–303. He is also mentioned in both Eileen Southern, *The Music of Black Americans: A History*, 2nd ed. (New York: W. W. Norton, 1983), 114, and Irene V. Jackson, "Music Among Blacks in the Episcopal Church: Some Preliminary Considerations," in Irene V. Jackson, ed., *More Than Dancing: Essays on Afro-American Music and Musicians* (Westport, Conn.: Greenwood Press, 1985), 113.

7. "Financial Report," *Vestry Minutes*, January 9, 1844, and subsequent years.

8. For Downing see John H. Hewitt, "Mr. Downing and his Oyster House: The

Life and Good Works of an African-American Entrepreneur," *New York History* (July 1993): 229–252; For Scott see Martin Robison Delany, *The Condition, Elevation, Emigration, and Destiny of the Colored People of the United States, Politically Considered* (Philadelphia: printed for the author, 1852), 102; *New York City Municipal Archives: Record of Assessments*, 1843.

9. For Rays, see John A. Kenney, *The Negro in Medicine* (n.p., 1912), 8–9; for Lyons, see unattributed obituary in possession of Evelyn Lane, a descendant of Albro Lyons, copy in Rhoda G. Freeman Manuscript and Research Collection, 1956–1985, Manuscripts, Archives, and Rare Books Division, Schomburg Center for Research in Black Culture, The New York Public Library, Astor, Lenox, and Tilden Foundations, box 7.

10. J. B. Wakeley, *Lost Chapters Recovered from the Early History of American Methodism* (New York: Printed for the Author, 1858), 446–447; obituary of Amy Matilda Remond, *National Anti-Slavery Standard*, August 30, 1856, 3.

11. "Financial Report," *Vestry Minutes*, January 9, 1844, and subsequent years.

12. DeCosta, *Three Score and Ten*, 41.

13. *New York City Municipal Archives: Record of Assessments*, 1843.

14. Benjamin Quarles, *Black Abolitionists* (New York: Oxford University Press, 1969), passim; George E. Walker, *The Afro-American in New York City, 1827–1860* (New York: Garland, 1993), 37, 77, 117, 151, 156–159; James Abajian, *Blacks in Selected Newspapers, Censuses, and Other Sources: An Index to Names and Subjects*, 3 vols. (Boston: G. K. Hall, 1977), 1:145–149.

15. Quarles, *Black Abolitionists*, 198; Walker, *Afro-American*, 56, 125, 173–174; Abajian, *Blacks in Selected Newspapers*, 3:95.

16. Eric Foner, *History of Black Americans*, 3 vols. (Westport, Conn.: Greenwood Press, 1975, 1983), 3:357–376.

19. *Economic Opportunity and Religious Choice*

1. "Appendix, table 1: Free Negro Population of New York City," in Rhoda Golden Freeman, *The Free Negro in New York City in the Era Before the Civil War* (Ph. D. diss., Columbia University, 1966), 439–443, see also 215–314, especially 218–219. See also Leonard P. Curry, *The Free Black in Urban America, 1800–1850* (Chicago: University of Chicago Press, 1981), 37–80; George E. Walker, *The Afro-American in New York City, 1827–1860* (New York: Garland, 1993), 9–10; Tyler Anbinder, *Five Points: The Nineteenth-Century New York City Neighborhood That Invented Tap Dancing, Stole Elections, and Became the World's Most Notorious Slum* (New York: Free Press, 2001), passim and especially 14–37; and Sule Greg C. Wilson, "Little Africa," in Kenneth T. Jackson, ed., *The Encyclopedia of New York City* (New Haven, Conn.: Yale University Press, 1995), 685.

2. *Reaching Out: An Epic of the People of St. Philip's Church* (Tappan, N.Y.: Custombook, for St. Philip's Church, 1986), 27, 33, 36–37.

3. Curry, *The Free Black*, 16–26, 258–266. Curry's categories are as follows:

   1: unskilled: laborer, mariner, woodsawyer

   2: semiskilled: sexton, gardener, well digger

   3: personal service: servant, barber, waiter

   4: transportation: carter, porter, drayman

   5: food service: cook, baker, pastry cook

   6: artisan: carpenter, tailor, blacksmith

   7: entrepreneurial/mercantile: fruit dealer, boardinghouse keeper, peddlar

   8: professional managerial, artistic, clerical, scientific, etc.: minister, teacher, musician

4. Curry, *The Free Black*, 258–261. He explains the Index of Occupational Opportunity thusly:"The two best indicators of black occupational achievement and opportunity for economic success are the proportion of the total employed black males following Group A (low opportunity) occupations and the proportion employed as artisans. Obviously, the greater the percentage of black males engaged in group A occupations in a city or a group of cities, the less likely it is that that particular population block will advance economically. Conversely, where a larger segment consists of artisans the chances of economic success are proportionately greater... . It is also possible to combine these two indicators into a single simple index of black occupational opportunity (I.O.O.). The formula for the construction of this index is: I.O.O. = % Artisan − % Group A + 100 / 200. If all blacks in a given city were artisans, the index figure would be 1.00; if all were employed in group A occupations, the index figure would be 0.00. Hence, the higher the index figure, the greater the degree of occupational achievement and opportunity."

5. Curry, *The Free Black*, 35–36: " The southern urban free black communities were created by selective manumission, not by mass emancipation... . Among southern slaves who were manumitted ... many earned the money to buy their freedom, some were freed as a reward for their labor or loyalty, and not a few were manumitted because of a familial relationship with their masters. Hence, it is apparent that many of the southern free blacks were drawn from the most able, energetic, and talented of the slave population, while many others had familial ties that were likely to make it easier for them to acquire education, training, and capital. It is hardly strange that such selectively manumitted slaves—many of whom had already successfully competed with free workmen—should exhibit a higher incidence of continued occupational achievement than a northern free black population that, to a much greater degree, included the weak as well as the strong, the indolent as well as the energetic, the inept as well as the able, and the unprepared as well as the experienced."

6. John Stauffer, *The Black Hearts of Men: Radical Abolitionists and the Transformation of Race* (Cambridge, Mass.: Harvard University Press, 2002), 125, asserts that his practice was interracial.

20. *Attentive to Their Devotions*

1. Quotations from the service of morning prayer are found in the *Book of Common Prayer*, 1–14. See note 6, chapter 7 for additional bibliographic information.

2. *Book of Common Prayer*, 24–31.

3. *Book of Common Prayer*, 208–228.

4. H. G. Adams, ed., *God's Image in Ebony: Being a Series of Biographical Sketches, Facts, and Anecdotes Demonstrative of the Mental Powers and Intellectual Capacities of the Negro Race* (London: Partridge and Oakley, 1854), 132–133, indexed and microfilmed in Randall K. Burkett, Nancy Hall Burkett, and Henry Louis Gates Jr., eds., *Black Biography 1790–1950: A Cumulative Index* (Alexandria, Va.: Chadwyck-Healey, 1991). The reference is to a visit during the tenure of Peter Williams.

5. *Freedom's Journal* 1, no. 7 (April 27, 1827): 26; *Vestry Minutes of St. Philip's Episcopal Church*, St. Philip's Episcopal Church Records, Manuscripts, Archives, and Rare Books Division, Schomburg Center for Research in Black Culture, The New York Public Library, Astor, Lenox, and Tilden Foundations, box 74, June 25, 1845.

6. For a discussion of the ways in which evangelical practices shaped regular worship services, see Ralph Gerald Gay, *A Study of the American Liturgical Revival, 1825–1860* (Ph.D. diss., Emory University, 1977), 80–87. This focuses in particular on two sources that advocated a congregational "Amen" at the end of prayers, "which would allow the worshipers to participate vocally" (84)—indicating that no such participation was usual.

7. John H. Hobart, *The Candidate for Confirmation Instructed* (New York: T. and J. Swords, 1816), 61, 83. Hobart's use of the term "regeneration," which comes from the prayer book baptismal service, invokes the debate between High Churchmen and evangelicals (of both Episcopal and other attachments) over the distinction and correspondence between baptism and conversion. For a full discussion of this issue, see Robert Bruce Mullin, *Episcopal Vision/American Reality: High Church Theology and Social Thought in Evangelical America* (New Haven, Conn.: Yale University Press, 1986), 63–66.

8. *Journals of the Conventions of the Diocese of New York: 1800–1819* (New York: E. French, 1846), 468–469; *Vestry Minutes*, September 12, 1843. For the catechism, see *Book of Common Prayer*, 246–251.

9. *Journal of the 59th Convention* (1843), 119; *Journal of the 60th Convention* (1843), 128. See note 5, chapter 1 for additional bibliographic information.

10. *Book of Common Prayer*, 568–572.

11. William S. Pelletreau, *New York Houses, with Historical and Genealogical Notes* (New York: Francis P. Harper, 1900), 3; *Vestry Minutes*, June 12, 1849; July 18, 1849; December 11, 1849; John Hewitt, "The Sacking of St. Philip's Church, New York," *Historical Magazine of the Protestant Episcopal Church* 49 (March 1980): 7.

12. See the financial reports in *Vestry Minutes* for the relevant years.

13. *Vestry Minutes*, December 10, 1850.

14. DeCosta, *Three Score and Ten: The Story of St. Philip's Church, New York City* (New York: Printed for the Parish, 1889), 15.

15. *Freedom's Journal*, September 28, 1827, 115. Regarding such concerts and their typical program, see Eileen Southern, *The Music of Black Americans: A History*, 2nd ed. (New York: W.W. Norton, 1983), 104–107.

16. *Vestry Minutes*, November 10, 1846.

17. *Vestry Minutes*, January 9 and February 3, 1855.

21. *The Express Wishes of Nearly All*

1. *Vestry Minutes of St. Philip's Episcopal Church*, St. Philip's Episcopal Church Records, Manuscripts, Archives, and Rare Books Division, Schomburg Center for Research in Black Culture, The New York Public Library, Astor, Lenox, and Tilden Foundations, box 74, September 14, 1847.

2. *Journal of the 63rd Convention* (1847), 65; Evan M. Johnson, letter to the Editor, *The Protestant Churchman* 5, no. 11 (October 16, 1847): 3. See note 5, chapter 1 for additional bibliographic information on the journals of the diocesan conventions.

3. *Vestry Minutes*, May 9, May 11, 1848.

4. *Vestry Minutes*, May 11, June 13, 1848.

5. *Vestry Minutes*, May 28, June 13, July 11, 1848.

6. *Vestry Minutes*, September 12, September 24, 1848.

7. *Vestry Minutes*, September 24, 1848.

8. *Vestry Minutes*, September 24, 1848.

9. William Jay, "The Episcopal Convention and Colored Churches," ms. (dated Bedford, ca. 1850), The Papers of John Jay, Rare Book and Manuscripts Library, Columbia University. George F. Bragg, *History of the Afro-American Group of the Episcopal Church* (1922; repr., Baltimore: Church Advocate Press, 1968), 121, dates this admission in 1856, and Harold T. Lewis, *Yet With a Steady Beat: The African American Struggle for Recognition in the Episcopal Church* (Valley Forge, Penn.: Trinity Press International, 1996), 191n, follows Bragg's assertion, but Jay's manuscript clearly states that it occurred in 1848.

10. *Vestry Minutes*, November 14, December 12, 1848.

11. William Jay, "The Episcopal Convention and Colored Churches."

12. *Vestry Minutes*, August 14, 1849; Edward S. Moffat, *Trinity School, New York City, 1709–1959* (Ph.D. diss., Columbia University, 1963), 147–148; Minutes of the Board of Trustees, May 15, 1856: Archives of Trinity School, New York City, box 2.

22. *Injurious to the Cause of Religion*

1. *Vestry Minutes of St. Philip's Episcopal Church*, St. Philip's Episcopal Church Records, Manuscripts, Archives, and Rare Books Division, Schomburg Center for

Research in Black Culture, The New York Public Library, Astor, Lenox, and Tilden Foundations, box 74, April 2, May 21, July 9, 1850. Lack of a quorum resulted in cancelled meetings in May, June, August, September, October, and November; substitute meetings were held in May, September, and November.

2. *Morning Courier*, September 27, 1850, 2. See also the *Protestant Churchman* 8, no. 10 (October 5, 1850): 2.

3. William Jay, "The Episcopal Convention and Colored Churches," The Papers of John Jay, Rare Book and Manuscripts Library, Columbia University.

4. *Vestry Minutes*, November 19, 1850; *Journal of the 67th Convention—Special Convention* (1850), 33. See note 5, chapter 1 for additional bibliographic information on the journals of the diocesan conventions.

5. *Journal of the 67th Convention—Special Convention* (1850), 33–36. See also the *Protestant Churchman* 8, no. 18 (November 30, 1850): 2.

6. John Jay to James Monroe, January 6, 1851, and James Monroe to John Jay, January 6, 1851, printed circular, John Jay II Scrapbook, John Jay Homestead, Katonah, N.Y.

7. *Journal of the 68th Convention* (1851), 36–40; *Churchman* 21, no. 32 (October 4, 1851): 2.

8. *Vestry Minutes*, September 23, 1851.

9. Robert Trendel, "John Jay II: Antislavery Conscience of the Episcopal Church," *Historical Magazine of the Protestant Episcopal Church* 45 (September 1976): 245–246; George E. Walker, *The Afro-American in New York City, 1827–1860* (New York: Garland, 1993), 106–109; John H. Hewitt, "Unresting the Waters: The Fight Against Racism in New York's Episcopal Establishment, 1845–1853," *Afro-Americans in New York Life and History* 18, no. 1 (January 1994); Jennifer P. McLean, *The Jays of Bedford* (Katonah, N.Y.: Friends of John Jay Homestead, Inc., 1984), 24; Rhoda Golden Freeman, *The Free Negro in New York City in the Era Before the Civil War* (Ph.D. diss., Columbia University, 1966), 396–400; and Allan Nevins and Milton Thomas, eds., *The Diary of George Templeton Strong*, 4 vols. (New York: Macmillan, 1952), 2:131.

10. *Vestry Minutes*, April 13, 1852.

11. *Vestry Minutes*, April 13, April 29, June 8, July 13, September 14, 1852.

12. *Vestry Minutes*, September 14, 1852; *Journal of the 69th Convention* (1852), 99.

13. *New-York Daily Times*, September 30, 1852, 8.

14. John Jay, "The admission of colored churches to the Convention of the Diocese of New York," ms. (labeled "draft"), November 1852, The Papers of John Jay.

15. *New-York Daily Times*, September 30, 1852, 8; *Morning Courier*, October 1, 1852, 2. The text of the resolution was also printed in the *Evening Post*, October 1, 2, and in the *Churchman*, October 9, 1852, 2. Jay's own account does not reproduce the resolution in full, but summarizes it.

16. Jay, "The admission of colored churches"; *Morning Courier*, October 1, 1852, 2.

17. Jay, "The admission of colored churches"; *Journal of the 69th Convention* (1852).

18. *Vestry Minutes*, October 12, 1852.

23. *A Fulness of Assent*

1. The diocesan convention journals from 1846 through 1851 designate St. Philip's and Messiah as "(colored)," and mark them with an asterisk signifying "not in union with the convention." This was not a canonically recognized status for a parish.

2. *Vestry Minutes of St. Philip's Episcopal Church*, St. Philip's Episcopal Church Records, Manuscripts, Archives, and Rare Books Division, Schomburg Center for Research in Black Culture, The New York Public Library, Astor, Lenox, and Tilden Foundations, box 74, May 10, July 12, 1853.

3. *Vestry Minutes*, September 13, 1853.

4. *Evening Post*, September 28, 1853, 2.

5. *Evening Post*, September 29, 1853, 2.

6. *New-York Daily Times*, September 29, 1853, 3; *New-York Commercial Advertiser*, September 29, 1853, 1.

7. *New-York Daily Times*, September 30, 1853, 4; *Protestant Churchman* 11, no. 11 (October 8, 1853): 2.

8. *Evening Post*, September 29, 1853, 2.

9. *Protestant Churchman* 11, no. 11 (October 8, 1853): 2; *Morning Courier*, September 30, 1853, 2; *Journal of the 70th Convention* (1853), 38–45; *New-York Daily Times*, September 30, 1853, 4. See note 5, chapter 1 for additional bibliographic information on the journals of the diocesan conventions.

10. *Journal of the 70th Convention* (1853), 38–45; *New-York Daily Times*, September 30, 1853, 4.

11. *Churchman* 23, no. 32 (October 8, 1853): 3; *Vestry Minutes*, October 11, November 8, 1853; Allan Nevins and Milton Thomas, eds., *The Diary of George Templeton Strong*, 4 vols. (New York: Macmillan, 1952), 2:131.

12. *Vestry Minutes*, October 11, 1853.

13. *Vestry Minutes*, September 12, September 28, October 10, 1854.

24. *But One Fold and One Chief Shepherd*

1. Letter from the Rt. Rev. William M. Green, dated April 2, 1883, cited in Appendix XI-9, "An Account of a conference held at Sewanee, Tenn., July 25 to 28, 1883, on the relation of the church to the coloured people," in *Journal of the General Convention of the Protestant Episcopal Church in the United States of America*, (Printed for the Convention, 1883), 595.

2. "Report of the Committee," *Journal of the General Convention*, 597.

3. "Report of the Committee," and "Canon: Of Missionary Organizations Within Constituted Episcopal Jurisdictions" [proposed], *Journal of the General Convention*, 597.

4. *Journal of the General Convention*, 251–252.

INDEX

The Religion and American Culture series explores the interaction between religion and culture throughout American history. Titles examine such issues as how religion functions in particular urban contexts, how it interacts with popular culture, its role in social and political conflicts, and its impact on regional identity. Series Editor Randall Balmer is the Ann Whitney Olin Professor of American Religion and former chair of the Department of Religion at Barnard College, Columbia University.

Michael E. Staub, *Torn at the Roots: The Crisis of Jewish Liberalsim in Postwar America*

Amy DeRogatis, *Moral Geography: Maps, Missionaries, and the American Frontier*

Arlene M. Sánchez Walsh, *Latino Pentecostal Identity: Evangelical Faith, Self, and Society*

Julie Byrne, *O God of Players: The Story of the Immaculata Mighty Macs*

Thomas E. Woods Jr., *The Church Confronts Modernity: Catholic Intellectuals and the Progressive Era*

Clyde R. Forsberg Jr., *Equal Rites: The Book of Mormon, Masonry, Gender, and American Culture*